PATHWAYS IN INTERNATIONAL LAW

A PERSONAL NARRATIVE

Pathways in International Law

A PERSONAL NARRATIVE BY

ARTHUR K. KUHN

GREENWOOD PRESS, PUBLISHERS
NEW YORK

What the world most needs today is a return to law, and to the orderly modes of action which the observance of law assures. In the national sphere, the alternative to law is despotism; in the international sphere, the alternative is anarchy. With law, let us have liberty; and with law and liberty, let us have peace.

—*The Collected Papers of John Bassett Moore*, VI, 490

Contents

Illustrations

Pathways Marked

Human life has been profoundly changed through the discoveries of modern science. The relative size of the planet on which we live has been diminished by reason of the speed of travel and communication. While science has been directed also toward a better understanding of psychologic forces, the conduct of men and nations is not adequately adjusted to the new conditions. Human interests and human problems do not stop at the border of any country, and the application of law to the affairs of men and nations can likewise not be territorially limited. The quest of these my pathways has been the advancement of the science which we call international law. I propose therefore to describe some of my activities along the way, both as a practitioner and as a participant in efforts to substitute law for war.

I was born in Philadelphia, the City of Brotherly Love, in the centennial year of our independence, on the day to be celebrated many years later by the national holiday of Armistice Day. My parents settled in Pennsylvania prior to the War Between the States. Before I reached school years, my family moved to New York, where I attended the public schools and City College, later transferring to advanced standing at Columbia College, where I graduated in 1895. The college was then situated on Forty-ninth Street, and it had not yet become a part of the great university on Morningside Heights known as Columbia University in the City of New York.

I seemed to have marked a pathway when still a sophomore at City College in 1893. My attention was drawn to an intercollegiate prize contest offered by the American Peace Society to undergraduates of colleges throughout the nation. The faculty of each college was requested to present the best essay written by one of its undergraduate students, upon an announced subject, to a national panel of judges, who were to select the three best essays. I believe it was the winning of one of these intercollegiate prizes that determined my future interest in international affairs and perhaps also in international law.

1. *The Economic Waste of War*

The announced subject for the year was "The Economic Waste of War." How different were the conditions of the world then from what they are at the beginning of the second half of the twentieth century. In what light did an undergraduate then view the world situation? I wrote: "The whole of Christendom is at present wrapped in the folds of profound peace. We perceive the benefits derived therefrom in the broad fields of a happier life, yet over the head of every civilized nation, especially in Europe, there hangs like the sword of Damocles the threat of future war. At such a time it behooves us, for the purpose of advancing the cause of peace, to examine into the evil effects of war and its accompaniments, and, by spreading far and wide the knowledge of those ethical and economic facts with which it is so entirely inconsistent, to arouse the human race to a consciousness of its unmitigated harm."

At the session of the Sixth General Assembly of the United Nations held in Paris during November and December, 1951, the subjects on the agenda were nominally political in character, and yet a great part of the discussions, especially the pleas and plans for disarmament, were motivated by the *economic* ruin facing all countries in the event that the expenditure for wars, past, present, and to come, should continue to increase in the geometric ratio of previous years. In 1893 I wrote:

"The loss which is probably the most evident, on account of the enormous proportions which it assumes, is the direct expenditure for war appliances. Especially is this true in these days of inventive science, when new firearms, new projectiles, new methods of naval construction and engineering apparatus are daily displacing the old. No nation is willing to be outdone by any other in the perfection of the material which it employs, and hence a governmental activity in this department is incessantly going on, the result of which is a factitious demand for a certain kind of manufacturing skill which the best scientific energy of the day finds it well worth while to satisfy, even at the expense of withdrawing itself from the remunerative fields of ordinary industrial activity. Thus the latest scientific results, the finest artistic contrivances, and the most exact mechanical appliances are, at the first moment of their discovery, impressed into the service of war, and render those previously in use, incapable of fulfilling the newly created ends. It needs not be pointed out how great a consumption of precious material and diversion of ingenuity all this involves, when it is multiplied over so many centuries and repeated in such interminable succession."

As I consider these reflections written more than half a century ago, I cannot avoid the thought that economic laws do not greatly change. Had the subject been one dealing with the influence of war on any phase of the political structure of states, the balance of power in the world, or of diplomatic policy, I am sure my conclusions would no longer have fitted the international scene. On the other hand, the economic effects of war on the human race at the end of the first half of the century have taken on enormously increased importance owing to the greater destructive power of war weapons and the direct participation in the conduct of any war by a much larger proportion of the population.

"As a result of all these losses and expenditures, the amount of taxation increases enormously, national debts are created and they are handed down as a legacy to posterity. No one generation ever sustains the cost of victory or defeat of the state. 'Mortgaged states their grandsires' wreaths regret, from age to age in everlasting debt.'

A writer in the *Edinburgh Review* shortly after the Napoleonic Wars complainingly remarks: 'The schoolboy whips his taxed top, the youth manages his taxed horse with a taxed bridle, the dying Englishman pouring his medicine taxed seven percent into a spoon taxed fifteen percent, flings himself back on his chintz bed taxed twenty-two percent and his whole property is, at his death, at once raised from two to ten percent. His virtues are handed down to posterity on taxed marble, and he is gathered to his fathers to be taxed no more.' Ludicrous as this may seem, it was no more than fact at the time." Unfortunately, history is repeating itself in the mid-century, and the facts no longer appear quite so ludicrous.

"As a result of the modern economic system of international investment, a blow struck by a state at property in its opponent's territory will often be found to react to the detriment of its own citizens. . . . Capital has become cosmopolitan. English capital made the Russian and American railways; the savings of France are invested in Austrian and Italian railways; while those of Germany are invested in Sweden and Spain. Thus it has become an impossibility for the wealth of any one country to be ruined, without dragging others into the destruction, and the clash of enemies portends a debtor's fall. From this standpoint, it becomes clear that modern war occasions loss, not merely to those directly engaged in it; its scope is far wider, its death-dealing arms subtend a broader field. A state of war wherever it exists implies universal harm and far-reaching misery."

It would be unfair to the reader of these pages were I to leave the impression that I had possessed unusual foresight for one so young. Quite the contrary seems to have been the truth of the matter, because I closed this otherwise acceptable study on the economic waste of war by a truly sophomoric statement which history was destined to turn into the bitterest irony. This was my peroration: "The roar of the cannon is growing fainter and fainter in the distance and in its stead is heard the approach of the chariot of universal peace in its onward course toward a higher and nobler future."

Such is the idealism of teenagers. History oft turns prophecy into irony.

2. *Diplomatic Relations with the Far East*

When I was an undergraduate at Columbia College, Seth Low was still its president. He was soon to become mayor of New York, not yet the greater city that it is today. This public-spirited leader was known not only for his amiable character but also because of his deep interest in the welfare of the students. Several times during the year he invited the members of the senior class to his home for a little social relaxation, and engaged many of us in conversation. This was a new experience for me, who had known only the Spartan discipline of General Alexander S. Webb, president of City College, who led his troops with gallantry at Gettysburg but, to my mind, had very little understanding of adolescent boys. I always had the impression that we represented to him only a body of raw recruits. Columbia moved to its present impressive site on Morningside Heights in the autumn of 1897. The graduates of the last five years at the old site organized a group known as "The Last of the Forty-Niners." Marching in a parade one day behind a large banner with this title, we heard a lady on the sidelines exclaim, "But these men are not old enough to have been digging for gold in California in 1849!"

The fortuitous circumstance of the peace-essay contest attracted me to make further studies in the problems of peace and war. I selected a number of courses in the School of Political Science and determined to compete for the annual James Gordon Bennett Award. The announced subject for the year was "The Past and Present Diplomatic Relations of the United States with China, Japan and Korea." The selection of this subject showed great foresight on the part of the faculty at a time when few could have anticipated the important role which our diplomatic relations with these countries was destined to play in the life of the nation. We were the first Western nation to recognize Japan (1854) and also the first to have concluded a treaty of amity and peace with Korea (May 22, 1882). My essay consisted mainly of historical research. Perhaps it is not without interest for us today to note that the consent of the Korean monarch to sign a treaty with the United States was influenced greatly by the advice of distinguished *Chinese* statesmen of that period who already had had opportunities for appraising the character of our friendship by reason of our relations with China during the preceding quarter-century. I pointed out that the treaty negotiations were brought to fruition by a document presented to the Court of Seoul by Kwo In Ken, adviser to the Chinese minister to Japan, in which he maintained that *Americans were the natural friends of Asiatic nations.* About the same time China's ofttime premier, Li Hung Chang, wrote a letter to an influential Korean statesman advising his country to seek the friendship of the United States and urging the signing of a treaty as a matter of national safety.

It is not without interest to us at the present day to take note of a result which I emphasized in my essay, that the steps which Chinese officials took at the time in encouraging the making of the treaty and assenting to it, actually constituted a waiver of the legal control over Korea which China had claimed over a long period.

My success in winning the James Gordon Bennett Essay resulted in an invitation from the city editor of the New York *Herald,* owned by Mr. Bennett, to become a cub reporter on the paper. This I accepted with alacrity. William C. Rieck was then city editor of the *Herald,* although later he became general manager of the New York *Times,* a position which he held for many years with great distinction. I remained on the staff only a few months, resuming my legal studies in the autumn.

3. *Law Studies at Home and Abroad*

The Law Department of Columbia University only a few years before this time had adopted the so-called Case System, following the appointment of William A. Keener, formerly of Harvard, as dean. This method of teaching law consisted in the reading and discussion of actual cases taken from the law reports. It had been developed at the Harvard Law School by Dean Christopher Langdell and his able associates, and supplanted the professorial or lecture method which had formerly prevailed. The Case System had the great advantage of calling upon the student's own resources of thinking and analysis. He was obliged to express himself upon the correctness of the decision of the court from the point of view of logic and justice. As a mental exercise it was probably unequaled by any other system. Chief Justice Arthur T. Vanderbilt of the Supreme Court of New Jersey, formerly dean of the Law School of New York University, recently pointed out that training in legal reasoning is essential but not enough. He said: "This sufficed in the long period of gradual economic and social development in this country, a period marked also by national isolation. But such training, outstanding though it was in many instances, will not satisfy the needs of a time when inventions, technology and a changing intellectual outlook on life are forcing developments in law at an unprecedented velocity."

The students of my day were generally well satisfied with the new system because it gave each of us an opportunity to express ourselves freely, as though already sitting upon the Bench, whereas it was only too obvious that we were mere neophytes in a difficult professional field requiring not only prior training but patient research and widespread experience with human affairs. The gentlemen of the faculty were well qualified to stimulate the young students through discussion of the cases on a basis of equality and without condescension. Some of the teachers, besides their professorial standing, had long experience in practice at the Bar. It is perhaps a purely personal reaction, but I had, and still have, a preference for law teachers who have been in active practice. I remember particularly George M. Cumming, who taught us contracts. He was a successful practitioner at the Bar and counsel to the United States Mortgage and Trust Company. Later he became vice president of the Erie Railroad. Though he did not devote all his time to teaching, he was nevertheless a most effective exponent of legal principles. He was tireless in his efforts to expound them with such force and eloquence that the student was convinced that after full discussion, on an equal basis with the teacher, we had arrived at a finality of decision which was sure to be upheld by a court of last resort.

Dean Keener himself was inclined to speak ex cathedra. I never lost the impression in attending his classes that he came with his mind fully made up on every case and that no matter what considerations were presented as a result of the general discussions in the classroom it would be impossible to shake him from the position which he had adopted at the outset. This is not to underrate his incisive and original mind. His work on quasi contracts is a classic. He was entitled to great credit for having successfully introduced what was then a new system of law teaching at Columbia.

It was in the first year of the Law School that I became acquainted with John Bassett Moore, who was destined to become the first American on the Permanent Court of International Justice. We shall leave to a later opportunity reference to the work of this great American authority on international law. I am proud of his lifelong friendship and grateful for his many kindnesses. At this time, curiously enough, he was teaching criminal law as well as international law. The latter subject was optional, and chosen only by a few students. The course in criminal law was given in leisurely fashion, more in the nature of a seminar. Judge Moore had come to the Law School from the State Department, where he had already served with great distinction and to which he was destined to return time and time again on leave of absence to accomplish specific tasks requiring his unique ability and experience. Some of the students thought Moore's courses rather dull because he made no attempt to be "dynamic" according to the custom of the period. This was a mistaken viewpoint, because he looked upon the administration of criminal justice from the larger angle of the welfare of the state and not as a mere application of legal principles drawn from the authority of earlier cases. He was particularly interesting in the discussion of criminal cases involving our relations with foreign countries, such as the Cutting Case with Mexico, with which he had an active part while in the State Department.

After graduation from the Law School, I entered the office of Samuel M. Fleischman as a law clerk, in order to obtain the experience with practice and procedure which could not be obtained at the Law School. As Chief Judge Arthur Vanderbilt of New Jersey said a few years ago, "Skill in the use of procedure—the lawyer's kit of tools—is still left to be acquired in the rigor of private practice, often at the client's expense." Fortunately for me, my employer was also my preceptor. Fleischman had a somewhat different background than most of the practitioners in the large city. He had come down from Albany, where the practice of the law was not then so specialized. He took pains to acquaint me with routine procedure, both office practice and the trial of cases. I assisted in trials as junior counsel and in the preparation of appeal briefs. As I look back, I am reminded that many of our opponents afterwards sat as Justices of the New York Supreme Court in the County of New York, so that the experience I was gaining at the Bar was in the best tradition. Charles C. Burlingham, speaking of a period of about twenty years earlier, says, "We law clerks—that's what we were called and what we were—were poorly paid, not more than ten dollars a week, but we were members of the Bar, and our elders treated us with courtesy as brethren, and we got to know them." This was also true of the period of which I write.

After one year I determined to open my law office. I had opportunities to join a firm but I preferred to remain independent, not wishing to be tied down by any routine of service. I knew that I would be obliged to be abroad frequently, for a number of my prospective clients lived abroad and others had branches in foreign countries. I was at once made aware of my woeful lack of knowledge of foreign legal terms, and though I could read French and German fairly well I had little speaking capacity in those languages and, worst of all, was greatly confused by correspondence using legal terminology of which a literal translation would prove more confusing than enlightening. I usually took my vacations in Europe and visited the great University of Heidelberg, which, in the first years of the present century, was attended by many American students, though not, of course, in law. I had only been in practice a few years when I determined to take up the study of law in some

European university in those selected branches which would be most likely to be useful in my own practice. Dean John W. Burgess was the head of the Political Science Department of Columbia during my student years. He was widely celebrated both here and abroad as a teacher of constitutional law. I had taken his excellent courses while at Columbia. I knew that he had studied at Göttingen University in his younger days, and, accordingly, consulted him about my plan. He warmly approved and advised me to go to Göttingen, where the celebrated authority in the field of private international law, Ludwig von Bar, was still living, although quite old. I went to Europe in the summer of 1903, and made inquiries about von Bar. Unfortunately, he had become inactive. Perhaps I should have said "fortunately," because this circumstance led me to visit some of the well known law teachers in Switzerland. I am sure that Switzerland was better suited to the needs of an American lawyer than Germany would have been. Switzerland has a federal constitutional system not very different from our own inasmuch as there are large fields of jurisdiction still reserved to the cantons. This was perhaps more true in 1903 than it is today because of the coming into force, in 1912, of the Swiss Civil Code applicable to the whole of Switzerland. However, the analogy still remains valid. Furthermore, the independence of the judiciary and the advanced liberal democratic system which pervades both law and society give to Switzerland an advantage over most other continental European countries as a place of study for American students in the fields of law and political science.

I enrolled as a graduate student in the Law Department of the University of Zurich in 1904. Law teaching was under the old system of lectures, without much cooperation demanded from the student. Some of the professors made notable exceptions. Friedrich Meili conducted courses in private international law and in comparative law. He was a jurist after my own heart. He had practiced actively at the Bar for twenty years. He was a gifted linguist and therefore also familiar with foreign legal systems as well as his own. Conflicts of law are frequent in the courts of Switzerland not only as between the laws of the several cantons but more particularly between Swiss and foreign law. Meili had also served for years as a judge of the highest court of his own canton. Meili's specialty was, of course, private international law or conflict of laws; but, like his eminent fellow countryman of a slightly earlier period, Professor J. C. Bluntschli, he was considered an authority also on questions of public international law. His opinions rendered in the Delagoa Bay controversy between Great Britain and Portugal and in the controversy between Germany and Russia over expropriations by the latter country during the Russo-Japanese War are well known and frequently referred to. The courses which I attended were in public and private international law and in comparative law. These courses were by no means lectures in the manner prevalent in European universities but were interspersed with discussion and comment between teacher and student. An American law student would have been immediately struck by the contrast in the method employed by even so progressive a jurist as Meili because of the predominance of reference to legislation rather than to jurisprudence.

The basic law of the countries of the Continent of Europe is derived mainly from the Roman civil law, particularly from codifications running back to the Corpus Juris Civilis promulgated in the sixth century by the Emperor Justinian. Our own Story and Kent were almost as much at home in the civil law as in the common law, but students of the period of which I speak, and perhaps even today, do not realize the essential difference of approach between the civil-law lawyer and the common-law lawyer. Accordingly, in order to understand the jurisprudence of European countries, it is necessary to be instructed in the fundamentals of the civil law of Rome. These courses are frequently referred to as instruction in the Pandects. To this research I now addressed myself by taking courses which might have seemed more like a study in legal antiquities than like a matter of practical interest to the average American lawyer. I was fortunate in being able to attend courses by a brilliant Roman-law scholar, Herman Hitzig. I also followed the courses of George Cohn in branches of early Germanic law. Curiously enough, the instruction of the latter-named was of particular interest to a common-law student because he had made a profound study of early Saxon law and especially of Saxon law terms which, when set in the proper light of etymological derivation, seemed not at all unfamiliar.

Before leaving New York for study abroad, I was given a letter by John Bassett Moore to Max Huber, professor of international law at Zurich. He had traveled extensively in the United States and had a wide acquaintance with the current problems of international politics as well as of international law. I followed his courses with the greatest interest. He later became a member of the Permanent Court of International Arbitration and for some years was also the Presiding Judge of the Permanent Court of International Justice at The Hague.

While pursuing these studies, Meili's well known treatise *Das internationale Civil und Handelsrecht auf Grund der Theorie, Gesetzgebung und Praxis,* which had appeared a year or two earlier, was the subject of frequent reference. With Meili's consent and warm encouragement I undertook to translate this work with my own additions of English and American law. More than twenty years had elapsed since any comprehensive work in this field had been translated into English. Savigny's treatise on modern Roman law had contained a part devoted to the conflict of laws which had been translated by William Guthrie. Von Bar's great work had been translated by Gillespie under the title *International Law, Private and Criminal,* published in 1883. Meili's work contained long extracts from French as well as from German authorities, and its translation into idiomatic English with the use of parallel English legal terminology served as a useful drill in foreign languages as well as in foreign law.

The completed work was brought out by Macmillan's in 1905 in New York and London under the title *International Civil and Commercial Law As Founded upon Theory, Legislation, and Practice. Translated and Supplemented with Additions of American and English Law.* It had a wider circulation than I could have expected, and after a number of years it was out of print. I think the reason for this was that Meili gave as much attention to the citation of cases as to the opinions of jurists. Of course my own additions followed the recognized method of legal commentaries in the Anglo-American sphere.

Reviews of my book appeared in most of the principal law reviews here and abroad. Its reception was more favorable than I had expected. Judge Simeon E. Baldwin, afterward governor of Connecticut, concluded his review in the *Yale Law Journal* for January, 1906, with the following remarks, which showed that at least the purpose of my work had been understood: "No lawyer can ever safely assume the conduct of a cause in a foreign country. He must rely on local counsel for the ultimate direction of its course; but a book like that under review will help him greatly, both in giving advice to such an associate and in understanding advice given by him. It is a good guidepost, and it is good to have guideposts as well as guides."

4. *The International Law Association*

While translating Meili's work, I was struck by the frequent references which it contained to the discussions and the draft statutes of the International Law Association. I became a member of the association and attended its 1905 conference held at Oslo, then Christiania. It was founded at Brussels in 1873, and was originally called the Association for the Reform and Codification of the Law of Nations. The idea for such an association was suggested by an American, Elihu Burritt, "the learned blacksmith." The idea reached fruition through the work of Dr. James Miles of the American Peace Society and a distinguished group of American and other jurists, prominent among whom was David Dudley Field, draftsman of the Civil Code of New York and also of a Code of International Law. Other distinguished American jurists and publicists who took part in its early activities were Senator Charles Sumner of Massachusetts, President Theodore Woolsey of Yale, and President Frederick Barnard of Columbia. When the association was organized in 1873, there was a strong belief, both among American as well as among foreign jurists, that a code of international law must precede any general resort to international arbitration and that the want of such a code was the great obstacle hindering the general substitution of arbitration for war.

As so frequently happens in the affairs of man, the institution developed in a manner quite different from the plan conceived by its founders. These men believed they were founding an organization which would be limited to problems of the law of nations and the maintenance of peace. It soon developed that there would be little hope for peaceful cooperation if the problems of private international trade on land and sea were to be left unsolved. Accordingly, along with subjects of the codification of international law, the association soon found itself dealing with maritime questions and the conflict of law between nations. Under its liberal rules of membership, the association welcomed not only specialists in these subjects but also laymen directly interested, such as shipowners, underwriters, delegates from chambers of commerce, and industrialists. In this it differed radically from the Institut de Droit International, which was founded in the same year (1873), at Ghent. The Institute was and still remains an academy of legal specialists with a strictly limited membership. I remember Wyndham Bewes of London saying that the inspiration of both organizations was to be traced to the successful termination, through the Geneva Arbitration, of the acrimonious dispute between Great Britain and the United States over the damage caused by the Confederate cruiser *Alabama*.

The Oslo Conference was held in the spacious building of the Nobel Committee of the Norwegian Parliament, the body designated by the founder of the Nobel Peace Prize to make this award. I was surprised to find that I was the only American lawyer in attendance excepting Cephas Brainerd. Brainerd was a fine representative of the old school of American lawyers of the period of Charles O'Conor and William M. Evarts. He brought a welcome current of humor and eloquence to the serious discussions of the conference. He had served on important finance committees in New York during the panic of

1873. Later, I had occasion to meet both Cephas and his son Ira in the course of my practice, not always on my side of the case. We became warm friends, as opponents frequently do, perhaps more in the law than in most other professions. American influence in the association had lessened over the three decades of its existence. In later years we were able to effect a change, and today the American branch is one of the most active of all.

The British members were the most numerous because the headquarters of the association were and still are in London. Their leader at this time was Sir Walter George Phillimore, son of Sir Robert Phillimore, the celebrated author of a treatise on international law. George Grenville Phillimore, cousin of Sir Walter, was general secretary of the association and devoted much of his time to its work. He was preparing a new and monumental edition of the well known work of William Burge on colonial and foreign laws. At his invitation I became editor of the material relating to American law for the new edition.

Sir Walter Phillimore exemplified the highest type of public service. Although he was at this time one of the judges of the Probate, Divorce, and Admiralty Division of the High Court of Justice, he devoted a large part of his time off the Bench to the various drafts and projects constituting the activities of the association with a view to the maintenance of peace upon a more firm foundation of law and justice. He was afterward elevated to the peerage and became one of the members of the Privy Council. He regarded these conferences as important because of the opportunity they presented of becoming better acquainted with the leaders of government and industry in the various capitals of the world. In this way a better understanding could be promoted and differences thrashed out by discussion and by pleasant social contacts. The country visited is likely to reciprocate the confidence implied in meeting within its borders. The ancient folkway of hospitality toward "the stranger within thy gates" is still a potent influence for the preservation of peace. It should be cultivated wherever possible.

Lord Phillimore prided himself upon understanding American

viewpoints and he was pleased to accentuate his American contacts. He informed me that he had come from the same family stock as our own President Fillmore. He was also proud as a young barrister to have served as junior counsel with Judah P. Benjamin, distinguished lawyer of New Orleans and successively Attorney General, Secretary of War, and Secretary of State of the Confederate States. Benjamin became an exile after the War Between the States and established himself in London, becoming one of the leaders of the English Bar. Lord Phillimore recounted some amusing anecdotes. In the argument of an important case before the Law Committee of the House of Lords, Benjamin was once interrupted in an abrupt manner by the presiding judge. He quickly brought the argument to a close and walked out of the room. He was recalled later, the judge making proper amends.

At the time we were meeting at Christiania, a serious crisis was being discussed at Karlsborg in Sweden near the border of Norway. These two Scandinavian countries had been connected through the person of the king. Norway had now demanded absolute separation, and commissioners from both countries were meeting at Karlsborg to arrange the terms. Our hosts showed considerable tension throughout the session but never had any doubt that the separation could be arranged peaceably. It was a fine exhibition, for all of us, of the highest qualities of good sense and public self-restraint.

In the autumn of 1905, I registered as a special student at the École de Droit in Paris. At that period the memory of the Franco-Prussian War had dimmed but was by no means eradicated. The statue of Strasbourg in the Place de la Concorde was still covered with mourning wreaths and black crepe. The courses in the Paris Law School which had to do with international law or foreign relations contained many references to the war and its results. Contrary to what I had been told, there was prevalent no spirit of revenge, but only one of confidence that this "injustice" would in due course be righted. Some of the professors took an exceedingly broad-minded view. I remember that Edmond Thaller, in his lectures on comparative commercial law, exhorted the students to forget past political differences and to cultivate a knowledge of the language and legal literature of Germany. This, he said, was in the direct interest of French legal science and of the French people. No one could ignore the importance of German world trade, and if the French were to compete upon equal terms, the French must not remain ignorant of the legal basis upon which this world-wide trade was conducted.

Instruction at the École was quite different from that which prevailed in Switzerland. The Law School was and still is in a large building near the Panthéon. The classes were extremely large, perhaps two or three hundred students. The classes always reminded me of pictures which I had seen of meetings of the French National Assembly in Revolutionary days. The seats were in tiers, and the professor, gowned in silk, was seated on a high podium below which was a bailiff in uniform who remained throughout the lecture. Under these circumstances there could be very little rapport between teacher and students. In all the courses which I attended, I never remember ever having heard a question asked by an auditor or any discussion initiated by the professor with any member of the class.

Besides the courses of Thaller, I took lectures in private international law under André Weiss and under Antoine Pillet. The latter I considered to be a particularly effective teacher because he regarded his subject not as a rigid system but as one capable of growth. He believed that it was the duty of jurists to develop it by interpretation and corrective legislation so as to meet the needs of international commerce and industry and of the private relations of persons under modern conditions.

The celebrated French authority in the field of public international law was then Louis Renault. He had also written a celebrated work on commercial law in collaboration with Charles Lyon-Caen. I had followed the latter's courses on this subject. Renault was at this period teaching international law at the École Libre des Sciences Politiques, which was an independent institution not connected with the university. The reputation of Renault as a publicist and teacher of international law was world-wide. He had long been adviser to the French Foreign Office. In looking around at the students in his class, one saw students representing many races and peoples not only from Europe but from Asia and northern Africa as well, some of them in their native dress. It was a unique picture in a classroom devoted to a subject which could scarcely be regarded as either colorful or romantic.

Renault always had before him a glass of water to which he added sugar from time to time, sipping it as the lecture proceeded. The material for his lectures was taken largely from his ripe experience in the French Foreign Office and was essentially a case method but with the discussion carried on only by the teacher. The students took no part, yet I came away from each lecture with the distinct feeling of having participated in the solution of real problems presented to the Foreign Office of a great state.

There were some other American students studying law in Paris at this time but not many. I remember Ellery Corey Stowell, who afterward taught international law at Columbia and later at the American University in Washington. I also remember Ramón Solorzano, who became a member of the Supreme Court of Nicaragua. I also met Serge de Chessin Chershevsky, a Russian student of great promise, whose mother was of French origin. Although trained in the law, he was interested more particularly in diplomacy. Though he came of an aristocratic family, he preferred the more democratic institutions of France, later becoming a professor at one of the universities in the south of France.

In the education of a lawyer interested in international practice, it is perhaps of equal importance to his technical training to become acquainted with the method of legal thought and practice of members of the Bar of other countries as well as of his own. I tried to cultivate friendship with French lawyers of standing and distinction. They were uniformly courteous and helpful. The Bar of the particular district holds a different relationship to judicial administration than do bar associations in the United States. In France the organized Bar as such is closely integrated with the courts, and its rules are strictly enforced. I became acquainted with some leaders of the Paris Bar, among others with Maître Fernand Labori, who had defended Captain Alfred Dreyfus at his second trial and through whose Herculean efforts Dreyfus's guilt was completely disproved. It was Maître Labori in person who was kind enough to take me through the Palais de Justice. I remember his explanation as to why the members of the Bar practicing before the Civil Tribunal could not practice before the Tribunal de Commerce. The branches of the former court are in the Palais, whereas the latter occupies a building of its own on the other side of the street. The barrister in France is compelled to appear before the court properly clothed in the costume of his office. This, therefore, made it inconvenient for the practitioner in one court to practice interchangeably before the other tribunal. This fortuitous circumstance was doubtless reinforced by another; namely, that the judges of the Tribunal de Commerce consist of lay judges as well as of those trained in the law. In a celebrated case in which I later had a part before the New York courts, it was contended by opposing counsel that for this reason the Tribunal de Commerce was really not a court at all. I shall have occasion to refer to the case later, but it is needless to say that the argument found no favor with the New York Court of Appeals.

5. *Reform of the Consular Service*

While in Paris I became a member of the American Chamber of Commerce, a body which for many years had prompted not only the trade interests of Americans in France but also conditions leading to more advanced legislation and more enlightened administration of laws affecting international commerce. At this period there was a strong demand for improvement in our consular service, and I was asked to analyze the bill introduced in the Senate by Senator Lodge of Massachusetts for the reorganization of the consular service. My paper was published in the bulletin of the American Chamber of Commerce for March, 1906. Americans at home and abroad complained of the lack of efficiency in the consular service. The details of import and export require a knowledge of technical matters not possessed by the usual political appointee. As a result of my paper,

I was appointed a delegate, together with the treasurer of the Chamber of Commerce to attend the convention held in Washington in support of the bill for reform of the consular service promoted by the various chambers of commerce throughout the United States. The bill as finally passed initiated many elements of much-needed reform. The report which we made to the Paris Chamber on our return in April, 1906, recognized that at least a beginning had been made, although the features of the bill relating to the necessity for preliminary examination for consular office and for direct promotion on a merit system had been eliminated. The members of the convention had made every effort to have these features retained and had invited Secretary of State Root, Senator Lodge, and Representative Adams to address the convention in person. These gentlemen appeared before the convention but were convinced that the reform in its weakened text was all that could be obtained and that half a loaf was better than no bread. We had the satisfaction of feeling that at least we had assisted in making a beginning of consular reform. The resolutions of the Convention of 1906, even with the progress made since that time, are still appropriate today.

"The rapid development of agricultural and industrial interests demand that we require a much larger share of the world's trade than that which we control today. If the enterprise, the initiative, the ability and the resources of our people were supplemented by that assistance in foreign markets which can be given by a body of thoroughly efficient consular representatives, it is unquestionable that it would facilitate in no small measure the efforts of the United States to achieve that prominence in foreign trade which they have in other directions. Unless we have that assistance, however, the development of our foreign commerce will be seriously retarded, to the great detriment of our people."

The consular service has been greatly improved since this early period, and it is now a part of the Foreign Service of the United States, under which officers within the State Department are frequently sent abroad either into the consular or into the diplomatic service, thus tending to create a career service in the true sense.

~~~ II ~~~

Pathways in Practice

1. *Legal Fictions*

The old saying "Out of sight, out of mind" applies as well to the legal profession as to others. My resumption of law practice in New York after an absence of three years abroad was not without its difficulties. However, I soon became drawn into matters involving conflicts of law or of jurisdiction.

A large number of stockholders in a Minnesota corporation were residents of New York State. The company had conducted a department store and had become insolvent. Under the Minnesota Constitution a stockholder of any corporation other than one carrying on a manufacturing or mechanical business is liable for its debts up to the amount of the par value of the stock held or owned by such stockholder. Similar provisions are contained in the Constitution of Kansas and perhaps of some other States. Legislation passed under the provisions of clauses such as these allows the receiver of an insolvent corporation to assess the joint liability of all the stockholders in an equity proceeding. The statute in Minnesota provided that the assessment thus levied should be conclusive against all stockholders "whether appearing or having notice thereof or not." The receiver of the Minnesota corporation obtained a decree of assessment from the Minnesota court and afterward proceeded against a large number of stockholders resident in New York. Some of these became my clients. I believed that there had been a failure of due process of law because the assessment proceedings assumed to bind stockholders in another State who were not parties properly under the jurisdiction of the Minnesota court. Even assuming that the receiver succeeded to the rights of the Minnesota corporation, he would then be an adverse party to its own stockholders, and the court certainly could not acquire jurisdiction as against stockholders merely by making their *adverse* party a party in the proceeding. We are looking at the matter from the interstate and international point of view. Residents of Minnesota might be bound, but surely a foreign court or the court of another State would protect its own citizens from liability under a procedure in which they were not properly represented. As a matter of fact, the courts of New York had taken this view. The receiver in other cases, however, brought actions in the *Federal* courts. Curiously enough, the issue was presented to the Supreme Court by a former classmate of mine, Laurence Tanzer. Action was brought in the United States District Court of New York by the receiver of a Minnesota corporation against one of his clients. Although most ably presented, the objections of the stockholder were overruled (Bernheimer *v.* Converse, 206 U.S. 516, Justice Holmes dissenting). The Court sanctioned the enforcement of the double liability of the stockholder as being "contractual in its nature," yet said it was "not entirely contractual and springs primarily from the law creating the obligation." This view I considered to be a clear violation of the usual rules of the conflict of laws, because if the cause of action could have arisen only in one place, namely Minnesota, it was not "transitory" from the point of view of interstate or international law. The Supreme Court of New Hampshire had expressed this view most aptly when it held that "the organic, or statute, or common law of no State in the Union has conferred upon its courts authority to put into active operative effect, efficient *per se*, the statutes of another State."

There is no other redress for a member of the Bar who finds his contention overruled by the Supreme Court of the United States than to draw attention to its error before a wider audience in the hope of subsequent correction. This gives to the loser at least a sort of mental surcease. I promptly sought this relief by publishing an article in the *Yale Law Journal* (April, 1908) entitled "The Extraterritorial Enforcement of Statutes Imposing Double Liability upon Stockholders." By this time my discussion of the subject in opposition to the rule adopted by the United States Supreme Court had become truly objective. Some of my clients had already agreed to a compromise settlement while, for another, I was able to escape liability for a different reason. This client had taken title to the stock as collateral for a loan although the stock was issued in the name of my client. However, by great good fortune, the secretary of the company had made a marginal note in the stockbook showing that the stock was held only as collateral. Although I was obliged to take the case to the Supreme Court of Minnesota, my client was saved from liability by this fortuitous circumstance.

The lesson which I attempted to draw from these cases was that courts sometimes carry to excess their power of so-called "judicial construction"—in other words, of setting up fictions to justify conclusions believed to be just. I said: "By this process, the most deeply rooted principles of jurisprudence may gradually be made to give way. A foreign receiver may now sue in a local jurisdiction, as constructive (*quasi*) assignee and successfully urge a conclusive assessment made in the foreign jurisdiction pursuant to a contract wholly constructive, against stockholders, in fact absent and without notice, but constructively represented by a corporation, in fact defunct, but constructively still able to represent its stockholders."

The decision of cases by the introduction of fictions is particularly objectionable when the result reached seems to be unjust. I had occasion some years later to call this to the attention of a wider audience while discussing the well known Ju Toy Case (198 U.S. 253) before the American Society of International Law. A person of the Mongolian race, claiming to have been born in the United States, was returning from a visit to China. Although his claim of United States citizenship was uncontradicted on the evidence, the administrative officials in California refused him reentry. He sued out a writ of habeas corpus, but the Supreme Court of the United States refused to review the denial of the writ under the fiction that he was not physically in the United States.

In my discussion I said (*Proceedings*, 1911, p. 211): "Now fictions are at best very dangerous proceedings. If fictions were adopted in science, I fear that the building of the Panama Canal would not be an easy problem, and if this hotel were built upon a fiction, I fear that none of us would sit here with the equanimity we all seem to have at the present moment. . . . We often speak of the 'inalienable right' of the citizen and yet it does appear to me that the right most inalienable of all is the right to prove citizenship before a judicial body."

Mr. Justice Brewer dissented from the opinion of the Court in the Ju Toy Case and referred to the result there reached as "abhorrent." I had the satisfaction some years later to observe that the Supreme Court corrected this "abhorrent" result in the Chin Yow Case (208 U.S. 8) under a different legal theory and without the assumption of any fiction.

There is an impression prevalent even today that questions involving the conflict of laws or the application of foreign law arise only infrequently in the practice of the law. This is a misapprehension. Perhaps another example of a case which came to me may prove interesting.

2. *Proof of Foreign Law*

While I was working one day in the office, a stranger strolled in without being announced. "I am Clarence Darrow and have a letter from a friend of yours. I am wondering whether you can help me." I knew Darrow, by reputation only, as one of the ablest trial lawyers of the Midwest. He afterward became nationally famous, if not world famous, by reason of his defense of Scopes, a teacher charged with implanting the "dangerously subversive" doctrine of the evolution of species in the minds of his students; William Jennings Bryan was for the prosecution. Darrow said that he had come from the

West to aid his friend William English Walling, or Walling English, as he was afterward better known. Action in the New York Supreme Court had been brought against him by Miss G. for breach of a promise of marriage alleged to have been made by him in Switzerland. There was evidence that the parties had lived together and used an American passport in which the defendant was described as being accompanied by "his wife." The defense relied upon was that the defendant, a prominent writer on socialism, had met the plaintiff in connection with their common studies abroad and, at her request, had agreed to accompany her back to her native Russia in order to visit her family there. This she would have been unable to do on a passport of her own because of the refusal of czarist Russia to grant visas to American citizens of Jewish origin. The specific question upon which Darrow wished to have my opinion was whether the law of Switzerland, more particularly of the Canton of Geneva in which the promise was made, would recognize an action for breach of contract to marry. This was important because an action for damages for a wrong committed in a foreign state or country is dependent upon the law of that state or country. I advised Darrow that under the law of Geneva, where the parties resided at the time of the alleged promise, no cause of action for unliquidated damages was recognized upon the breach of a promise to marry, but only for the specific expenses which had been paid or incurred by reason of the promise. At the trial of the action, I appeared as a witness learned in the law of Switzerland. Foreign law must be proved as facts are proved. In corroboration of my testimony, I was able to present official copies of the codes applicable to this question under Swiss law. The case went to the jury upon all the facts adduced at the trial and not specifically upon any of the expert testimony. The two issues, first, as to the making of the promise and its consequences, and second, as to the foreign law applicable, might have been separated, but they were not. The verdict of the jury was for the defendant.

The New York evening newspapers of March 3, 1911, reported the trial at considerable length, doubtless because of its sensational features and the prominence of the defendant and his counsel Clarence Darrow. The case attracted attention because the law of another country had become involved in the trial of an action of so personal a nature as the breach of a promise to marry. The publicity which the case received resulted in my receiving many requests to testify as a witness on the law of certain European countries. Some of the other cases I shall have occasion to mention, but I was not anxious to accept requests of this kind. An expert witness on a question of foreign law must be very sure of his ground because otherwise he may be confronted with some unpleasant surprises on cross-examination. On the other hand, it is sometimes a professional duty to respond in cases of this kind in order to assist in reaching a just result. Under our present system it is very difficult to present proof of a foreign law in open court, for there are few persons available who have been admitted to the Bar of the particular foreign jurisdiction or who are qualified by training or experience to be acceptable for expert testimony.

The presentation of testimony on foreign law is related to the general problem of obtaining the testimony of foreign witnesses for use in legal proceedings within the United States. This problem is sometimes referred to as "international judicial assistance." It has become more acute today than it was a quarter-century ago because, since the close of World War II, our courts have received a large number of cases with international or extraterritorial ramifications. Harry Leroy Jones of the Department of Justice discussed the problem unofficially before the 1951 meeting of the American Society of International Law. He said:

"The large number of cases in our courts in which proof of foreign law is necessary makes that problem a considerable one. The difficulty of finding, and the expense of retaining, expert witnesses, and their uncertainty of proof of foreign law as a fact, particularly in view of the paucity of legal materials from abroad in most of our libraries, make proof of foreign law a real challenge."

The Harvard Research in International Law prepared a draft convention in 1939 which contains a provision for obtaining information on foreign law through an official certificate to be issued by a designated agency of the particular foreign government. This is a common practice in European countries, and it might be adopted with advantage under proper restrictions by legislation in the United States.

~ III ~

Pathways in the Public Interest

1. *Beginning of International Air Law*

While in Europe during the summer of 1908, I had occasion to visit my old teachers at the Law School in Zurich. Max Huber and Meili were still active with their classes. Meili was known for his reliance upon the most ancient as well as the most modern precedents. He once exclaimed that a solution of a new problem without reference to the old authorities invited the danger of establishing principles "without roots." John Bassett Moore knew Meili very well as a colleague of the Institut de Droit International. He told me once of a visit which he paid at Meili's home, when he was ushered in without being announced. He saw the old gentleman sitting near the window with a great quarto volume of the Corpus Juris Civilis, and so absorbed in study that he did not become aware of his visitor's presence for some time. It would be wrong to conclude from this that his interests were those of an antiquary. Quite the contrary was true, because he was one of the earliest jurists to write on the law of the automobile and also of wireless telegraphy in international commerce.

On the occasion of my visit to him in 1908, Meili very proudly presented me with a copy of his most recent monograph *Das Luftschiff im internen Recht und Völkerrecht* (The Airship in Municipal Law and in International Law). He explained that he was impelled to deal with the subject, having witnessed a successful flight by Count von Zeppelin in his new airship. "I felt that I had to follow him," he said. The international problems relating to air navigation had already been considered by the Institute of International Law particularly in the notable report of Paul Fauchille. However, Meili carried his investigations much further and dealt not only with the international law but also with the domestic law. This, he held, must be relied upon to assure the airworthiness of any aircraft, whether undertaking flight within the state or beyond it. In developing his ideas, he referred to the ancient law of Rome, where airships were undreamt of, and of course to the modern private law of the principal European states.

When I returned home, I felt that something of the kind ought to be attempted from the point of view of American law and administrative procedure. Accordingly, I prepared a paper to be read before the American Political Science Association at its annual meeting held at Johns Hopkins University in Baltimore in December, 1908. Whenever physical, chemical, or electrical science introduces new forces into the life of man, it may reasonably be conceived to be the task of jurisprudence to adjust and coordinate the legal relations both of states and of individuals under the new conditions. In 1908 air navigation was, of course, only in its infancy, and it was only with much diffidence, indeed, in an apologetic mood, that I ventured to present the subject for consideration. I said, "Whether it may ultimately serve the purposes of commerce in a larger sense, though not negatived, has not yet been demonstrated, nor is it necessary for the purpose of the present discussion." If I apologized then for having discussed the subject, I feel apologetic now for not having realized the enormous, almost dominant role, which its development has brought about in the affairs of the human race. At least I realized that air navigation was in its infancy and almost sure to make rapid progress. "Jurisprudence follows the path of science as the flag of a nation follows the territorial explorations of its subjects."

The members of the Political Science Association received the paper with courteous attention but with no great enthusiasm. There was no discussion whatever, and no questions were asked of the speaker. My old political-science teacher, Frank J. Goodnow, afterward president of Johns Hopkins remarked, as we left the hall, "It is all very interesting but, I am afraid, long ahead of the game." I suppose it was. Charles Warren, author of the standard work on the history of the Supreme Court of the United States, remarked some years later that I had pioneered the subject, and John C. Cooper, director of the Institute of International Air Law, in his comprehensive work on the law of aircraft, suggests that my address was perhaps the first publication in the English language on international air law. He credits me with having been the first to suggest a system of governmental inspection for aircraft like that prevailing over ships of the sea, together with registration of all aircraft within a given state in a particular locality established by law.

I was soon deluged with requests to enlarge upon the ideas presented in 1908. The art of air navigation was making more rapid strides than could have been anticipated. In the following year I prepared a more extended paper for the *American Journal of International Law*. In less than two years it was necessary to take note of the fact that "longer and more regular flights have been recorded by both the dirigible balloon and the aeroplane type of aircraft. . . . A great number and variety of aircraft are being built for state as well as private uses in large establishments. . . . Great nations have established a special aeronautic service for use in conjunction with both the army and the navy." On the other hand, I was obliged to admit that there was as yet little attention devoted to the subject in the United States. Before 1910 there was not much air navigation practiced on American soil by American pilots. Furthermore, the wide expanse of our home territory and its isolation by two great oceans postponed the international and military problems which had already become practical in Europe. This isolataion of the American continent from the danger of air bombardment was to disappear only too soon. The first Hague Peace Conference of 1899 had adopted a proposal prohibiting the "throwing of projectiles or explosives of any kind from balloons, or by any similar means." A treaty was later ratified by many nations to this effect, providing a time limit of five years for the prohibition. By the end of 1909, the time limit had expired, and many of the nations, including France, Germany, and Russia, which had ratified the first treaty, refused to ratify its extension. Great Britain, which had failed to ratify the first treaty, ratified the second. This induced me to say: "Reluctant as we may be in arriving at such a conclusion, the change of front can be satisfactorily explained only by the change in the technical position of the respective Powers in their land and naval forces and the relative advance that each has made in aeronautics." The military isolation of Great Britain could no longer be assumed, since it was demonstrated that airplanes could cross the English Channel.

I have gone to some length in reviewing the situation of this early period because it is by no means without its serious lesson to all nations at the present day. Regulations of the conduct of warfare sufficient to control the use of new weapons will depend upon the technical position of the respective Powers at the particular moment. A notable exception was made at the end of the Second World War by the United States through its generous offer to place the control of the atomic bomb under international supervision before it was believed that any other nation was in full possession of the secrets of the bomb. The result of a policy of opportunism with respect to the laws of war has resulted in the lamentable peril which now threatens the human race.

2. *The Treaty-Making Power of the United States*

During the period in which I first became interested in the control of the state over its airspace, I had reason to inquire how far the Federal Government could go in making treaties having a binding character over the separate States. The treaty-making power granted by the Constitution had never been elucidated in any comprehensive manner. The treaty power is still controversial. Up to this time it could fairly be said that disputes had been comparatively few in respect to the interpretation of our organic law under Article VI of the Constitution. In 1907 a serious question had arisen under the Treaty with Japan of 1894, which assured residents of both parties in the territory of the other, rights of residence under the most-favored-nation clause. A denial of access of children of Japanese residents in California to the same schools frequented by the children of citizens and alien whites brought up the question of the treaty-making power. This question I endeavored to explore in an article in the *Columbia Law Review* (1908) under the title "The Treaty-Making Power and the Reserved Sovereignty of the States." The scope of such power was widely discussed at the time in California, although in reality the question was one of the interpretation of the treaty. The limitations upon the treaty-making power, if any, had never been authoritatively defined. Now that we have passed the mid-century mark, the scope of the power is still problematic, although the United States has exercised the treaty power over a vast field in which the States formerly considered themselves to be sovereign. This is especially true now, when so many specialized agencies created under the authority of the League of Nations and the United Nations deal with social and economic problems which ordinarily remain academic unless embodied in conventional international agreements.

The issue was brought to a head through the Draft Covenant on Human Rights, which recognizes a large number of social and economic so-called "rights" which, if embodied in a convention, might tend to upset the recognized constitutional limitations of State and Federal power under our Constitution. A similar objection has been raised with reference to a proposed convention for establishing a Permanent Court of Criminal Justice. Although the powers of the court are to be strictly limited to crimes definable as being international, fear has been expressed that State courts might lose their freedom to act in behalf of the protection of due process of law. It has even been proposed that the Constitution should be amended to change the automatic effect of treaties as part of the law of the land, and to require executory legislation from Congress. This will remain a subject of controversy for some time to come.

Without discussing the merits of these contentions, the main judicial test is, as indicated in the case of the Japanese treaty, whether the subject matter is a proper subject for regulation by treaty according to the custom and practice of nations. The treaty-making power should not attempt to engage upon indirect methods of social reform through treaty legislation without proper reservations within the treaty for submission to the proper legislative authority.

3. *Founding of the American Society of International Law*

The treaty power had been the subject of discussion at the very first annual meeting of the American Society of International Law, held in April, 1907, in connection with the wider topic of "The Rights of Foreigners in the United States in Case of Conflict Between Federal Treaties and State Laws." I digress here to mention the organization of this important body which has played so great a role in the education of students interested in international law both public and private. The inspiration for the formation of a society for the advancement of international law and for the establishment of a journal as the organ of the society must be traced to the meetings of the Lake Mohonk Conference on International Arbitration, to which I shall have occasion to refer later. As a result of an exchange of views in the course of its 1905 meeting at Lake Mohonk, an informal committee met on a number of occasions at the residence of former Ambassador Oscar S. Straus. The laboring oar was taken by James Brown Scott, a member of the Columbia law faculty. There were also present John Bassett Moore, George W. Kirchwey, Chandler P. Anderson, and others. A constitutive meeting was called to be held at the Association of the Bar in the City of New York on January 12, 1906, to which I was invited. I took part in the discussions. Others who were present and took part, besides the organizing committee, were William M. Ivins, Judge William L. Penfield, Frederic R. Coudert, and Everett P. Wheeler. The need for a distinctively American organization was argued on a high intellectual level. However, I remember at least one amusing incident which indicated that not all those present appreciated the various phases of the legal problems in international life. One speaker thought that the International Law Association founded at Brussels in 1873 was "honeycombed with commercialism" because, forsooth, some of its membership consisted of groups active in international trade, such as chambers of commerce, shipowners, maritime committees, and the like.

From the very beginning of our national existence, the people of the United States were keenly interested in the common law of nations. In the Ordinance of 1781, passed before the recognition of our independence, Congress professed obedience to the law of nations "according to the general usages of Europe," and in being admitted to the family of nations the new Republic recognized international law as binding. The Constitution conferred upon Congress the power to punish "offenses against the law of nations." The Supreme Court has repeatedly declared that "international law is a part of our law, and must be ascertained and administered by the courts of justice of appropriate jurisdiction as often as questions of right depending upon it are duly presented for their determination." (*The Paquete Habana*, 1899, 175 U.S. 677, 700).

Elihu Root became the first president of this society. Its first annual meeting took place on April 19, 1907, and it was at this meeting that one of the principal subjects discussed was the rights of foreigners under treaties. President Root indicated that a mere colorable exercise of the treaty power would not be upheld. This, of course, referred to an attempt to make provisions regarding matters not the proper subjects of international agreement. President Root had dealt with the Japanese treaty in his usual statesmanlike manner, and I took part in order to reinforce the points made by quoting a letter from Hamilton to Washington in which Hamilton said, "There are no express limits to the treaty-making power, and it was a reasonable presumption that it was meant to extend to all treaties usual among nations and so to be commensurate with the variety of exigencies and objects of intercourse which might occur between nation and nation."

At the present time the problem of the treaty power has again been raised in connection with the Charter of the United Nations. Certain conventions elaborated under its authority have been opposed by some on the ground of possible trespass upon the criminal jurisdiction of the separate States. Without enlarging upon it, I may reiterate what I wrote in 1908: "If, however, owing to the peculiar structure of our political system, such limitations do exist, it is plain that the consequences may be serious; for the Federal Government may either find itself incapable of maintaining the integrity of a compact regularly entered into with some foreign power for the benefit of citizens or subjects of that power residing or sojourning in the United States, or as a corollary, it may find that it is powerless to enforce reciprocal provisions beneficial to our own citizens residing or sojourning within the territory of that power."

The lesson to be learned is that the United States should exercise great discretion at the time of the elaboration and drafting of treaties, especially of multilateral treaties such as those worked out under the auspices of the United Nations or its specialized agencies. The Declaration of Human Rights and the proposed Covenant to follow are excellent examples of the dangers which can follow from negotiations with a large number of countries whose public laws and whose ways of life are so different from our own. Undertakings no matter how high-minded in purpose must be scrupulously scanned with a view to avoid any which are not properly within the functions of our own Federal Government. This will avoid impinging on the powers and functions reserved to the several States. It is on this account that I have found the Genocide Convention acceptable for adoption as well within the functions of the Federal Government, whereas the broad and often ambiguous undertakings in the Human Rights Drafts may cause stresses and strains within our own political structure.

4. Teaching Law at Columbia University Law School

In 1909 I was invited to become a member of the teaching staff at Columbia Law School. The university had by this time become well established on Morningside Heights. John Bassett Moore had been granted a leave of absence in order to serve on the International Commission of Jurists appointed under the authority of the Pan American Union. This necessitated long periods of absence in Washington and in Latin American capitals. Accordingly, George Winfield Scott took over his courses in public international law while I was invited to give the course in conflict of laws, or, as it is sometimes called, private international law. At this period the dean of the Law School was George W. Kirchwey. He was not only a capable lawyer but a man of broad human interests. He was deeply interested in the cause of world peace, and although I had known him as a teacher of the law of real property he became one of the founders of the American Society of International Law. In later years he gave up his position at Columbia to become warden of Sing Sing Prison in order to demonstrate the advanced new methods of penology and prison reform advocated by Thomas M. Osborne.

When I began to teach at Columbia, the method had not greatly changed since my time as a student. The classes were much larger, however. Conflict of Laws was a third-year course. It was not a required subject and, accordingly, my classes were not so large as those of the first two years. The students were more mature, thus making the discussion much more interesting. The contact with young minds well trained in the underlying principles of the law and eager to discuss new and progressive pathways in the administration of justice should never be undervalued by practitioners at the Bar. Among students of outstanding ability I remember Wellington Koo, ambassador of China to the United States, Charles E. Martin, now professor at the University of Washington, Eustace Seligman, son of Edwin R. A. Seligman, my former teacher of economics, Samuel C. Coleman, now judge of the City Court of New York, and Hamilton Vreeland, Jr., afterward professor at New York University. The students found that the course served as a review of their other courses. Thus, one case might involve a conflict in the law of contracts, another of wrongs, and another in marriage and divorce.

5. *Abrogating the Russian Treaty Because of Religious Discrimination*

It was a coincidence but a strange one. Within one month after the trial in the celebrated Walling Case, which I have already described, the practice of Russia in discriminating upon religious grounds in granting visas to citizens of the United States became the subject of vigorous objection in Congress. It will be remembered that this discrimination gave rise to the chain of events leading up to the Walling trial. I was now to take part in helping to combat these discriminations. Complaints against the practice of Russia's interpretation of the Treaty of 1832 had been made over a long period of years to the President, to the Secretary of State, and to both Houses of Congress. The treaty regulated the rights of entry and of residence to be mutually enjoyed by the inhabitants of Russia and the United States in their respective territories. Secretaries of State Evarts, Blaine, Bayard, Olney, Hay, and Root had all declared the Russian position to be indefensible, and had sent various diplomatic notes in protest as being contrary to the American concept of equal rights of citizenship. The protests of individuals and groups within the United States now began to be more articulate, and vigorous insistence was heard that something definite be accomplished to remove these discriminations. Secretary Root expressed a sympathetic point of view but recommended revision of the treaty rather than its complete abrogation. On the other hand, the well known dilatory diplomacy of Russia induced members of the Committee on Foreign

Affairs of the House of Representatives to consider the abrogation of the treaty by the adoption of a joint resolution.

Russia claimed in defense of her practice that the treaty granted no greater rights to United States citizens than is accorded to Russian citizens of the same "class" in Russia.

In order to meet this and all other legal objections before the hearings to be held by the Committee on Foreign Affairs, the Board of Delegates on Civil Rights of the Union of American Hebrew Congregations and the Independent Order of B'nai B'rith prepared to take part in the hearings. My friend Max J. Kohler, always a valiant defender of civil rights irrespective of race, color, or creed, took an active part in collecting a record of the discriminations practiced by Russia under the treaty. The two groups determined to demand the abrogation of the treaty which had, by Russia's own interpretation, become unacceptable because it was inconsistent with the American way of life under the Constitution. I was requested to prepare a brief on the appropriate precedents of international law. Louis Marshall, one of the leaders of the New York Bar, presented my brief and made the chief argument in favor of the abrogation of the treaty.

The chairman of the Committee on Foreign Affairs was William Sulzer, who afterward became governor of the State of New York. In the report adopted by the committee, a joint resolution was approved in which it was declared "that the Government of the United States concludes its treaties for the equal protection of all classes of its citizens, without regard to race or religion." The committee set forth the main facts developed by the hearings and incorporated my brief in full without any changes as a part of its report. I was, of course, much gratified. It was published as a separate Congressional document, and I received an appreciative letter from the chairman of the Committee on Foreign Affairs.

The joint resolution was adopted by the House with only one member voting negatively. It was thought almost certain to pass the Senate. However, President Taft believed that the terms of the joint resolution would be offensive to Russia and that our relations might become strained. Accordingly, he gave notice to Russia of the intention of the United States to terminate the treaty. This was adopted and ratified by both Houses by a joint resolution approved on December 31, 1911.

The interpretation of treaties of entry and residence often raises serious disputes. It is of interest, therefore, to recount some of the points which I urged with reference to the Russian treaty. "The most meager reflection leads inevitably to the conclusion that if this [Russia's] contention were permitted to prevail as a guiding principle of international relations, not a single treaty in force with reference to the protection of the rights of citizens of one country within the territory of another could be deemed any longer the source of any definite rights or privileges. However definite might be the right or privilege granted by treaty to the citizens of a foreign state, it could be rendered nugatory simply by denying the right or privilege to native citizens. The acceptance of any such principle would revolutionize the relations of states upon the basis of conventions, and would extend the class distinctions made in one nation, beyond the borders of that nation to the territory of every other nation with which it had treaty relations affecting aliens."

My brief cited diplomatic history as far back as the administration of President Fillmore. The discriminations then complained of were practiced, strangely enough, by Switzerland. President Fillmore insisted that the proposed treaty being negotiated with Switzerland in 1855 should obviate the application of the same discriminations in the treatment of American citizens as were applied to native Swiss subjects. Great Britain, although recognizing the equality principle, did not insist on its enforcement abroad. Very different was the attitude of the French Government toward Switzerland with respect to discriminations of certain Swiss cantons toward French citizens because of creed. The French Government of the Second Empire repudiated treaties with Switzerland because of their failure to guarantee equal treatment to all French citizens without distinction of faith or worship. As a result the Swiss authorities reversed their original stand so that our minister there, George Fogg, wrote that they had taken a step "imperatively demanded by the spirit of the age and their own position as the vanguard of liberty in Europe."

The normal relation of states, especially under conditions of modern life, is one of free intercourse. This was recognized by Emmerich von Vattel as early as the eighteenth century. He contrasted the condition of China and Japan with that of Europe, where "the access is everywhere free to every person who is not an enemy of the state." If he were writing today, he would have to exclude Soviet Russia and the satellite states.

Continuing the argument, I said: "We would not wish to be understood as denying the theory of international law that in the absence of treaty, each state has the right to exclude aliens from its soil. This right is commonly spoken of as one of the essential attributes of sovereignty. However, when rights of entry or residence have been extended by treaty to the subjects of a foreign nation, all the subjects of that nation are entitled to the benefit of the treaty, even though incidentally they receive greater privileges under it than native subjects. . . . Furthermore, if distinctions of race or creed are permitted to enter into the status of our citizenship in foreign countries in respect of rights and privileges, it is inevitable that distinctions will likewise arise on the side of duties and obligations. The relationship of allegiance between the citizen and state is a mutual one. Thus, for example, a treaty of amity and friendship between two nations is binding upon all citizens and no distinctions among them ought to be or is permissible. . . . If every citizen is to be equally and personally pledged to abide by a treaty of amity and friendship, every citizen should likewise be equally and personally benefited without discrimination under treaties relating to the citizens of his country. . . . The treaty thus involves fundamental danger to the equality involved in republican institutions."

6. *At an Ancient Seat of Learning*

During the summer of 1911, I attended the Conference of the Internationale Vereinigung für Vergleichende Rechtswissenschaft

(International Union for Comparative Law) held in the halls of the University of Heidelberg, Germany. As I look back, I am startled when I realize how quickly the political atmosphere changes in the relationship of peoples and nations. So far as an American delegate could observe, all was sweetness and light in Germany at that time. There was not the slightest indication at Heidelberg that within three years there would come general upheaval and war between the principal countries of Europe, ultimately involving the United States and the whole world. There was only the best of good will manifested toward the members of the conference who came from foreign countries.

I was invited to speak before the conference and took as my subject "The Doctrines of Private International Law in England and America Contrasted with Those of Continental Europe." I pointed out that while it is not essential nor perhaps even desirable that the laws of all jurisdictions should tend toward uniformity throughout, yet the *system* of law applicable to a given state of facts or legal relationship should be the same, no matter in what forum a judgment concerning it is eventually pronounced. Although this seems to lie in a sphere remote from foreign affairs, I have always felt that wherever there is a very lively interchange of personal and industrial activities the diversity in law and in the administration of justice have a marked influence on the continuance of peaceful relations. The comity of nations played and still plays a great role in England and in the United States in determining what system of law should apply to a private controversy; and yet comity is a political concept and originally belonged entirely within the law of nations. It has lost much of its earlier friendly significance. On the Continent of Europe, the national law of the parties (*lex patriae*) still plays a predominant role in the application of law in a controversy between private individuals where there is a foreign element in the case. This also tends toward a narrowness of view and a barrier in the way of cooperation in the administration of justice. Discussing some of the technical questions involved, I concluded: "In an age when physical barriers between nations have been broken down by ever more efficient means of transportation and intercommunication and when guarantees for permanent friendship and peace are daily multiplying, a closer bond of interest in the administration of private justice, though long delayed, would seem to be inevitable."

I am afraid that in view of what happened only a few years later, I had not displayed any great foresight. Perhaps because the German Foreign Office was already trying to beguile the world with a show of friendly cooperation, it supported this conclusion. I was much surprised to have the paper, which I feared would be criticized, warmly received and discussed by the legal adviser to the German Foreign Office, Dr. Walther Simons. He admitted, indeed, that he personally was inclined to prefer the Anglo-Saxon principle of domicile for the application of law to that of nationality, which was only recently adopted by German law. It is interesting to recall that Dr. Simons afterward became Chief Justice of the German Reichsgericht. During the Hitler régime he resigned from the Court because of political interference with the independence of the judiciary. He was a guest of honor of the American Bar Association at its annual meeting held at Memphis, Tennessee, in 1929. His son Hans became president of the New School of Social Research.

Based upon my paper, I made three proposals, all of which were accepted by the section before which the paper was read:

I. That the Anglo-American and Continental spheres of jurisprudence, by making mutual concessions, should tend toward harmony in the rules for solving conflicts of law.

II. That an international commission be appointed to deliberate and report upon the best plan for effecting progress in this direction.

III. That Great Britain and the United States should send delegates to future conferences to be held at The Hague upon private international law, for the purpose of reporting thereon to their respective governments.

7. Legislative Drafting

While teaching at Columbia Law School, I took part in the early activities of the Legislative Drafting Research Bureau which first took form, I think, in the fertile mind of George Winfield Scott. He had been impressed with the excellent results accomplished in the field of scientific legislative drafting as carried on for the Houses of Parliament in England under the supervision of Sir Courtenay Ilbert. No comparable bureau existed in the United States at that time, although efforts had been made in some of the States, notably in Wisconsin. Winfield Scott was a man of learning, but his talents were never fully exercised. He could conceive a project and expound it eloquently to others, but seldom undertook himself to do the spadework necessary for its execution. He associated with the project Joseph P. Chamberlain, Thomas I. Parkinson, and Middleton Beaman. They were able scholars of politics inspired by Scott's conviction that here was a public service that needed to be done. I was asked to join the project but, though convinced of its importance, I was unable to devote the necessary time away from my practice. However, I assisted in research and drafting in some of the fields undertaken in the early days of the bureau.

One of these projects was the preparation of legislation improving our navigation and admiralty laws. This had been found to be necessary after the public had been aroused and profoundly shocked at the great loss of life in the sinking of the British steamship *Titanic,* on her maiden voyage from Southampton to New York, on April 14, 1912. She had collided with an iceberg on the high seas and sunk within a few hours, causing the loss of about two thousand lives and a total loss of vessel, cargo, personal effects, mails, and everything connected with the ship except certain lifeboats. The Senatorial committee which investigated the disaster, both as to the facts and as to need of change in our laws, was headed by Senator William Alden Smith of Michigan. He was energetic and eager to accomplish results but woefully ignorant of the custom of the sea. Senator Smith consulted the Drafting Bureau. I attended some of these consultations and remember the active part that was taken by Dr. William Draper Lewis, of the University of Pennsylvania Law School, who afterward performed such notable service as director of the American Institute of Law in its preparation of the Restatement of American Law. Senator Smith's investigation was thorough in its determination to bring out the facts. His lack of knowledge of the sea, however, sometimes proved ludicrous in the examination of the witnesses. One of the questions put to a sailor who had manned one of the lifeboats was something to this effect: "Now tell me what icebergs are made of"; to which the sailor laconically replied, "Ice, your honor." On another occasion he asked whether any of the passengers had been seen going into any of the airtight compartments of the ship. He afterward explained this question by saying that he knew that the passengers could not save themselves in that way but that they might prefer to go down with the ship. However these trivia did not prevent the results of the investigation from having great value, and much-needed legislation was passed for the greater safety of life at sea.

My own contribution to this movement, if it could be called a contribution, was through my contention that there should be a greater responsibility on the part of the shipowner for damages where the vessel was a total loss. The United States statute limited the liability of the shipowner to the value of the remnants of the vessel and pending freight, unless the accident was due to the direct negligence of the owner in person. I felt that it would be useful to make a comparison of this law with the statutes in other maritime countries, especially Great Britain. Under British law also, there is a limitation of liability, not beyond a certain amount of money for each ton of the ship's tonnage. Accordingly, in the case of the *Titanic* there would have been a very substantial fund for possible compensation to the families of those who had lost their lives in the disaster. As a matter of fact, the claimants endeavored to have the British law apply because the loss occurred on a British vessel upon the high seas and they therefore argued that the United States statute should not apply. The United States Supreme Court thought otherwise and applied the absolute limitation of our own statute, although the *Titanic* had never at any time entered the territory of the United States. My feeling was that, although some limitation of the shipowner's liability is just and reasonable, an absolute exemption after abandonment of the wreck was not likely to make shipowners take all possible precautions for the safety of life at sea. I pointed out that shippers and shipowners are almost invariably protected by insurance, whereas passengers seldom provide for the contingency of accident and are often of a class unfamiliar with the risk incurred or with the principle of insurance. As John Bassett Moore pointed out: "The preparation of legislation amendatory of our navigation and admiralty laws has also necessarily required an accurate knowledge both of the laws of other countries and of their operation. For the fact is always to be borne in mind that a knowledge of law, such as a draftsman should possess, signifies an acquaintance not only with the text of statutes and decisions, but also with the methods and results of their administration."

The Senatorial investigation of the *Titanic* disaster preceded the final decision by our courts of the shipowner's liability. In 1914 the United States Supreme Court decided that the shipowner was entitled to the exemption and limitation provided by United States law and statutes and that a United States court would entertain the proceeding to enforce the limitation of his liability (233 U.S. 718). I felt that an injustice had been done and that the application of United States law was unjustified. British law, though recognizing some limitation, would have been much more favorable. I undertook to review both the law and the proposals for change in an article in the *American Journal of International Law* (April, 1915) entitled "International Aspects of the Titanic Case." Mr. Justice Holmes, who wrote the opinion, recognized that the law of the flag, the British law, was the foundation for recovery against the shipowner, but that the law of the forum, United States law, could decline to enforce the obligation as being contrary to domestic policy. Without going into the technical details, it suffices that my reaction was as follows: "If then the rule in the *Titanic* must rest upon public policy, the result is indeed bizarre, for the principle thus forces the application of a *domestic* statute to the liability arising in respect of a *foreign* vessel foundering upon the *high seas,* so as to grant exemption in favor of an *alien* shipowner as against rights of action of *citizens* of the *United States.*"

There was some satisfaction in knowing that some of the rigid results reached in the Titanic Case were later changed by amendments to the United States statutes.

8. *The Lake Mohonk Conferences on Peace and Arbitration*

In the years just prior to World War I, I was a regular attendant at the Lake Mohonk Conference on International Arbitration. This organization was founded in 1895, through the vision and generosity of Albert K. Smiley, for the purpose of creating and directing public sentiment in favor of international arbitration and an international judicial system. Mr. Smiley was a Friend, or Quaker, a group which has done so much over the years in the cause of peace and mutual understanding. My own father, Herman Kuhn, lived among the Quakers when he came to this country as a young man in 1850, and, indeed, became an instructor at a small Quaker college at London Grove, Chester County, Pennsylvania. Accordingly, I felt and still feel deeply sympathetic with their point of view relating to the basis of peace.

Membership in the Lake Mohonk conferences was entirely by invitation. Mr. Smiley and his brother, Daniel Smiley, were accustomed to act as hosts at their Lake Mohonk Mountain House in Ulster County, New York, in May of each year, the conferences usually lasting about four or five days. The members of the conference were representative of all walks of life, education, business, labor, the Army and Navy, journalists, clergymen and leaders of public opinion generally, here and abroad. The Mohonk House was situated in the center of a landed holding of the Smileys of about 5,000 acres, consisting of mountain and forest scenery of supreme beauty, unspoiled by the inroads of our mechanistic civilization. The effectiveness of the conference lay in the fact that the addresses and discussions did not deal with peace propaganda but rather with the particular ideas which the members presented for overcoming impediments and devising machinery which would make less likely the recurrence of war. President Nicholas Murray Butler of Columbia, who frequently presided at the Mohonk conferences, once expressed this idea as follows: "Peace is not an ideal at all; it is a state attendant upon the achievement of an ideal."

At the 1915 session of this peace Olympiad, I made the following contribution: "It is with facts that life has to deal, and though abstract principles, noble sentiments, fine visions, glorious dreams should occupy us from time to time, there comes a time when it is right also to apply in some administrative way, the faith which we are willing not only to confess in the abstract but also to apply in the concrete." I then endeavored to be more "concrete" by applying my remarks to the war that had broken out in Europe just nine months previously but which had not yet attained the scope of a world-wide conflict. I tried to compare the causes of this war with those of previous wars. The South African War arose out of the dissatisfactions of the Uitlanders. The Serbs considered themselves the object of planned racial and political aggression. Both wars might have been averted if the clash of interests had been dealt with in time. It is dangerous to wait until a controversy reaches the critical state. Unrest may grow to be so menacing as not to be adjustable by peaceful means. I made a plea for organization and machinery so that practical questions, not merely moot ones, could be brought up for discussion. If the question of the Transvaal and the dispute between Austria and Serbia had been discussed in time before official conferences meeting regularly, and then followed up by necessary governmental action, these wars might have been averted.

The middle of the twentieth century still finds us grappling with the problem of how to supply deeds instead of words, but now at least the machinery is more adequate. The Security Council of the United Nations is a permanent body to explore conflicts endangering peace before they become critical. The General Assembly may be called on short notice, and represents all Member States. It operates without the veto. We have also learned that dialectics are often used in order to conceal true intent and, indeed, may become the real enemy of peace.

The Lake Mohonk conferences gave the first impetus to the organization of the American Society of International Law. It was also at Mohonk that the first steps were taken leading to the Carnegie Endowment for International Peace. Andrew Carnegie repeatedly visited the conferences. I was present upon one occasion when he made a most vigorous defense against the popular accusation that he had made his fortune by supplying armament and munitions of war. He emphatically asserted the greatest distaste for executing contracts of this nature even for the United States. He could not refuse them because that would have been distinctly unpatriotic. The Mohonk Conference undoubtedly supplied the main part of the inspiration for his later benefactions in the cause of peace, and particularly the huge expenditures made in the field of peace education through his friendship for Dr. Butler. If peace has not yet been attained, notwithstanding the huge expenditures made for disseminating the cause of peace, the blame does not lie with benefactors like Carnegie and Nobel who did so much to achieve it.

IV

Wartime Pathways

1. *Teaching Law in Switzerland*

The fateful year of 1914 changed the face of civilization upon our planet. I remember the remark made by Dr. Butler shortly after the outbreak of the war, when he said, "The world will never be the same again." The effect of his remarks did not sink in at the time. As we read of wars in history, we are apt to take for granted the profound changes they cause in the life of nations; those who lived through them seldom realized the scope of their influence upon the state of civilization of their own day and age.

The law faculty of the University of Zurich had honored me with an invitation to deliver a course of lectures at the university during the spring and summer semester of 1914. A number of special courses in the various faculties were projected for the inauguration of the splendid new buildings completed on the heights overlooking the city and the Lake of Zurich. When I was at the Zurich Law School some ten years previously, instruction was given at the Villa Rechberg, a fine old private residence in the rococo style. It had a lovely garden, and the surroundings were more homelike than those of a great academy might be expected to be. The new buildings were much more commodious, and of impressive architectural style.

During the winter of 1914, we made an extensive tour of the Mediterranean, including Palestine, still under Turkish domination, and Egypt up the Nile to the borders of Abyssinia. On reaching Zurich I was invited to take part in the impressive ceremonies in connection with the inauguration of the new buildings. The subject of my course was to be a general survey of the principles of Anglo-American private law and procedure compared with the systems in force on the Continent of Europe. A comparison of this nature could be pursued more fruitfully at this time than during previous decades, because the particularism of the laws was beginning to disappear gradually in many countries of the world. The most recent example was in Switzerland itself, where the adoption of the Swiss Civil Code in 1912 had unified the private law of the twenty-two cantons to a very great extent. The German Civil Code unifying the private law of the German Reich was a monumental task which occupied a commission of jurists for the better part of two decades. It had come into force on January 1, 1900. Some progress toward unification had even been made in the United States through the work of the Commissioners on Uniform State Laws. The plan of the faculty was to present a functional survey of the administration of justice in England and the United States in addition to a comparison of substantive law in these branches of law which were of greatest importance in personal and business relations resulting from international intercourse.

When I arrived at Zurich, I was confronted with some startling news. The cantonal authorities having supervision over all matters of higher education had decided that my lectures were to be given in German and not in English. The reason for this was that it was intended to have officials of the administration attend the lectures as well as students of the Law School, and it was felt that not all would have a sufficient linguistic knowledge of English to gain much from the lectures if they were delivered in English. Accordingly, I had the not easy task of translating all the lectures into German. I am sure that I could not have done so without the invaluable aid of my wife, who was born in Switzerland of American parents.

The presence of an American lawyer delivering a series of lectures at a European law school in the language of the country was something of a novelty. Perhaps it was for this reason alone, although I hope it was not, that the lectures were fully attended not only by the student body but also by practicing lawyers and officials of the canton who were in the administrative service. No women were admitted for law studies, although the University of Zurich had established a reputation for its liberality in admitting women in certain other branches, notably in its School of Medicine. Zurich of that day was filled with women students, particularly from Russia, where they held no such privilege until a later date.

The method I employed was partly European and partly American. The class would be opened by the reading of lecture notes followed by general discussion upon questions asked by students. Linguistic differences presented a problem, as they frequently do in speaking of one system in the language of another. The use of an English or American legal term would frequently have to be explained rather than merely translated. This is particularly true in the field of equity, which is a system peculiar to English law and which has no well defined parallel in the systems of the Continent of Europe. It is for this reason that the law of trusts represents an enigma to the mind of the lawyer trained in the modern Roman law of the Continent of Europe. Some jurists see in the trust a resemblance to the law of *mandatum* of the Roman law; others, to the *fideicommissa*. The better view is to regard it as an institution *sui generis* of English law. I found it easier to explain the principles of the trust by a historical account of the growth of equity law and equity procedure and their control over fiduciary relationships. There was great interest in this subject during the lectures because of the intimate financial relations between Switzerland and the United States. Switzerland is a country of investors, and accordingly information affecting their financial investments in the United States is of the greatest importance, especially to bank officers, almost all of whom are trained in the law of Switzerland and in that of other countries of the Continent.

Referring again to our linguistic difficulties, I remember some amusing incidents. On one occasion a student asked whether there

was no body of codification in the law of the United States. I has-
tened to explain that in many of the States, more particularly in the
State of New York, we had a thick volume constituting our Code of
Civil Procedure. This I translated something as follows, *"In New
York haben wir eine dicke Bande."* At this there was a shout of
laughter from the audience. It occurred to me promptly that what
I had said was that in New York we had a "fine gang." It is needless to say that the Swiss are well aware of the corruption of our
municipal politics. However, the lecturer was equally well aware of
it, and joined in the laughter. I should have said that we had *"einen
dicken Band,"* signifying that we had a thick volume of civil procedural law.

The course was drawing to a close when one day a student asked
about the strained political conditions between Mexico and the
United States. At that time General Pershing had been placed at
the head of forces to prevent further incursions by Pancho Villa. I
explained that under prevailing conditions Mexico was a source of
tension but not really of any threat or danger such as so frequently
existed for Europe in the Balkans. At the time I was speaking, all
was yet serene, but the very next day the world was shocked by the
assassination of the Austrian crown prince in the Balkans. At first
few believed that this act, deplored by right-thinking persons in
every country, could possibly lead to war. No one could be justified
in saying that prompt diplomatic steps were not taken to avert it.
However, the sinister influence exercised by governmental circles in
Germany over the steps being taken by the Austrian Foreign Office
in seeking retribution gradually led to the final tragedy of a world
war.

The lectures I had delivered in Zurich appeared later in book
form substantially as they had been given. After the war some of
my friends at the French Bar suggested that they should appear also
in a French edition, dealing more particularly with French and
Belgian legislation and jurisprudence. I was fortunate in obtaining
the cooperation of Max Petitpierre, a young lawyer of Neuchâtel,
Switzerland, who agreed to translate the German text with my

collaboration. Accordingly, I enlarged the text so as to take particular account of French and Belgian law, and Petitpierre's excellent translation appeared in Paris in its French format, under the title *"Principes de droit anglo-américain, droit privé et procédure."* Petitpierre has since had a distinguished career. He became a professor of law of the University of Neuchâtel and afterward was elected a member of the Swiss Federal Council, serving as President of Switzerland in 1950, under the system of rotation which prevails in accordance with the Swiss Constitution.

I was, of course, gratified with the favorable reception which the French edition received. I did not realize that it was destined to become known in Asia as well. In 1948 Professor Tcheng Tchao-Pie of the National University of Amoy, China, a graduate of the Catholic University of Louvain, Belgium, published a Chinese translation with explanatory notes of his own. The Minister of Public Instruction of the Nationalist Chinese Government had made the instruction in the law of England and America an obligatory course for the fourth year in the law schools of all Chinese universities. Dr. Tcheng had been using the French edition of my book as a basis of his course given at the University of Amoy, and he desired to have the book made available in Chinese. It is regrettable that a dissemination of the principles of Anglo-American law, especially of our judicial system, had not been sooner undertaken with the encouragement of the many American educators who were influential in China before the communist régime. There were Chinese students pursuing law studies in the United States. Wellington Koo had been a student of mine at Columbia. Beneficial and widespread influence of American free institutions could have been expected to flow from regular instruction to Chinese students in China.

In the Foreword which I was asked to write for the Chinese translation, I emphasized the most characteristic feature of English law accepted by the new American Republic after its separation from the mother country; namely, the supremacy of law itself over every other governmental power. I quoted Henry de Bracton, who, as early as the thirteenth century, stated, "The king himself ought not to be subject to any man but he ought to be subject to God and the law, since law makes the king." I pointed out that this concept was not so very different from that which had prevailed in China for a very long time, though with a different approach. Professor John H. Wigmore, who knew the Far East well, expressed this approach as follows: "The ruler should frame the laws to voice the best sentiments and wants of the people—not to impose his personal will upon an unwilling people; else there can be no contentment." I also pointed out that English law served free peoples not only in the British Isles where it was first developed, but in countries formerly under British dominion all over the world. Even when all political connection has been severed with the parent country, the maintenance of English law has been and still is considered as one of the precious possessions of the people. "The study of the Anglo-American system should, therefore, not be regarded as entirely foreign to the Chinese environment, but as a development from simpler forms to the more complex, a problem which is presented to China of the present day. Human nature, human reason, and the love of liberty remain as common elements throughout."

The Chinese translation was the first book of mine which I could not read, the first which begins at what for us would be the back of the book, and the first in which the words run in vertical columns instead of horizontal lines. The book reached the Chinese law schools before the advent of communism, but it had come too late. If instruction in Anglo-American constitutional and legal institutions had been brought to China at an earlier date, this country of a great people, but the unfortunate heritors of an amorphous system of government, might have successfully resisted the inroads of the new totalitarianism.

2. *Wartime Practice*

The return to the United States after the outbreak of the war in 1914, was a matter of considerable complication for Americans caught in the maelstrom in various European countries. Many land frontiers were barred, and most of the shipping lines, especially the important British, French, and German companies, canceled the sailing of their passenger steamers. Fortunately, the frontier between Switzerland and Italy was not closed because Italy had not yet entered the war. Accordingly, we determined to leave through Italy if at all possible. I shall always remember the congestion in Genoa caused by the large number of American tourists endeavoring to engage passage on the few Italian ships that were available. We had some good friends there, and we were able to sail for home within five days on the small Italian ship *Taormina*.

Upon arrival in New York, I prepared to resume my work at Columbia and continue my law practice which had been taken care of for me by my office associate, Harlan Moore. He was a member of one of the old families of Kentucky, and although we often fought over again the War Between the States I do not remember a single incident during twenty-five years of office association characterized by anything but warm understanding and good will. He once reminded me of the remark made by a member of his family when he had made up his mind to leave the South and practice in New York: "Harlan, remember this, if the climate doesn't freeze you, the Yankees will." I remembered defending myself upon this occasion by reminding him that while I admired the loyalty of the people of the South to their homeland, I was always impressed by the fact that such a large number of Southerners made their home permanently in New York. I had attended the delightful banquets of the Southern Society in New York and found more of my acquaintances there than in the Pennsylvania Society of my own native State.

The outbreak of the war created much legal business and litigation within the fields of public and private international law. This fortunately kept me very busy for a long time. Perhaps some of the problems will be of interest. When hostilities broke out in Europe, neutral merchants were in the position of awaiting merchandise from oversea countries and ports, to be shipped in vessels of which many belonged to owners in belligerent countries, especially Great Britain and Germany. Submarines and other commerce raiders were a very real and immediate risk which few of the parties had contemplated. It is well known that marine insurance covers only the ordinary perils of the sea and not the risk of destruction or capture by the enemy. If insurance could have been effected at reasonable rates, the problems would have been comparatively simple, but in the early months of the conflict war-risk insurance was quoted at enormously high rates and in many cases could not be effected at all. To meet this situation, neutral governments, that of the United States, for instance, established governmental war-risk bureaus; but this was not accomplished for some time. Upon whom should the cost of insurance fall, and who should bear the loss in case of destruction or capture of the merchandise?

American merchants had a large number of contracts for the shipment of produce from Asiatic ports to ports in the United States and Europe. Of course, where the contract provided that one or the other of the parties was to bear all the risks of transportation the question was clear. Thus, where the goods had been sold and shipped from the Far East to be delivered at New York during certain months named, or where the contracts read f.o.b. a certain port, the seller must be assumed to have taken the risk, even the unexpected risk arising out of conditions of war. A more difficult question arose where, for example, the contract read that the goods were sold at a certain price, "c.i.f., to be shipped from the East to New York." The terms "c.i.f." (cost, insurance, freight) are exceedingly common in oversea commerce and indicate that the price mentioned includes not only the cost of the goods but also freight and insurance. Both by the custom of trade and by the decision of the courts in England and the United States, under these terms the seller does not take the risk of transportation.

In the law of England and of the United States, just as in the law of Continental European countries, the ownership of the goods passes to the buyer as soon as the goods are delivered to the carrier designated in the contract, even though the carrier receives the goods at the seller's domicile and not at the buyer's. It is only where the contract specifies delivery at some other place, such as the buyer's domicile, that the seller takes the risk of transportation. Of course parties to a contract may, and frequently do, vary the terms of their agreements by mutual consent ex post facto. Thus many Italian firms with contracts for shipment from North and South American ports arrived at understandings with their shippers after the outbreak of the war, so as to avoid all dispute. In this manner large quantities of merchandise destined for Italy and Switzerland were promptly delivered upon reasonable terms.

In the examples already given, the outbreak of war did not vary the obligations of the parties. The question was simply one of interpretation. We now come to a totally different class of cases; namely, those in which dealing with an enemy is involved in the performance of the contract by one of the parties and in which, therefore, the obligation of both parties is affected by a state of war.

A very large part of the business of exporting grain from the United States and from countries of South America is transacted through sales made in London on forms of contracts known as "Grain Contracts of the London Corn Trade Association." At the outbreak of the war, commercial firms in the United States and countries of South America had pending contracts for the sale and shipment of grain from American ports to European ports such as Antwerp, Rotterdam, Trieste, and Fiume.

Upon the outbreak of the European War, unusual conditions existed in all North and South American ports, making it extremely difficult to obtain shipping facilities to European ports. German and Austrian ships canceled their sailings; British ships, of course, did not clear for ports of their enemies and freight rates rose to an almost prohibitive price. Under these unusual conditions the owners of the grain who were under contract to deliver in European ports were most unwilling to carry out their contracts, especially since the market price of the merchandise also increased by reason of the war.

A notable distinction must be mentioned between the Anglo-American doctrine of contract and those prevailing in countries of the Continent of Europe. Generally speaking, the common law of England does not recognize relative impossibility as an excuse for nonperformance unless performance was made impossible by "act of God or the public enemy." In other words, it is only a particular kind of *vis major* which excuses the nonperformance of contracts under the English and American law. A contract is prevented by an "act of God" only where the impossibility results directly or proximately from some superhuman power such as the action of the elements. The conditions caused by the outbreak of war could not possibly come under this head; nor could they come under the second exception because they were not the result of acts of an enemy of the United States or of any South American country, for these countries were at peace with all the world. Thus the Continental theory adopts only a subjective impossibility; the Anglo-American theory inclines toward the objective.

The breach of these grain contracts might have been a serious matter for the neutral sellers. But now there entered an entirely new element. By their terms the contracts were to be governed by the law of England. And if, before the time for performance arrives, English law has made performance unlawful, either party could treat the contract as dissolved. In relying upon the English law to justify an excuse as well as to impose an obligation, the neutral seller might very well be heard to say with Schiller's Maria Stuart:

> *"Wenn man mich denn so streng nach englischem Recht*
> *Behandelt wo dies Recht mich unterdrückt,*
> *Warum dasselbe Landesrecht umgehen,*
> *Wenn es mir Wohltat werden kann?"*

(If I am thus to be so strictly governed by English law where this law constrains me, why circumvent this same law when it could vantage me?)

Who could have anticipated that a clause ostensibly made for the benefit of the English or other purchaser, acting through London agents, would have had just the contrary effect? Who could have anticipated that legislation subsequently passed in England under Trading with the Enemy Proclamations would subvert the obligations of an English contract?

Some time later I brought the problem to the attention of John Bassett Moore, who did not completely agree with my conclusion, although he may have misunderstood the status of the parties. He wrote to me under date of May 18, 1917:

Concerning grain shipments under contracts containing a stipulation that any questions arising under them should be governed by English law, I observe that you give to that stipulation a broader effect than I had been accustomed to ascribe to it. I had not supposed that it would have the effect of placing a contract between a neutral and an enemy of Great Britain in the same category as a contract between a British subject and such enemy. Without much reflection, it had seemed to me that the effect of the stipulation was merely to apply the principles of English law to the actual situation of the parties, and not to treat a citizen of a neutral country as if he were a British subject, in respect of his contracts with citizens or subjects of third powers.

In my reply I explained that the contracts were made between American neutrals and English purchasers, and that if any principal possessed an enemy character he was certainly at all times "undisclosed" both in the legal and in the literal sense. Judge Moore's opinion would have been entirely right if there had been a change in the status of any of the parties owing to the war. I reached my conclusion under principles of contract law. It was not necessary to draw the broader conclusion that the stipulation for applying English law should give to the American neutral the same exemptions that a British subject might have with respect to an enemy.

3. *Postwar Litigation*

After hostilities had ceased, the dislocations of the war resulted in much litigation. I recount some cases which are not too technical to be of interest to the general reader.

The French Line had delivered a shipment of merchandise from New York to parties in France on presentation of a bill of lading which happened to be a mere non-negotiable copy. The plaintiff was the assignee of the *negotiable* copy and, because of the wrong delivery, sued the French Line before the Tribunal de Commerce at Paris. The court held in favor of the French Line because under French law it was justified in delivering the goods against a bill of lading ostensibly valid without gross negligence or fraud on its part.

The defeated plaintiff brought a new action before the Supreme Court of New York on the same state of facts, and when the French judgment was set up as a defense the plaintiff argued that the judgment was not binding on an American court under the ruling in Hilton *v.* Guyot (159 U.S. 113). In that case action had been brought in a United States court on a money judgment obtained in France. The Supreme Court by a five to four decision held that because no foreign judgment could be enforced in France without a review of the merits of the case, an American court should not be bound by a French judgment because of this want of reciprocity for our own judgments.

I was drawn into the case under peculiar circumstances. While the point was being argued before Judge Robert F. Wagner (later Senator), an old acquaintance, Benjamin Tuska, happened to be waiting for a case of his own to be reached on the calendar. During a recess he was speaking to Joseph Nolan, who was trying the case for the French Line. Nolan expressed doubt as to the accuracy of the rule of French law as stated by the plaintiff, but said that he did not know of any available witness to testify as an expert. Tuska suggested that perhaps I might be able to qualify because he knew that I had testified as to the French law in another case. The issues there were somewhat different owing to the peculiar state of facts. However, the general subject to be covered was the same. Nolan asked me to act as expert witness on the French law, and handed me a string of cases which had been relied on by a French *avocat* who had testified for the plaintiff. I took the stand on the following day and was able to show that the cases cited did not at all establish the proposition that a French court would reexamine the cause of action of every foreign judgment on the merits of the case before granting execution. The opposing trial counsel for the plaintiff had been a classmate of mine at Columbia Law School. He was plainly upset at the introduction of a new witness in the midst of the trial. However, on cross-examination he treated me with great courtesy, and, curiously enough, transferred his resentment from the witness to the judge. Pointing his finger menacingly at Judge Wagner, a particularly mild-mannered jurist, he warned him against recognizing the validity of any French judgment without a reexamination of the merits. In a tone hardly suited to proper decorum in a courtroom, he cried, "If you do that, I will reverse you." I was told that my classmate was an unusually successful trial lawyer, especially in negligence cases. He was successful here too. Judge Wagner would not dismiss the complaint and allowed the case to go to the jury and the jury found for the full amount.

The French Line immediately carried the judgment up on appeal. Mr. Nolan asked me to write a memorandum to assist him in preparing the case on appeal. In this memorandum I maintained that the case of Hilton v. Guyot was not binding on a New York court and that there had never been any change in the common law under which a foreign judgment was regarded as conclusive upon the merits unless the foreign court lacked jurisdiction or the judgment had been procured by means of fraud. I prepared these notes carefully and left them with Mr. Nolan before going to Europe on my vacation. Upon my return I was greatly disappointed to learn that the case had come on for argument before the Appelate Division and that the judgment had been affirmed with one dissenting opinion. To my astonishment Mr. Nolan explained that he had not made use of my notes because they had been mislaid in his office. In extenuation he informed me that the French Line was going to appeal to the Court of Appeals and that this time he would have me write the brief on the law, and asked me to make my argument on the only theory which promised any chance of victory, namely, that the case in the Supreme Court of the United States was not conclusive upon the courts of New York.

The case was finally argued upon my brief and resulted in a unanimous opinion of the Court of Appeals, reversing the judgments of the Appellate Division and of the Supreme Court and dismissing the complaint with costs in all courts (Johnston *v.* Compagnie Générale Trans-Atlantique, 242 N.Y. 381). Judge Pound, who wrote the opinion, refused to follow Hilton *v.* Guyot. He held that the reciprocity of the French courts was not a pertinent issue as there was no question of international relations; that the issue was strictly one of private, and not of public, international law; of private right and not of public relations, and that our courts recognize judgments of foreign courts having jurisdiction of the parties and subject matter. Comity rests, not on reciprocity, but on the persuasiveness of the foreign judgment. In other words, the New York Court of Appeals decided to follow the rule of the English common law rather than the judicial legislation represented in the opinion of the United States Supreme Court which Judge Pound said might be regarded as "magnificent dictum." I was not personally acquainted with Judge Pound at the time. Many years later I became acquainted with him through his son-in-law Ralph Taylor. Taylor had been designated as my assistant at a round table which I was conducting at the Institute of Politics. I reminded Judge Pound of the case of the French Line, which he recalled very well. He said he had been surprised to learn that a number of States of the Union had been following the authority of the Federal decision, when there was not the slightest reason for departing from the common-law doctrine, and thus injecting the element of reciprocity without legislative authority. Judge Pound had become Chief Judge by that time. He was not only a jurist of wide learning but of warm human sympathies, and one of the most modest personalities to be found anywhere in high office.

Shortly after the decision in the Court of Appeals was rendered, I received a congratulatory letter, dated June 17, 1926, from Judge John Bassett Moore, who was then sitting as a Judge on the World Court at The Hague, written in his own handwriting. He expressed satisfaction that the State of New York had finally recovered "from the thraldom or menace of the decision thirty years ago in Hilton vs. Guyot." He continued as follows: "In my lectures I usually adverted to the circumstance that the opinion in that case was not filed until five months or more after the decision was announced. An old friend, who was exceptionally well informed in such matters, told me that the delay was caused by the difficulty in framing an opinion to support the decision. It happens that, one day in September or October last, when I was working at the Bar Association, I re-examined the record, arguments and opinion, and had my impressions as to the misconceptions and distortions running through the case completely confirmed. One amusing feature, as I recall, was the fact that, while counsel for plaintiff in error assailed—one may say, ridiculed, —the Tribunal of Commerce because it was composed of commercial men, the French Court of Appeal, composed of lawyers, actually increased some of the amounts which the plaintiff in error, whose counsel specially assailed the Lower Court, was condemned to pay." The lectures to which Judge Moore referred in this letter were, of course, those on the Conflict of Laws, a subject which he taught for many years at Columbia Law School.

Another interesting case with which I was connected, and which grew out of war conditions, was an action brought by the Victor Talking Machine Company against the Opera Disc Company and others, before the United States District Court in Brooklyn, to obtain an injunction against the import from Germany and the sale within the United States of gramophone records made by a German corporation from matrices loaned by a British company but belonging to the Victor Company. During the war with Germany, the German Government seized and eventually sold the matrices in Germany as alien property. The defendants were purchasers and distributors of the commercial records printed from these matrices. The defendants were acting in perfect good faith, but the Victor Company, after the Treaty of Versailles was signed, sought to enjoin the importation and sale of any records made from the matrices on the ground that the defendants had not acquired a good title and, in any event, that the distribution of the records violated the intangible rights of the plaintiffs in the renditions.

I was retained to write only so much of the brief as involved questions of international law. I was put upon my mettle because the plaintiffs had retained Mr. Elihu Root to cover this portion of the issue for their side. My main contention was that when the matrices were physically seized and later sold by the German Government, the purchaser acquired full title, good against the whole world, by virtue of successive "acts of state." An effort was made to distinguish between a government sale in time of peace from one made in time of war. However, the Treaty of Versailles laid this question at rest by confirming all such sales when taken pursuant to war measures. The United States Treaty of Peace with Germany adopted the pertinent provisions of the Treaty of Versailles, thus confirming titles obtained under authority of an act of state in Germany during the pendency of the war.

In my research for precedents, I came upon a peculiar case in our own courts which happened in the War of 1812. An American ship, *The Star*, was captured by Great Britain and condemned by a British prize court and sold to a British subject. During the war it was recaptured by an American privateer. The question involved was whether the ship was to be restored to the American owner, just as though the British condemnation had no effect, or whether it was to be condemned by our government as an ordinary prize of the enemy. The Supreme Court held that the American owner had no right to restoration (*The Star*, 1818, 3 Wheat. 78). It still remained an open question as to whether the intangible rights of reproduction involved in the use of the gramophone records also passed with the seized property.

It was an interesting case because of the application of basic principles of international law to the products of modern science. So far as I know, the case did not reach the higher courts for decision. I believe the issues were settled by compromise.

4. *The League of Small and Subject Nationalities*

After the attempt to arrange a negotiated peace had failed in 1916, the smaller nationalities, especially those which had remained neutral, began to suffer intensely from the war. Groups in this country having cultural and other ties with these smaller countries endeavored to bring their plight as well as their future aims for security to the attention of friendly great Powers. After the United States had entered the war in April, 1917, a congress of groups and individuals who were subjects of a number of these smaller countries, but living in the United States, met in New York City and organized a permanent body under the title of the League of Small and Subject Nationalities. Senator Henri La Fontaine of Belgium was one of the moving spirits. Other nations unofficially represented at the congress were Holland, Ireland, Romania, Serbia, Switzerland, the Scandinavian countries, and certain countries of Central America and of the Near East.

I was invited to represent the Swiss point of view at the congress. This I consented to do with the express understanding that while endeavoring to approach what I believed to be the aspirations of the people of Switzerland, my ideas would represent only personal views for which I would hold myself alone responsible. However, I went just a little further than this, because at the time of meeting of the congress Professor William E. Rappard, well known publicist of Geneva, was in the United States serving as high commissioner for Switzerland. He was endeavoring to arrange terms with our government, as well as with other belligerents, under which foodstuffs and certain raw materials would be allowed to enter Switzerland and thus prevent suffering and possible starvation as a result of the blockade. Accordingly, I made it my business to call upon the high commissioner and explain what I proposed to say at the congress, obtaining from him his approval and warm support.

At the opening of World War I in 1914, there were only three nations whose territorial integrity was perpetually guaranteed by the treaties of the Powers and enforced by long-continued assent. Of these three, the neutrality of two, Belgium and Luxembourg, was violated at the outset; that of Switzerland was maintained partly by the action of the belligerents, but also by the preparedness of the Swiss and the strategic advantages which great rivers and high mountains still represented in 1914–1918.

I pointed out that neither international agreements nor natural barriers were absolute guarantees. The Treaty of Vienna of 1815 established the perpetual neutrality of the Helvetic state as demanded by "the general interest," and yet hardly were the words dry upon the written page when the armies of Austria and Russia crossed the Rhine into France over Swiss territory in order to meet the armies of Napoleon after his return from Elba. Switzerland was taught then by experience what she has since learned by observation: the neutral nation must also rely largely upon self-help.

I drew attention to a consideration which is often neglected at the present time; namely, that the political independence of small states such as Switzerland is inadequate when not accompanied by economic independence. Switzerland produces only enough food to last its population three or four months in each year. It has neither coal, iron, copper, nor tin. It must import all its raw cotton, its silk, its wood pulp, all of which it requires in large quantity for its manufactures. I pointed out that at the time I was speaking it was "an island entirely surrounded by war," a condition repeated in World War II. Whether neutrality is a status to be recognized under the conditions created by the Charter of the United Nations may be a moot point but there is no doubt that even today Switzerland relies largely, if not entirely, upon its neutralized status. At the time I was speaking, Switzerland wished to bring before the congress that it had been threatened with starvation precisely because it determined to remain true to its obligations. My presentation before the congress concluded as follows:

"As an example of what may be termed the psychologic entity of the Swiss people, it should be recorded that they have displayed an equal generosity toward the wounded and the interned civilians of both groups of belligerents, exchanged through Swiss mediation. Every part of Swiss territory has been a refuge for the war-torn people of Europe, regardless of nationality. The Swiss are loath to speak of this, and yet it is proof that the people are truly Swiss at heart and not merely Latins or Teutons as the case may be. Though the temptation for friction between the elements of the population during the present struggle has been tremendous, the French, German, Italian and Romance Swiss have all been of one mind in defense of their traditional liberty and the integrity of their neutrality. Had they not been so, the course of this war might have been different. A people whose separate existence has been recognized since the days of Caesar and Tacitus, and whose capacity for liberty and self-government has been demonstrated through six centuries, should not remain dependent upon the will of neighbors for the right to feed themselves and to market the product of their toil."

5. *Should International Law Be Codified?*

During the first year of World War I, complaints multiplied from both sides because of alleged violations of international law. The United States, during this period of neutrality, suffered from the belligerent acts of both parties. It was natural that strong differences should arise as to what constituted the positive rules of war and neutrality, an uncertainty which stemmed not only from the fact that new weapons of destruction had been devised but also because international law was not to be found in any codes or written documents, except in fragmentary form and concerning a few isolated principles. Elihu Root, who was then president of the American Society of International Law, pointed out, with his keen and practical insight, that international law was made not by any kind of legislation but by agreement. "The agreement is based upon customs, but the ascertainment and recognition of the customs is the subject of the agreement; and how can agreement be possible unless the subject-matter of the agreement is definite and certain?" He pointed out that the development of international problems, owing to the multitude of new situations, could not be adequately dealt with by customary law, and that "if you wait for customs without any effort to translate the custom into definite statements from year to year, you will never get any law settled except by bitter controversy."

At this time I was invited to speak on the subject of whether international law should be codified, and if so, whether it should be done through governmental agencies or by private scientific societies. I had no panacea to offer and I did not oppose codification per se, but I did strongly insist that in order to be effective, codification must proceed hand in hand with the establishment of an international forum. "If nations are unwilling to surrender a part of their sovereign will by placing the interpretation of the code within the competence of independent jurisdiction, the code will tend toward becoming in the stress of actual events only a standard of ethical ideals to which all are willing to subscribe but none to observe."

As I look back over the decades since 1915, when codification was being considered as a pillar of law and security, I am struck by the fact that the problem still confronts us very much as it did at that time. Efforts toward codification have been made under the auspices of the League of Nations by the creation and work of the Committee of Experts for the Progressive Codification of International Law, by the official Diplomatic Conference of The Hague of 1930, by scientific societies and groups, and now by the International Law Commission under the auspices of the United Nations. There has, of course, been progress, first by the establishment of the Permanent Court of International Justice and now by its successor, the International Court of Justice. There has been, however, comparatively little inclination toward a submission of really critical issues to the Court. This is by no means the result of the lack of any codified body of law binding upon the Court. The cause must be sought elsewhere, especially in the political stresses and moral retrogression in the diplomacy of the present period.

The long disputes over interpretation of the principles of international conduct contained in such documents as the League of Nations Covenant and the Charter of the United Nations show that my contention is as true today as I believed it to be true in 1915, when I said:

"The codification of an international system as an entirety must remain a task of academic achievement until the sovereignties of the world are willing to limit the 'national idea' by the surrender of part of their sovereign powers in the interest of the common good. So long as imperialistic ambitions flourish in the councils of great Powers, just so long will even the most energetic efforts toward codification be thwarted by a play for advantages. In the absence of world federation, codification must depend upon *uberrima fides* not only in the elaboration of the system but also in its subsequent interpretation. When that fails, the whole structure collapses like a house of cards. So long as national self-interest alone rules the conduct of states, codification can neither be satisfactory nor permanent. Indeed it may sometimes be dangerous, for if the discussion of the minutiae of a code of international law is to be accompanied by considerations of the effect of each rule upon the political situation of the individual state, the elaboration of such a code, at least after it has passed the academic stage, is apt to be the cause of suspicion and friction, tending toward dissension where before there was none."

To illustrate my point, I gave the example of an incident that had occurred only a few months earlier. On September 24, 1915, the Austro-Hungarian minister of foreign affairs delivered a diplomatic note to the ambassador of the United States at Vienna complaining about shipments of munitions of war to Great Britain and France. As part of the note, he maintained that a certain danger attaches to the codification of international law, inasmuch as the wording of the conventions bringing this about might be considered more important than the elementary principles underlying these laws before codification. However, if the code is not to be final, what *is* to be final? It was true then, as it is true even today, that when codified law clashes with momentary national self-interest there is no assurance of finality at any point in the system. The best example that we can give today consists in the many disputes over the meaning of the Charter which occur in the Security Council and in the General Assembly of the United Nations. The Charter is not a code, but it certainly is legislation of an international character laying down certain principles of international law, especially with respect to threats to the peace, breaches of the peace, acts of aggression, the treatment of territories that do not possess self-government, and other matters. There is no judicial body competent to settle disputes of interpretation except the International Court of Justice, to which it would be quite impractical to refer legal questions requiring immediate decision, not to speak of the misunderstanding or lack of respect of certain nations for the judicial process as such.

There was a more hopeful side to codification which I sought to emphasize. In the broad field of law regulating the international commerce of the world in times of peace, political considerations are not so important. Consider for a moment the administration of criminal justice. "Does not the security of society in all countries suffer for lack of uniform and certain processes existing between all nations for the extradition of criminals? A codification in this field, even though resulting first in only modest accomplishments, would tend to elevate the majesty of law in all countries and draw together the governments of the world in the execution of a common purpose." Another field which I believed was ripe for codification was that of international maritime law. Here scientific societies had already rendered great service. The work of the International Law Association and of the International Maritime Committee has contributed to the drafting of treaties relating to collision, assistance and salvage and safety at sea, later adopted by maritime nations. So too, codification more or less complete has been accomplished in the field of international air law, the preparatory work having first been undertaken by many unofficial scientific organizations over the years and elaborated into final form by the International Civil Aviation Conference composed of official delegates meeting in Chicago in 1944.

We shall have occasion to refer to work in the field of codification from time to time. In 1915 I summed up my views by insisting that the desirability of codification depends upon whether, in the particular branch, enforcement agencies already exist or whether interpretation will lie only in the sovereign will of the individual nation:

"The nature of law is generally dependent upon the organic character of institutions. Codification in the field mentioned, in order to be permanently effective, must receive its direction and character from the structure and *modus agendi* of the agencies intended to enforce it. In those branches of international law which do not concern the rights and duties of nations *qua sovereigns*, no international agency or forum is essential to its obligatory character. Accordingly, codification may proceed there without danger of political arrières pensées either in elaboration or construction. Codification combines uniformity with certainty, and is particularly desirable, therefore, in the regulation of peaceful commerce between nations and in the coordination of the national systems of justice. It promotes the advent of an international basis of civilized society."

6. *Pan American Friendship*

During the period of our neutrality in World War I, it seemed to me to be of the utmost importance to maintain and strengthen strong and friendly diplomatic contacts with nations outside the European sphere. This is particularly true now, as it was then, with our neighbors in Latin America. It is not generally realized that the peoples of our neighbors to the south have stronger cultural ties with the countries of Europe than they have with us. This may change with the years, but it can only change by affirmative efforts on our part to cultivate better understanding and stronger friendship by educational, scientific, and social activities between the United States and our neighbors to the south. Accordingly, I took the opportunity of expressing my views on Pan American friendship in speeches and addresses.

On Lincoln's Day, February 12, 1916, I was invited to address the members of the Lincoln Society of Peekskill, New York. I was wondering how I could bring the subject of Pan Americanism into a discussion on the life of a great leader who was probably too much absorbed with domestic problems ever to have given it particular attention. However, I introduced the subject by saying that the name of Lincoln usually raised in the minds of foreign peoples an enthusiasm experienced for few others in our history. Furthermore, Lincoln had expressed his admiration for Henry Clay's policy of cultivating natural friendships and closer contacts with South America. I called attention to the fact that the Latin American countries had established their independence at periods averaging about forty years after our own, and had patterned their various Constitutions after ours. Then came the Monroe Doctrine in 1823, which, though not having the force of international law, was at least recognized and respected by the European Powers. "At first the difference between the power of the United States and these weak republics to the south was so great that none could conceive of anything else than that the Monroe Doctrine was a form of guardianship. But over the passage of years have come greater power and greater self-reliance among our neighbors to the south, so that now the promise is great that in time some of them will become as prosperous, perhaps as powerful as any others in the Western Hemisphere." The representatives of the Latin American countries at The Hague Conference of 1907 had insisted upon absolute equality as the only principle upon which they were willing to participate. The Monroe Doctrine was being transformed into a policy of equal cooperation in the work of the Pan American conferences, dealing with questions affecting the nations of the Pan American Union, including problems of public and private international law, and the regulation of financial and business intercourse.

"Peculiarly enough, the great cataclysm that had fallen upon humanity by the outbreak of the war in Europe has served to bring closer together the nations of the American Continent. In the last analysis, prosperity tends to separate men and adversity often brings them together. The differences between us and our American neighbors to the South are superficial; the agreements between us are deep and fundamental." In retrospect, this has been our experience during the expansion since World War II. Jealousies and tensions have arisen which must again be allayed in the face of new dangers.

7. Studies in Foreign and Comparative Law

One of the pleasant incidents of teaching at the Law School of Columbia University was the opportunity of fruitful exchanges of viewpoint with other members of the faculty, some of whom were my former preceptors. Professor Munroe Smith was a member of the brilliant galaxy of teachers brought to the School of Political Science by Dean Burgess. Munroe Smith was recognized as one of America's brilliant scholars of Roman law and comparative jurisprudence. He had been a student at Göttingen, and as I was anxious to continue training in the Latin texts of the Roman law I enrolled in his courses. He suggested that I qualify for the degree of Doctor of Philosophy. I remember hearing a friend at the Bar saying that he never admitted being a Doctor south of Fourteenth Street. However, I took the risk!

The importance of the comparative method and of the relationship between foreign and international law is only now beginning to be understood. The Belgian jurist Rolin-Jaequemyns insisted that foreign law helps to throw light upon the principles of domestic law. Sir Henry Maine pointed out that by the time Rome had entered the period of vast conquest and the incorporation of other peoples into the Empire, the system out of which grew our first concepts of international law had become part of the Roman system. The Roman state thus recognized the diversification of law in the dealings between its own citizens and aliens. The American Bar Association has given practical recognition of this relationship by creating a Section on International and Comparative Law.

When it came to writing my thesis, I thought that perhaps academic study could be combined with experience in the practice of law. I therefore chose as its subject "A Comparative Study of the Law of Corporations with Particular Reference to the Protection of Creditors and Shareholders." The thesis was afterward published (1912) by Longmans, Green & Company and Columbia University as one of the Columbia University Studies in History, Economics and Public Law. Legislation throughout the United States was fragmentary and inadequate to protect creditors and investors from the abuse in the use of the corporate form. It was useful, therefore, to explore what other industrial nations had done to prevent these abuses. I gave particular attention to the English system with its emphasis on the prospectus:

"If, as was said after the Civil War, the best way to resume is to resume, the best way to prevent overcapitalization is to prohibit the issue of capital stock in excess of the actual market value of the resources supporting such capital stock. . . . Though English law is thus much in advance of prevailing legislation in most of the American states, it still permits wide latitude in the organization of companies partly or wholly capitalized upon the value of property transferred, insisting only that the disclosure of pertinent facts be full and truthful."

There is some satisfaction in the thought that when the abuses of corporate organization resulted in a national scandal during the depression of the thirties, the curative legislation which emerged in the formation of the Securities and Exchange Commission relied very largely upon disclosure through the issuance of a comprehensive prospectus in order to prevent fraud and wildcat speculation under the corporate form.

The importance of systematic investigation of foreign systems of law had been given recognition by the American Bar Association through its establishment of a Comparative Law Bureau in 1908. As stated in its first *Bulletin*, the bureau was called into existence by the growing conviction among practicing lawyers and teachers of the law in this country that we need more than a mere knowledge of how to conduct litigation by the aid of *stare decisis*. The staff for the preparation of the *Bulletin* was made up of some of the most prominent lawyers and teachers in the field of international and foreign law, such as Judge (afterward Governor) Simeon E. Baldwin of Connecticut, Roscoe Pound and Samuel Williston of Harvard, William W. Smithers of Philadelphia, and others. The country assigned to me was Belgium, and it became my duty to make regular reports upon its law and legislation from year to year.

After the Kerensky revolution in Russia in March, 1917, one of the earliest subjects for legislation was that of Workmen's Courts, which was supposed to be a new idea. However, my research in Belgian law proved that the legislation of the Russian Congress was by no means a novelty. It was anticipated by the Belgian law of 1910 which represented an extension and perfection of an older system to a degree never before attained. Accordingly, I presented a paper on the Workmen's Courts of Belgium which was commented on in the New York newspapers.

It is surprising that the provisions of the Belgian law have not been taken into account as a possible model for similar legislation in the United States even at the present time, because the law is well adapted to many of the problems which are presented under our industrial situation.

"The judges of these workmen's courts are composed of workmen and employers sitting jointly, elected by an electorate consisting of both classes, under a system of proportionate representation. It is notable also that since 1910, women are not only permitted to vote in the election of the judges, but are even eligible to sit as judges themselves. Another novel feature is the separation of each of the workmen's courts into two chambers, one for disputes respecting workmen engaged in manual labor, and one for employees engaged in intellectual labor. This is a wise separation, and well conceived to serve the different classes of labor. It avoids placing all kinds of workmen upon the same dead level. The separation is maintained not only in the determination of the dispute, but also in the personnel of the judges who are to determine it. The workmen's courts do not have jurisdiction in claims for compensation growing out of accidents but nearly all conceivable disputes arising out of the interpretation of the contract of labor and its performance, and the incidental relationships between employer and employee, are covered by the jurisdiction assigned to these courts. Appeals from the decisions of the courts formerly went to the Tribunal of Commerce, or, in case of employment in mines, to the Civil Tribunal of First Instance. Now appeals are heard by a special Workmen's Appeal Court, com-

posed of employers and employees who have had long experience in
the lower courts, the president only being appointed by the king.

"Sufficient has been stated to give an idea of the operation of
these courts and their salutary effect in reducing strikes, industrial
unrest, and friction between employer and employee. It may well be
urged that the law leaves out of account the making of the contract
and the fixing of the terms of labor. In other words, collective bar-
gaining, the minimum wage and other devices familiar to modern
industrial experience are left without supervision. This is explained
by the fact that the Legislature is here dealing with a judicial system,
and has purposely left to the parties full freedom of action. But if
it has not thus endeavored to accomplish the millennium, it has,
nevertheless succeeded in eradicating the cause of a large number
of strikes. Our own experience teaches us that a surprisingly large
number of important strikes in the State of New York and on the
Pacific Coast, originated in disputes between the employers and a
small number of their employees, which might have been finally
settled by workmen's courts such as we have been describing. The
tremendous cohesion now existing between the various classes of our
industrial system lends to these disputes, at first petty, their final
huge proportions. Belgium is a country with an area not quite that
of the State of Maryland, but with a population approximately that
of the whole of Canada. There were, it is true, strikes in Belgium, as
in other countries, but, considering its highly complex industrial
organization, they were surprisingly few. May not the legislation of
this enlightened little country serve as a valuable model in solving
some of our own industrial problems?"

V

Pathways from War to Peacemaking

1. *Military Field Director in the American Red Cross*

The end of the year 1917 found the country fully mobilizing for the great struggle. I was informed that I was beyond the age for acceptance in any of the combat divisions of the services. I therefore continued with my lectures at the Law School of Columbia. In the meantime I had filed an application for a commission in the Judge Advocate's Department with Professor Eugene Wambaugh of the Harvard Law School, who was then a colonel in the Office of the Judge Advocate General in Washington. I made a trip to Washington to interview him, and he assisted me in the formalities of my application.

Because I was anxious to be on active duty, I approached the dean of the Law School, who was then Harlan F. Stone, afterward Chief Justice of the United States Supreme Court. Dean Stone explained the disruption caused in the work of the Law School by the war, and begged me to carry through my work to the end of the academic year in the following spring. As no action had yet been taken on my application for a commission, I continued my work until the end of May and then applied for an appointment with the Military Division of the American Red Cross. I was soon after appointed assistant field director in the service of military hospitals. I was first assigned to Base Hospital No. 1, known as the Columbia

University Unit, in order to become familiar with the work. Later I was sent to the Base Hospital of Camp Upton, at Yaphank, Long Island, where I became familiar with all the activities of a great war hospital. The hospital was situated within the general confines of the camp, which, at the time I was there, contained over 60,000 soldiers in the various services. The hospital itself was a one-story wooden structure with floor space of wards, halls, and auxiliary rooms approximating the almost incredible area of fifty acres and having a capacity of about 2,500 beds.

Under the provisions of the War Department General Order No. 17, dated February 13, 1918, a Red Cross field director in the Military Division enjoyed the status of a commissioned officer in the United States Army. I found the officers of the Medical Corps to be most cooperative and anxious to promote the humanitarian services of the Red Cross in every possible way. At the time I was serving at Yaphank, the hospital beds were practically all occupied because of a virulent epidemic of Spanish influenza then raging in many of the camps. The losses which we sustained as the result of this terrible epidemic were comparable to our casualties on the battlefield.

At the end of the summer I was promoted to the rank of full field director and ordered to proceed to Long Beach, Long Island, where a fine hotel-building was being remodeled and equipped as a new receiving hospital to be known as Debarkation Hospital No. 4. There I could start from the ground up. With the help of the Construction Division of the American Red Cross and with the approval of the Medical Corps, we built a glass-enclosed sun porch for convalescent wounded soldiers brought home from the battlefields. In addition to my routine duties, I was asked by the commanding officer to deliver a number of lectures to the personnel of the hospital on their legal rights and privileges under the Civil Rights Law enacted by Congress.

The end of the war was approaching. Soon after Armistice Day, I applied for my discharge, for I was desirous to be of service in the solution of the many legal problems within the field in which I had

Major Larson, Commanding Officer, and the author as Field Director A.R.C. at the United States Army Hospital in Long Beach, N.Y., 1918.

had special training. The old adage has it that in time of war the laws are silent. Now the tocsins were hushed and the law was again to be heard, with what voice remained to be seen. I was invited to go to Paris as a member of the Committee on Public Information, and to serve on the President's press-staff party. I was not informed as to precisely what my duties were to be. Indeed, I was given to understand that they were likely to be legal as well as journalistic. As a member of the board of editors of the *American Journal of International Law,* I was anxious to obtain as much material as possible bearing upon all proposed new developments for the pacific settlement of international disputes.

I sailed early in December, 1918, on board the French Line SS *Chicago,* one of the smaller vessels that had survived destruction during the war. Among those whom I met on board were William Allen White of Emporia, Kansas, Edna Ferber, well known novelist, K. P. Tsolainos, one of the secretaries of Prime Minister Venizelos of Greece, and others. In my cabin was a young French army officer who had been serving as a liason officer in Washington. On the way over, he had developed symptoms which I recognized only too well from my experience in the military hospitals as indicating Spanish influenza. I called the attention of the ship's doctor to his case with a view to having him removed to the clinic, but I was told that the clinic was already full. Unfortunately, he rapidly became worse and was finally removed, but died shortly before reaching Bordeaux. We were four in the cabin, with the ship being greatly overcrowded owing to war conditions. One of my cabin mates was Nahum Slouschz, a distinguished authority in the field of ethnology who had acted for the French Government in matters of race relations in the French colonies of North Africa and the Near East. Professor Slouschz was very much worried at having been for so long a period subjected to the danger of contagion. I was not free from anxiety myself, but the experience I had had in the military hospitals had taught me that above all it was necessary to avoid worry and maintain serenity.

Upon arrival in Paris, I presented myself at once to the chief of the Committee on Public Information, George Creel. President Wilson was not then in Paris, since he was making a tour preparatory to engaging in the actual negotiations to come. As no specific duties had been assigned to me, I made an extensive tour of the battlefields under the auspices of the American Red Cross, which had placed an automobile with suitable military guidance at the disposal of two or three others who had been in the service. As hostilities had ceased only little more than a month previously, the trip was made practically under war conditions, except for the shooting. The roads and fields were pitted with enormous shellholes, unexploded shells and bombs were to be seen everywhere, and the more horrifying aspects of the battlefields were in process of being removed. We slept in partially wrecked buildings.

When I returned to Paris, the President had arrived, but the real work of the conference did not begin until after the turn of the year. However, the preparatory work was in full swing. It was well known that the President's major interest was in the establishment of a league for a permanent and lasting peace. Just what form this was to take was, of course, not known. I discussed some general problems with James Brown Scott of the legal staff of the American Mission at Hotel Crillon headquarters. He was not favorably disposed toward the idea of a league. This was quite understandable, for he had been closely associated with Elihu Root at the Second Hague Peace Conference of 1907, and they preferred reliance upon the method of war prevention developed at the Hague Conferences. It must be admitted that the Hague Conferences had gone beyond the mere limitation of armaments and the humanization of warfare. The draft treaties elaborated at The Hague dealt also with plans for reducing the probability of war by the prohibition of force for the collection of contract debts, by provisions for mediation and commissions of inquiry, and by a statute for a permanent tribunal of arbitration. The continuation of progress along these lines rather than through a league was in the minds of Dr. Scott and of other members of a school of thought influenced by him. Elihu Root seemed to favor a league, but one without strong commitments.

The celebration of the advent of the New Year of 1919 found expression everywhere of new hope for a better world. It was not known at this time in what precise form the league idea was crystallizing in the minds of President Wilson and his advisers. Inquiry at American headquarters in Paris gave no clue. Shortly after the turn of the year, I came across a little book by General Jan Christian Smuts then being sold in Paris. It was called *The League of Nations: A Practical Suggestion.* Although much had been written on both sides of the Atlantic on plans for a league, I was deeply impressed by the statesmanship and practical foresight compressed within a compass of about seventy-five pages in this brochure. It pointed out that if the league was ever to be a success, it would have to occupy a much greater position and perform many other functions than those ordinarily assigned to it. In his Foreword General Smuts said: "Peace and war are resultants of many complex forces, and those forces will have to be gripped at an early stage of their growth, if peace is to be effectively maintained. . . . The League should be put into the very forefront of the programme of the Peace Conference, and be made the point of departure for the solution of many of the grave problems with which it will be confronted."

What impressed me most about the suggestion of General Smuts was that he did not restrict himself to the discussion of the reasonableness and necessity of the idea of a league, but proceeded directly to its Constitution. He pointed out that no scheme could be a final solution: "Our Constitution should avoid all rigidity, should be elastic and capable of growth, expansion, and adaptation to the needs which the new organ of government will have to meet in the process of the years." He advised that while the quality of a super-sovereign should be avoided, the league should not be a mere ineffective debating society, but should be effective as "a system of world-government." He referred to a certain scheme he had seen (he did not identify it) that required representatives of all the States to discuss the most thorny subjects, while their decisions to be binding must be unanimous. To this he objected vigorously, saying that if unanimity were required, nobody would take the League seriously, that it would not even serve as camouflage and that it would "soon be dead and buried, leaving the world worse than it found it." How prophetic of the fate of the body which actually did emerge! Moreover, although he strongly favored economic boycotts against those who would go to war without submitting a dispute to peaceful settlement by arbitration or by the organs of the league, he emphasized that economic measure would not be enough if not supported by military and naval action.

2. *At the Peace Conference in Paris*

Early in January, 1919, while I was still acting as a member of the Committee on Public Information I received a communication from Oscar S. Straus, former Secretary of Commerce and Labor and a member of the Permanent Court of Arbitration at The Hague. He wanted me to act as secretary and counsel to a delegation appointed by the League to Enforce Peace which was about to meet in Paris with similar delegations from other voluntary associations of various Allied and Associated Nations. Their object was to cooperate in every possible way with President Wilson and the official delegates to the Peace Conference in endeavoring to organize a League of Nations that would be an effective organ for the maintenance of peace in the world and at the same time meet with general approval of public opinion among peace-loving nations. Mr. Straus, who was still in New York, was to become chairman of the American delegation, and Hamilton Holt, vice chairman. Mr. Holt, whom I had known while he was editor of the *Independent*, was already in Paris with some of the other delegates. I accepted the invitation with avidity, for it was precisely in line with the work in which I was engaged.

I was not a member of the League to Enforce Peace nor had I taken any part in its activities prior to this time. I believe that I was selected because in the previous year I had been bold enough to draft a tentative plan for the organization of a league of nations. There was nothing remarkable about it, because it was all more or less "in the air." Lawyers with experience in international law or diplomacy were making suggestions and outlining plans much as young lovers are supposed to turn to poetry in the spring. The only merit I could claim was that I had drafted the actual *text* of a plan. I think I did this as the result of a remark which Elihu Root once made that the only sure test of a plan or project was after it had been reduced to precise language in the form of a text.

Perhaps I may digress here sufficiently to mention only a few features of my plan. The principal organs of the league were to consist of the International Council, the International Court, the Council of Ministers, and six Commissions of Inquiry and Concilation for the six geographical divisions of the world to be more particularly delimited by the International Council. Without going into the details of the plan, which consisted of twenty-three articles, it will be sufficient to quote two of the articles because they related to the pacific settlement of international disputes.

"Article VIII. The International Council shall have power to formulate rules of international law and to consider and recommend action upon questions affecting the peace of the world and the relations of peoples and nations, whether members of the League or not. The resolutions adopted by it upon such questions shall be binding upon each nation respectively from the time of ratification.

Article IX. The International Council shall also have power to hear and determine disputes not within the jurisdiction of the International Court, arising between the nations of the League. It shall also have power to hear and determine disputes between such nations and non-sovereign political entities or ethnic or racial groups, provided a recommendation in favor of hearing the dispute be first made by the Council of Ministers, or by the Council of Inquiry and Conciliation having jurisdiction thereof, and further provided that the dispute be not within the jurisdiction of the International Court. The judgment and determination of the International Council upon any matters within its jurisdiction under this Article IX shall require the concurrence of an absolute majority of all of the representatives."

The League to Enforce Peace had been doing notable work in arousing the American public to the importance of creating some international organization, not a superstate, with permanent existence and exercising specific functions for the maintenance of peace. Its president was former President William Howard Taft, its vice president, Judge Alton B. Parker of the New York Court of Appeals. The chairman of its Executive Committee was President A. Lawrence Lowell of Harvard University. The Peace Conference Committee, besides Mr. Straus and Mr. Holt, consisted of Raymond V. Ingersoll, who later became president of the Borough of Brooklyn, Dr. Henry C. King, president of Oberlin College, Ohio, Frederick Lynch, executive secretary of the Federation of the Churches of Christ in America, Mrs. Fannie Fern Andrews, educator and publicist, of Boston, Judge William H. Wadhams of New York, and myself.

The British delegates represented the League of Nations Union, a very strong and representative organization which, though unofficial, was supported by some of the most influential persons in British public life. The head of the delegation was Lord Shaw of Dunfermline, one of the Law Lords of the House of Lords. Other active members of the British group were Sir Willoughby Dickinson (afterward Lord Dickinson), Major David Davies (afterward Lord Davies), Lord Robert Cecil (afterward Viscount Cecil), Mr. J. H. Thomas, a leading Labor Member of Parliament, Sir A. Shirley Benn, M.P., Sir Paul Vinogradoff, and Professor Gilbert Murray.

The French delegation was headed by Léon Bourgeois, several times Premier of France, who was one of the official members of the French delegation at the Peace Conference. M. Bourgeois was promptly elected president of the Allied Societies, and as he was one of Premier Clemenceau's chief collaborators he formed the liaison between our meetings of the Allied Societies, and the Peace Conference. The executive secretary of the Allied Societies was Baron d'Estournelles de Constant, who had acted for many years as representative of the Carnegie Endowment for International Peace in its European activities. Other active members of the

French delegation were Paul Appell, president of the Sorbonne, Paul Renaudel, and Paul Doumer (afterward to become President of the French Republic).

The active members of the Italian delegation to the Conference of the Allied Societies were Professor G. Ferrero, historian; Professor C. Salvemini, socialist, and Mario Borsa, editor of the *Secolo* of Milan. M. Émile Vandervelde was one of the official delegates of Belgium and Mr. S. Tchou Wei represented China.

3. *Preview of the League Covenant*

The first working meeting of the delegates of the Allied Societies was held on January 26, 1919, at special headquarters at 254 Boulevard Saint-Germain. At the very first meeting there was general agreement upon a resolution calling upon the Allied Governments to concentrate their efforts toward the establishment of a League of Nations. I was deeply impressed by the fervent appeal of Léon Bourgeois that all the Allies should make some necessary sacrifices toward this end. He pointed out the importance of a League in preserving the rights of smaller nations, "small perhaps in territory or population, but great in ideals and equal in the right to justice." Lord Shaw was equally eloquent. "No war in all history ever represented as this one did the moral forces of the world against bad faith; and now the opportunity should not be lost of perpetuating the cooperative forces of international good faith."

The French delegation objected to the title-word "League," insisting that historically speaking a league was a *"union pour combattre,"* and would suggest too much the idea of war. It was agreed that while the word "League" would be retained in English, the equivalent in French should be the word *Société.* This solution was in fact later adopted officially by the Peace Conference. The French objection had distinct merit and was of influence in the adoption of the title of "United Nations" in 1945.

The American delegation in the Allied Societies made a distinct contribution at this time by calling attention to the fact that the maintenance of permanent peace carried with it the necessity for the establishment of machinery for the pacific settlement of international disputes. The independent function of the judiciary is not appreciated as much in other countries as it is within the Anglo-American sphere. Accordingly, in addition to the jurisdiction of the International Court, the American delegation recommended that the Council should provide for the development of international law and also have among its functions the duty of examining all disputes or differences between the states that do not fall within the competence of the Court. It also recommended an Executive Committee of the Council able to speak with authority in the name of the members of the League and to initiate action in the event of danger to the peace of the world.

Reference to these discussions of so many years ago would seem historic rather than practical were it not for the fact that the issues are still with us in the functioning of the United Nations at the present time. Such differences as arose between the various delegations centered around the immediate readiness of the League to act in case of danger. Léon Bourgeois stated it quite simply when he said: "Suppose a nation is guilty of a sudden act of violence. Must not the League take action at once?" This reflected not only his own view but, as it later appeared, also the demands of the official French Mission to the Peace Conference. In other words, the official French delegation demanded that the League should control the manufacture of all armaments and war industries; and also that it should have an international military force to defend aggression, especially the French frontier, which President Wilson had once described as "the frontier of civilization."

By this time Mr. Oscar Straus had arrived in Paris, and the issue as developed within the Allied Societies was laid before him by Mr. Holt and myself. As an old and tried diplomat, he took hold courageously. We were informed that President Wilson was not ready to go so far in the draft of the League statutes. Straus then proposed that we call on Bourgeois to see if this issue could not be ironed out. He informed Colonel House of his intentions, which were approved enthusiastically. Accordingly, we arranged to have M. Bourgeois and Baron d'Estournelles meet with Mr. Straus, Mr. Holt, and myself at the residence of Mr. Straus. We explained the effect of the United States Constitution which lodged the war-making power exclusively in Congress and insisted that there was danger in making the League too strong to have the approval of the American public, since the League idea was still a new and strange proposal. Bourgeois finally assured us that while the two points mentioned would be insisted upon as part of the draft provisionally presented by the fourteen nations which had participated in its preparation, there was no intention on the part of the French to make this an impossible barrier for the acceptance of the League draft. Mr. Straus was later informed that it was a great relief to President Wilson that we had been able to remove the impasse by inducing the French delegates to agree to support the draft as preliminarily accepted by the Committee of the Fourteen Nations.

Two plenary sessions had been held by the Peace Conference. The second took place on January 25, 1919, at which a resolution was unanimously adopted to the effect that "It is essential to the maintenance of the world settlement which the Associated Nations are now met to establish, that a League of Nations be created to promote international coöperation, to insure the fulfillment of accepted international obligations, and to provide safeguards against war." The resolution also provided that the League should be treated as an integral part of the general Treaty of Peace. It was not until February 14th that the Covenant of the League was presented in tentative form as prepared by the subcommittee under the chairmanship of Lord Robert Cecil. Oscar Straus and I were in the office of former Ambassador Henry White, one of the official American Peace Commissioners, shortly before the plenary session was to assemble. Mr. White invited us to come to the meeting as his assistants.

The presentation of the Covenant to the plenary session on February 14, 1919, took place in the famous clock room of the French Foreign Office on the Quai D'Orsay. It was indeed a historic occasion. The representatives of the great and small Powers there assembled presented an unforgettable scene. There were Prime Minister Clemenceau, the presiding officer; Lord Robert Cecil in place of Lloyd George who was absent; Premier Venizelos, with his fine features resembling those of a Greek statesman of the classic period, and Asiatic representatives, who wore native costume adding distinction and color to the significant moment. It marked the initial acceptance of the first world-wide permanent organization for the maintenance of peace.

The draft of the Covenant was read word for word by President Wilson, who interrupted his reading from time to time to explain the meaning of certain clauses. This he did with great dignity and fervor. M. Bourgeois, while approving the document, gave notice of two amendments which his delegation reserved for later discussion. The first related to the organization of a system of armament inspection to ascertain whether the disarmament clauses of the Covenant were being complied with; the second related to the creation of an international force large enough to cope with any sudden situation or crisis until national forces of Member States could arrive. M. Bourgeois had explained the need for these requirements at our meetings of the Allied Societies. I remember the subject coming up at our meeting at Mr. Straus's residence. M. Bourgeois complained that the United States representatives had objected to the word "control" as applied to armaments on the part of the League. I called attention to the fact that the French word *controle* is not the equivalent of our English verb "to control," but signified a meaning more like that of "surveillance," which has the same meaning in French as in English. This was a clarification which he readily accepted. Besides these reservations of M. Bourgeois, several other delegates, including Baron Makino of Japan and Premier Venizelos of Greece, made brief speeches. The tentative draft of the Covenant was promptly adopted and sent for further consideration to the special committee of the Peace Conference. That same night President Wilson left Paris for his first return to the United States.

*To Dr. Arthur K. Kuhn
with every good wish for
his success in his lectures
on Greece*   *E. K. Veniselo*

Paris, 28th July. 1920

A day or two after this session, I was surprised by a personal invitation from Premier Venizelos to lunch with him at the headquarters of the Hellenic Delegation in the Hotel Mercedes. I arrived at his hotel fully expecting to meet with a small group of other guests. Much to my surprise, I learned that I was to have the honor of lunching with the Premier quite alone in his private suite. I think I owed this honor to the fact that I had been of some little assistance to the secretaries of the Greek Delegation in clearing up some questions of English legal procedure and supplying English equivalents for technical legal terms in connection with the settlement of problems of the Near East. We talked about recent events of Greek history, especially his relations with the king and the fate of the Greek settlements on the littoral of Asia Minor. He explained that the Greeks in the islands of the Aegean Sea were of purer ethnic stock than those of the European mainland because they had succeeded better in avoiding the inroads of successive Ottoman invasions over the centuries. I asked him whether it was possible for the modern Greek to read the literature of the ancient Greeks in the original. He replied that he saw no reason why an educated Greek should not do so with facility, although he might not catch the significance of certain idioms without special training. I reminded him that there was a special bond of interest between Greece and the United States because we were one of the first nations to recognize the independence of Greece. Indeed, this step was announced by President James Monroe in the same message to the Congress in which he had made the famous declaration afterward known as the Monroe Doctrine. Mr. Venizelos was pleased to have this information, which, he said, had never been brought to his attention. He told me that he was at work on a commentary on Thucydides. We also discussed the sessions of the Allied Societies, and he expressed the hope of being able to attend some of their future meetings.

As it proved, I was to meet Mr. Venizelos again shortly in London and later in New York and in Switzerland. I had every reason to appreciate his towering intellectual ability and also how well he merited the commendation once given him by President Nicholas Murray Butler, who said that he was one of the few great statesmen produced by the diplomacy of the period of World War I.

As the Allied Societies reconvened after the plenary session, it was planned to discontinue further sessions in Paris for the time being and to accept the invitation of the British delegates to continue discussions on the League in London. There was still much to be done to improve the Covenant. The American group deplored the absence in the Covenant of any provision for the codification or development of international law. The British group, or at least a number of its members, favored the establishment of an international police force. The Italian group wanted some detailed provisions for control of arms and munitions of war and the limitation of armed forces. It was also decided that there should be a discussion with reference to incorporation in the Covenant of the Bill of Rights.

All these subjects were in fact taken up when the Allied Societies convened on March 10th at Caxton Hall in London. We felt that our meetings were being held at a psychological moment during which opinion for or against the League was crystallizing, and when there was still opportunity of reforming the first draft before President Wilson returned to Paris.

The demand of the French delegation for an international police force was one of the first brought up at Caxton Hall. The American group was individually in favor of the principle, for it represented what we called the "teeth of the Covenant." However, because of Constitutional objections, we recognized that at least at the beginning it would have to be made up of joint national forces as employed during the war, and not of an international force. As I look back on this supposed objection on Constitutional grounds, I cannot help contrasting the ready solution found in 1945 in San Francisco in the drafting of the Charter of the United Nations, and also at the time of our adherence to the Atlantic Treaty of Mutual Defense. Because Congress still retains the inherent power to declare war, even though there remains the moral obligation of carrying out a duty imposed by a treaty to repel aggression. Lord Shaw's witticism made at Caxton Hall in this connection comes to my mind. He said that if a man disregard his constitution, he grows reckless and goes wrong; but if he is obsessed by it he grows hypochondriacal and also goes wrong. "Were not constitutions made for man, not man for constitutions?"

Another subject dealt with at the sessions in London was the absence from the Covenant of anything in the nature of a Bill of Rights. Ordinarily such rights are under the jurisdiction of national sovereignty, but in view of the fact that the denial of such rights to individuals of a minority group is a potent cause of international unrest and instability, it is eminently proper and desirable to effectuate an international sanction. This problem is still with us today in the United Nations, and while it was intended to make progress along these lines by the adoption of a Declaration of Human Rights at the General Assembly of 1948, it will still take much time and labor to effectuate wider recognition throughout the world of even the limited category of rights recognized in our own Constitution.

At the London meeting Oscar Straus and I both urged the adoption of a clause that the Member States would make no law prohibiting or interfering with the free exercise of religion or discriminating against members of any religious minority in the protection of their fundamental liberties. Curiously enough, Mr. Venizelos, representing the Greek Association for a League of Nations, opposed its adoption as part of the Covenant, although personally in favor of the principle. He gave as his reasons that the official representatives of Japan, Viscount Chinda and Baron Makino, objected at the Peace Conference to the insertion of the clause unless some analogous guarantee against *racial* discrimination were also adopted. President Wilson preferred to withdraw the clause entirely rather than run the risk of imperiling the traditional policy in regard to Asiatic immigration into the United States. Curiously, our proposal was adopted at London because of the support given by the delegate of the Chinese League of Nations Association, Mr. Tcheng, who pointed out that the Asiatic question in the United States was more economic than racial. If the restriction of Asiatic immigration should be linked with the principle of religious liberty, a grave in-justice would have been committed. This was indeed a remarkable example of fair-mindedness and sacrifice of immediate advantage to the common good. It is regrettable that the same spirit did not prevail generally during the peace negotiations in Paris. Mr. Tcheng's view was supported by Mr. J. H. Thomas, one of Eng-land's most influential Labor Members of Parliament, who insisted that it was most impolitic to lose the opportunity of getting out of the way *one* of the most fruitful causes of international unrest simply because it seemed to be more difficult to do the same with another one.

The objections of the Japanese delegates to the Peace Conference finally prevailed, however, and the clause for the protection of minorities was omitted from the Covenant as finally adopted. In-stead, minority clauses were inserted in the separate peace treaties with the new states, such as Poland, Czechoslovakia, and Yugo-slavia, created under the provisions of the Treaty of Versailles. However, as we pointed out in London, we should sharply distin-guish between the insertion of such clauses in an ordinary treaty and their incorporation in a constitutive charter like the Covenant. We warned that the history of the Berlin Treaty of 1878 would be repeated if religious liberty were to rest solely upon the conditions upon which the new states of Europe were to be created. Under the Berlin Treaty, Romania was admitted into the family of nations under the express condition of maintaining the broadest guarantees of religious liberty; but Romania persistently violated these guar-antees with impunity because the Powers were too jealous or too fearful of one another to raise an issue.

As we look back, we see that this prophecy of evil was to be real-ized only too soon. We shall have occasion to comment upon this later. The lesson learned after World War I had to be relearned after World War II. The clauses for the protection of human rights and fundamental freedoms contained in the treaties of 1947 with Bulgaria, Hungary, and Romania were soon ruthlessly violated. Complaints were presented to the United Nations General Assembly in 1949, and advisory opinions concerning these alleged violations were requested of the International Court of Justice. The trial of Cardinal Mindszenty in Hungary, the trial of fifteen Protestant pastors in Bulgaria, and the suppression of churches were some of the items of the complaint.

The sessions of the Allied Societies in Caxton Hall were successful in so far as they called attention to some of the weaknesses and omissions in the Covenant. Ambassador Straus returned to Paris after the adjournment, and on March 24 made a report to President Wilson on the work of the Conference. I think it was partly owing to his efforts that President Wilson offered the revised text of Article XXI containing the special provision relating to the Monroe Doctrine. Mr. Root and Mr. Taft had both been strongly critical of the Covenant draft in this respect.

I did not return to Paris with Mr. Straus because I felt that the main task had been accomplished in recommending improvements in drafting the Covenant. I felt that the most valuable contribution that I could make would be to take some part in the difficult task which now loomed ahead, that of educating the great mass of our citizens in the principles of the Covenant and in explaining the new direction in world affairs which was about to be inaugurated through a League of Nations.

I sailed for home on March 17th aboard the *Olympic,* which was carrying home several thousand Canadian soldiers from the fields of battle. I had only recently visited Vimy Ridge, which will always be connected with their heroic exploits. There were only about fifty regular passengers aboard, including Bernard Baruch and his charming wife. His father had been our family physician when I was a boy. Sir Charles Henry, one of the members of Lord Mersey's committee which had conducted the investigation into the *Titanic* disaster, was another passenger. We were taking a course considerably further north than the usual ship lanes at this season because our destination was Halifax. As might have been expected, we were soon passing near ice-infested waters, and conversation at table turned to the circumstances causing the loss of the *Titanic*. Sir Charles Henry of course defended the findings of his committee, and was inclined to ridicule some of the proceedings of the Smith Senatorial investigation. He was much disturbed, I think, when I disclosed that I had been somewhat connected with the investigation. An American fellow passenger came to my rescue by remarking that although he was not qualified to render a technical judgment, he felt that the American committee, though made up of landlubbers, was anxious to arrive at the truth, whereas the British committee was determined on a whitewash. To be quite objective, I must add that shortly after the *Titanic* disaster I had occasion to travel on board the German S.S. *Kronprinzessin Cecilie*. The captain, although having no reason to favor a rival British line, frankly admitted that had he been in command of the *Titanic* on the tragic night of the accident, under the conditions of moonlight, wind, and sea which prevailed at the time, he would have taken the same course as did the captain of the *Titanic*.

~VI~

Pathways of Discussion

1. *In Defense of the League of Nations*

When I arrived in the United States in the spring of 1919, the country was in the throes of discussion over the terms of the peace and particularly of the role which the proposed League of Nations was to play. I was called upon for interviews with members of the press concerning the negotiations in Paris. I was also asked to speak upon the Covenant of the League in schools, colleges and churches and before trade and labor organizations and other groups interested in public affairs. The League to Enforce Peace at first undertook to supply speakers for widening discussion. However, this organization did not contemplate a continuance of its labors after the close of the Peace Conference. A new and permanent group for this purpose had been organized under the title of the League of Nations Association. This association was sponsored by a large number of public-minded citizens under the able direction of James G. McDonald later destined to be our first ambassador to Israel. As time went on, so much interest was taken in problems relating to the League that regular luncheons of the society were held with prominent speakers invited to discuss special topics, its work being later continued as the Foreign Policy Association.

I was assigned from time to time as a speaker, both in New York and in neighboring sections of the country. My purpose was primarily not to be a propagandist for the League but to give information upon subjects which the general public could not very well be expected to understand without some elucidation. One of the points which I tried to stress was that the League should not be expected at the beginning to develop an international police force but that if force were necessary it would have to be a joint national force such as had been so successful in bringing the First World War to a close. As I look back upon this problem in the light of present-day experiences with the United Nations, I feel that this view was essentially correct. If the nations had consistently developed the use of contingents of force, maintaining them under national control but with a view to emergencies to be brought to the service of the first League, the subject would not have been left in a state of disorganization to plague the peace-loving nations of the world in the organization and operation of the United Nations. Instead, the question was allowed to drift, and still remains with us to be solved by such improvisations as the Atlantic Pact and the united action of nations who are willing to respond to a call of the Security Council or of the General Assembly of the United Nations.

Another point, which I expressed in an interview given to the press on April 5, 1919, was that our committee had definitely recommended "the establishment of an international representative body capable of representing peoples as well as their governments." This proposal would sound visionary without further elucidation. Accordingly, at the meeting of the Academy of Political Science held at Columbia University on June 5, 1919, I enlarged upon this proposal of the committee. I maintained that the foreign policy of the United States tends in the direction of the protection of the weak against aggression by the strong. This is reflected in the Monroe Doctrine, and it is more or less academic to consider whether it is based upon pure altruism or merely upon an enlightened self-interest. World War I was begun by aggression on the part of two powerful empires against two of the small states of Europe. Thus the enfranchisement of the smaller states came to be one of the avowed objects for which the war was waged. This object was reflected in the League, as indeed it is in the United Nations, because in principle both organizations recognize the equality of the members, grant to each equal representation in the Assembly and, at least in the League, adopted a requisite of unanimity except as to certain specified matters. Both the League and the United Nations disappointed the hopes of the minor Powers because of the lack of adequate representation in the Council.

In my address before the Academy of Political Science, I recommended that all the members of the League could be presumptively represented by slightly enlarging the Council and by forming the minor Powers into groups or panels from which each member would serve for a fixed period in rotation according to permanent rules. This plan has been adopted in some measure by the rules of the United Nations, and with excellent results. However, the movement has not gone far enough.

"When it is said that the League of Nations is to represent the 'organized peoples' of the world and not merely their governments, some further clarifying exposition is necessary. Peoples are organized in and through the state. The state articulates and functions only through government. Even the freest governments are frequently controlled by officials who represent only a bare majority and indeed often an actual minority. As public opinion is not static but in a constant condition of flux, there can be no absolute assurance that a government, or an administration, no matter how democratically selected, will represent the majority at all times. Nor is it of vital importance that it always should. The people cannot act except through their representatives and it is to be assumed that in all states deemed eligible to a league of free nations, there will be a constitutional structure by which the majority may, within a reasonable period, assert its will and oust the minority from control. The vital point is that in a league the primary object of which is not to carry on any international government but to promote peace and international cooperation between sovereign states, the theory should not be merely to assure representation in the league by the majority within each state, but to reflect as many responsible elements of public opinion as possible."

In my address I applied these principles to the Covenant, but they apply equally well to the Charter. The Council is frankly and intentionally the reflection of the executive power of the governments represented in it. It is an organized body of governmental executives. Where a Council member represents a parliamentary system of government, his responsibility will be to the people through the majority of their legislative representatives. In a system like that of the United States, his responsibility will be primarily to the Chief Executive. It is plain that so far as the Council is concerned, there is no representation of the people except through the government or administration.

The Assembly, both in the League and in the United Nations, could be referred to as the deliberative body, and yet its functions are not so different from those of the Council in many respects. It will be a numerous body always and common observation teaches us that a numerous body acts only after much deliberation. Of course, in the case of the United Nations the difficulty was to get the Council to act at all on some matters, but that was due to special circumstances. In my address I pointed out that if the Assembly is to be chosen only by governments, there will not be the slightest difference in the complexion of its membership from that of the Council, except in that part which represents nations not represented on the Council; namely, the minor Powers. I pointed out a danger which, indeed, has appeared on several occasions in sessions of the Assembly of the United Nations; namely, that such restriction permits a continuing element within the Assembly to endeavor to impose the opinion, if not the will, of the Council upon the Assembly, thus encroaching upon its independence and lessening its value as a coordinate body.

Minority representation in the Assembly of the United Nations or in any future international deliberative body is more vital to the effective expression of the public opinion of the people of the United

States than to most other nations. Under a parliamentary system like that of the United Kingdom, immediate control is exercised over the appointment of representatives, and thus the administration finds it advantageous to conciliate various currents of opinion. Under the American system, however, the administration may have lost its majority long prior to the appointment of national representatives, and party policy may dictate a narrow view. It is true that the President has often met the problem by appointing a delegate of the opposition party. However, he is not obliged to do so, and even when he makes such a designation his appointee feels himself governed by the policies of the Executive rather than by the large forces of minority public opinion, the expression of which it is equally important to have understood by an international deliberative body. It is curious to observe that at the time of my address in June, 1919, the differences between President Wilson and the leaders of the opposition party induced me to say, "We are confronted at the present moment with some of the dangers to which international negotiations may be subjected through neglect of the wishes of the opposition in the appointment of negotiators." After an interval of over three decades, and in the light of the differences in foreign policy existing between the President and the opposition party in much more critical situations, I could repeat my observation with equal force.

While the principle of minority representation in our delegations was intended to present a strictly objective viewpoint, it appealed naturally to many *partisan* groups. Because my views upon the subject were well known, I was invited to discuss it further. In April, 1919, I was the guest of the Women's Republican Club of New York. I had no hesitation in expressing disappointment that some active leader of the party was not included in President Wilson's delegation to the Peace Conference. I cited Lincoln's War Cabinet and McKinley's appointments during the Spanish-American War as examples of patriotism above party. I admit that I was speaking to a receptive body, but I was none the less sincere when I said: "Mr. Wilson is alone. He does not know how anybody else feels or what anyone else thinks [on subjects before the Conference]. I have it on high authority that Colonel House, when some decision was to be made, said that he never initiated anything but took his orders from and reported to Mr. Wilson." I closed my address with a reference to political conditions then existing but which have not changed much in the course of three decades. As reported in the New York *World* of April 23, 1919, I expressed grave fears that Bolshevism was threatening the peace of the world and that this threat hung like the sword of Damocles over the Peace Conference. "It is no longer a question of whether the world will be safe for democracy, but whether democracy will be safe for the individual." Perhaps my oratorical excitement of the moment was induced in part by the charm and sympathy of my audience.

2. *Nonpolitical Functions of the League*

As I had originally served in Paris on the United States Committee on Public Information, I felt it my duty to speak on implications of the Covenant other than political ones. Accordingly, in an address delivered on May 15, 1919, before the Brooklyn Chamber of Commerce, I endeavored to explain how the general plan affected Labor, how the control of disease was to be made more efficient through international cooperation, how backward governments were to be assisted through a system of trusteeship, and, above all, what steps were to be taken to control the traffic in arms. Such information was needed for an understanding of the Covenant, for often the scope of the Covenant was lost in the maze of discussion over political issues.

Whenever I spoke on the control of armaments I was confronted with expressions of a widespread belief that the conduct of the belligerents during World War I had already dealt a death blow to much of international law. I wanted to bring this question into the open and have it discussed both by jurists and by military men from a more technical angle.

At the thirtieth conference of the International Law Association held at The Hague from August to September, 1921, I presented a paper "The Laws of War and the Future." I pointed out that in the midst of the war, Viscount Bryce insisted, "Unless an effort is made as soon as ever the present conflict ends, to regulate the conduct of hostilities between combatant forces, and, which is of even greater importance, to provide more effective safeguards for non-combatants, there may be a terrible relapse toward barbarism everywhere." Lord Phillimore in his book *Three Centuries of Treaties of Peace*, written in 1917, proposed that the amendment of the laws of war and the provisions of means for their enforcement should constitute part of the work of the Peace Conference "for two reasons: First, to make war less inhuman; secondly, to prevent war by taking away from some nations the temptation to rely on their superior capacity of committing atrocious acts as an element of success in war." To the two reasons mentioned by Lord Phillimore, I ventured to add five more which I believe to be as valid today as they were then:

3. To uphold the respect for law in international relations both in war and peace, because those who violate their obligations in war time and who are guilty of barbarous practices cannot be trusted to fulfil their treaty obligations in time of peace.

4. To make possible the resumption of peaceful relations again after the war, which is for a long period rendered practically impossible by a war carried on à outrance.

5. To prevent the extension of damage to non-combatants and neutrals.

6. To permit the localising of the conflict; or, conversely to prevent the spread of the conflict to other countries, so that each war shall not tend to become a world war.

7. To protect our present civilisation from a relapse into barbarism.

The main objection usually raised by the uninitiated toward attempts to regulate the conduct of hostilities is the lack of any authority adequate for enforcement. As we look at the situation today, notable progress has been made through the adoption of the principles of the London Agreement of August 8, 1945, with its Charter for the punishment of the Axis war criminals, followed by the subsequent military trials in Germany and in Japan. The Genocide Treaty which came into effect between signatories of the Agreement on January 11, 1951, also constitutes notable progress although ratification by the United States has been delayed. In my address at The Hague, I considered the question of sanctions generally and not merely for the laws of war. These we are still fighting to maintain, and the future alone can tell whether the wider implications of international law will have a positive sanction. In 1921 I said: "Progress in establishing and defining the laws of war will go hand in hand hereafter with the development of the sanctions of international law. The laws of war will no longer be merely the pious wish of nations in the quiet hour of peace and good will. Furthermore, there should be some definite recognition of the interest of all states whether members of the League of Nations or not, in the violations of international law. Mr. Elihu Root has pointed out that, up to the present time, breaches of international law have been treated as we treat wrongs in civil procedure, as if they concerned nobody except the particular nation upon which the injury was inflicted and the nation inflicting it. He deemed it essential that there should be developed a real public opinion of the world responding to the duty of preserving the law inviolate."

Many of the things which I was bold enough to recommend must have seemed visionary. It is gratifying after three decades to realize how much progress has been achieved, even though the establishment of sanctions against aggression and other violations of both customary and conventional law are still short of accomplishment. The war in Korea represented the public will of the free world to make progress in this direction, but it also reminded us of the barriers yet to be overcome.

3. *Debating the League of Nations*

In the years immediately after World War I, I endeavored to reach as many cross sections of public opinion as possible. Because it was known that I was a protaganist for the League, I began to receive challenges to debate the issues publicly. One of these debates occurred toward the end of 1919 in Earl Hall, Columbia University. My opponent was Walter Lippmann, who has since become one of our most widely read commentators on foreign affairs. He had returned from the Peace Conference greatly dissatisfied with the conduct of our foreign policy there. At all events, he expressed strong doubt as to the advantages of the League. Like many others, he changed his opinions as the years went by, and as the functional value of the League became more apparent he became one of its supporters, perhaps for no other reason than that of the intransigeance of its enemies.

A much more menacing challenge was that which I received from the Workers' Educational Forum of Brooklyn. This was a left-wing Labor organization which had selected for a subject "Will the League of Nations Benefit Labor?" George R. Kirkpatrick, who had been candidate in 1916 on the Socialist party ticket for Vice President of the United States, was selected to argue the negative. I had been warned that the followers of the group were "radicals" and that I was in for an acrimonious debate. I did not have long to wait for proof that my informants were right. As I entered Arcadia Hall at Halsey Street and Broadway in Brooklyn, on January 30, 1920, I found the hall lined all the way round with policemen.

I had made it a point in public discussions always to give my opponent the benefit of sincerity and good faith. On the other hand, I pulled no punches and hit Mr. Kirkpatrick's arguments against the League as hard as I could. He relied upon certain benefits which labor was supposed to be receiving in Russia under the Bolshevist system. Curiously enough, I had armed myself with some letters which had been written about the League and current international affairs by Samuel Gompers, president of the American Federation of Labor. One of these referred to the long hours of labor prevalent in Russia. I had met Mr. Gompers in Paris. His signature was characteristically written with very large letters and, as an evidence of good faith, I held up one of these letters so that the audience, at least in the first ten rows, could actually see his signature. Much to my consternation, my reliance on Gompers did not mollify the crowd, but on the contrary seemed to infuriate them. This was something of a surprise to me, as I was not informed on matters of the inner council of labor groups. However, I continued with arguments on the economic destruction wrought by war and the consequences of inflation, which usually fell with particular force upon all wage-workers.

Quoting from the report of my argument in the Brooklyn *Daily Eagle* of January 31, 1920, I said: "The workers represent the vigor of the community and their needs must be met. Through the cooperation brought about by the League of Nations, Labor of all nations will be looked after and treated alike. Let us always remember that Labor is not a commodity nor an article of commerce." Referring to what I called the Charter for Labor in the International Labor Organization allied to the League, I continued: "The foremost considerations of this Charter consist as follows: The right of association equally between employee and employer, the payment of just compensation or wages to meet living conditions of the times, an eight-hour day or a 48-hour week, a weekly rest of 24 hours, the abolition of child labor, the consideration that men and women get equal pay for equal work, each country to treat the workers on an equal basis, not putting the foreign workers at a disadvantage."

The newspaper report continued: "Mr. Kuhn offered three questions which he wished answered by Mr. Kirkpatrick. They were: 'First, do you believe that the prospect of more war is in the interest of Labor? Secondly, if not, do you favor the old system of competitive armaments and also the old system of diplomacy? Thirdly, if you do not favor these two systems how do you expect to maintain peace and favor Labor without the League of Nations?'"

The tide of the debate seemed to turn from this point onward. During the few moments of intermission, my opponent crossed over to my side of the "ring" and grasped my hand in very friendly fashion, asking whether I was not Irish. I told him that I was not, but that I had fought both with and against Irishmen before, having grown up in New York among Irish boys. We parted the best of friends. As I left the hall and went out into the street, a large crowd followed, the police following the crowd. I motioned the police that no protection was necessary as I welcomed further questions. One of the officers asked me whether I desired an escort, which I emphatically refused as being wholly unnecessary. I frankly enjoyed the evening, although I confess that when I reached home my wife said that she had had great fears that something untoward would happen at the meeting.

Heated debates were not the only methods employed for putting over the League idea. Mr. Justice John H. Clarke of the Supreme Court of the United States had resigned from the Court with the express idea of devoting the remainder of his life to promoting measures to avert further destructive wars. This high-minded and capable jurist addressed meetings in all parts of the Eastern States in favor of joining the League. On some of these missions I had the privilege of accompanying him. On November 14, 1923, we spoke before the convention of the Connecticut League of Women Voters at Waterbury. Justice Clarke favored bringing in both Germany and Russia as members of the League. My part of the program was to speak on the establishment of an International Court. The impact of threatened evil was too strong upon Justice Clarke for him to retain his seat on the Court without himself making a major contribution toward better organization of human society. "Civilization and modern war," said he, "cannot exist together; one of them must perish." The answer of the Sphinx to the question "Which?" still remains to be given.

~~~ VII ~~~

Pathways in Coordination

1. *Organizing the American Branch of the International Law Association*

The 1921 Conference of the International Law Association was held at the Peace Palace at The Hague under particularly happy auspices. The war had come to an end. Both the place of meeting and the spirit of the delegates combined to inspire the hope of permanent peace which springs eternal in the human breast. The American members in attendance determined to organize an American branch similar to those already functioning in some of the European countries as well as in Argentina and in Japan. Our group consisted of Judge Charles B. Elliott of Minneapolis, Hollis R. Bailey of Boston, Oliver H. Dean of Kansas City, Professor Edwin R. Keedy of the University of Pennsylvania, and myself. I was requested to undertake the organization.

Accordingly, when I returned to the United States, I corresponded with a large number of the American members and visited some others, with the object of explaining the plans of our constitutive committee. The American branch came into being on January 27, 1922, when we held our first meeting followed by a banquet in New York City. Chief Justice William Howard Taft graciously consented to be honorary president, Mr. Hollis R. Bailey, president, while I became secretary. I quote from the speech of Mr. Frederic R. Coudert, toastmaster:

"Our amiable Secretary has asked me to preside, I suppose because I knew less about the subject than anyone else present and he therefore thought that I would talk more briefly than anyone else. In that, however, he is entirely mistaken. I have probably known the International Law Association longer than anyone here tonight, because when I first made its acquaintance, I was not far removed from the cradle. It was in the year 1880 that I accompanied my father to the Conference which was then being held at Berne, Switzerland, and I saw there an assemblage of very venerable and exceedingly formidable old gentlemen, sitting about in a large hall, and I wondered then what it was all about. I heard them talking about the sea, and I turned around and said to my father, 'Father, are these men not too old to be sailors?' He looked down on me and said, 'They only talk about the sea, but there isn't one of them that wouldn't be terribly sea-sick if he had to go to sea.' "

In the same year in which the American branch was organized, the parent association held a conference at Buenos Aires in August. This furnished a fine opportunity for some of the American members to visit the countries of South America. Brazil was at this time celebrating its centenary of independence from Portugal with a fine exposition at Rio de Janeiro. My wife and I stopped off there and also visited the cities of Santos and São Paulo. In the latter city I presented a letter of introduction to Senhor Mesquita, distinguished editor of the liberal newspaper *Estado de São Paulo*, who was kind enough to invite us to visit his coffee *estância* about one hundred miles in the uplands above São Paulo. It was a rare experience to watch the cultivation, harvesting, and processing of the coffee bean, the most important industry of the country. Our host explained that he had a small cup of carefully brewed coffee in the black brought to him every half-hour during his working day in the editorial rooms of his paper. Seemingly it had no bad effect upon his system, and at the time we were there all informants agreed that he was one of the most effective political commentators of São Paulo.

At Rio de Janeiro we had a most amusing experience. Professor Keedy, afterward dean of the Law School of the University of Pennsylvania, was traveling with us. He expressed a desire to a member of the Bar whom we visited to observe at firsthand the workings of the Brazilian criminal courts. This was arranged and, with a competent guide to explain matters of procedure, we spent part of an afternoon visiting trials of petty and major offenses, courtrooms for appeal arguments, and jury rooms. The building was certainly not modern, but we thought nothing of it until the next morning, when the story of our visit appeared with prominent headlines in the morning papers together with a series of complaints by members of the Bar and others against our having been taken to see such a dilapidated building. It was said that in this manner two Yankee jurists had been allowed to receive a very false idea of Brazilian criminal justice. We certainly drew no such conclusions, and we tried to assure our hosts that the facilities were no worse than could be found in many cities of the United States. We learned some years afterward that our visit and the local reaction toward it had a very definite influence in obtaining a new criminal court building for Rio de Janeiro.

Because we arrived in Buenos Aires about two weeks ahead of the date set for the conference, we were able to cross the Andes and spend the week in Santiago and Valparaiso, Chile. The train crosses the mountains at an altitude of over ten thousand feet, and a number of the passengers became ill. Reaching the highest point on the line, one sees the famous statue of the Christ of the Andes, high up in the snows. The high point of the line is at Puenta del Inca, and there one meets the train coming up in the opposite direction. On the station platform I was surprised to meet one of our American colleagues, Mr. Hollis Bailey, who had come down the west coast and was on his way to the conference. He said that there was a group of tourists on the train traveling under the auspices of the Brooklyn *Daily Eagle* and led by H. V. Kaltenborn. Saying that he wanted us to meet, he called Mr. Kaltenborn out of the train. Shaking hands at that isolated spot, I could think of nothing more appropriate than, "Dr. Livingstone, I presume."

While in Chile, we were surprised by an unseasonable fall of snow in Santiago, a *temporal,* as they called it, which closed down the rail-road line over which we had just come and delayed our return to Argentina five days. I understand that this line is no longer regu-larly used and that transportation across the Andes is now either by air or by a railroad line running further south over a much lower pass.

The conference at Buenos Aires was a very successful one. The Argentine Government spared neither money nor pains to entertain the delegates, who indeed represented almost every country of the world. It was the first (and still remains the only) conference of the International Law Association to be held in a Latin American capi-tal. Free passes were presented by the railway companies to all mem-bers over the whole of the railway systems of the Argentine, and special excursions were arranged to various points of interest. After a stay of over a week at one of the best hotels with my wife and son, I was surprised when the manager would not allow me to pay any-thing.

I was called upon at the inaugural session to respond on behalf of the United States members of the conference. As I look back upon what I said on that occasion, I am struck with the thought of how quickly in the life of nations conditions change so as to make wholly inappropriate the emotions felt and the words spoken. I said: "We of the North rejoice in the spirit of freedom and progress which we find to prevail here. Furthermore, though our culture is derived from different historical sources, we feel a strong sense of unity with you because your political and constitutional system so closely resembles ours." I closed my remarks by quoting from Juan Cruz Varela:

> *"Buenos Aires es patria de libres*
> *Y esta gloria le dieron sus hechos.*

A los hombres que tienen derechos,
Buenos Aires es patria comun."

I presented no paper of my own at the conference, but I read and discussed at his request, a paper prepared by Charles Cheney Hyde, afterward Solicitor of the State Department, "The Negotiation of External Loans with Foreign Governments," which was well received by our Argentine hosts. It met with opposition by a British member and a German member because of its liberality toward debtor countries. I endeavored to defend the position of Mr. Hyde, and remarked, "It is most significant that a paper of this kind should have been presented from a *creditor* nation."

One of the most interesting excursions which the delegates made was the visit paid to the great Argentine liberal newspaper *La Prensa*. We were escorted through every department of this great enterprise by Señor Paz, the director, and by Dr. Zeballos, the able president of the conference. The building in which the newspaper is published was not a mere newspaper factory, but contained a large hall, a replica of one of the salons of the Palace of Versailles, which was regularly used by the Instituto Popular for public lectures on political, social, and economic science. This institute, which invited eminent public men and scholars from all parts of the world, played a great part in the intellectual, social, and moral life of Buenos Aires. I cannot refrain from contrasting the situation in which this great organ of public expression has found itself during recent years, when its director has been forced into exile and its publication made impossible by a semitotalitarian régime. It is to be hoped that the spirit of freedom will soon again be as characteristic of Argentine life as it then was.

2. *Double Nationality and Statelessness*

The next conference of the International Law Association was held two years later, in September, 1924, at Stockholm, Sweden. The Swedish capital is an admirable place in which to hold a conference dealing with problems of international law and relations not only because of the neutral and objective position for which the Swedish Government has been celebrated for so many years but also because of the generous hospitality accorded visitors. The cordiality of the reception given the delegates both at private and at public functions, and the interest shown by the royal family, the government, and the municipality of Stockholm made the conference a notable one.

I remember the reception given at the Royal Palace on the opening day by Sweden's beloved King Gustaf and members of the royal family. The delegates were presented individually, though first gathered together in small groups by nationality. There were not many American members, and the king seemed to enjoy chatting with each for a considerable time. He asked me whether the Swedes were well thought of in the States where they lived together in groups, as in some places in Minnesota and Wisconsin. I responded that all Americans would agree that the Swedish elements of our population were of the very best. He said that he was pleased to hear this, because while he understood that most of them had become American citizens the people at home still wished to feel that their cultural ties had not been lost. I assured him that from my own experience, there was no danger of this, at least in the early generations, before those born in the United States had lost identity with local cultural groups. I reminded him that in some places street signs could be found in two languages, English and Swedish. He laughed, and said that he had heard about it.

A curious incident worth recounting occurred on this occasion. A member of the British delegation was chatting with the crown prince while waiting to be received by the king. Though the British member knew that he was speaking to a member of the entourage, he had not been introduced. The crown prince asked whether he was a barrister or a solicitor. Wishing to be polite, the member in return asked the occupation of his inquirer. The crown prince smiled and responded blandly that he would have to confess that he had never had any other occupation than that of being the son of his father.

During the proceedings of the conference I took part in the debate on the effect of marriage on nationality. This constitutes part of the larger problem of statelessness and double nationality. The so-called Cable Act had been enacted by the United States two years previously, and was already beginning to show inadequacies, although based upon correct principles. I pointed out that the object was not to lay down any fixed rules which should govern any country in its test of nationality, but to bring into harmony the legislation of different countries so as to avoid multiple nationality and statelessness. I pointed out that the French rule was to recognize the loss of nationality for married women only if they had acquired a new nationality upon marriage. It is plain that such a provision avoids the danger of statelessness where the statute of the husband's country also recognizes a separate nationality for married women.

I said, "The Committee has evidently not regarded marriage—as, I am afraid, many in these modern days are apt to regard it—as an embattled field of the sexes, but rather regarded it as a natural union of two individuals willing and desiring to live more or less a common life." I pointed out that under the Cable Act a married woman is by special privilege allowed to acquire American nationality after one year by reason of her marriage to an American citizen. This of itself does not cure the danger of her losing the nationality of origin. Accordingly, I suggested that she should not lose the nationality of origin "unless or until, by reason of such marriage, she becomes a citizen of such other state either automatically or by naturalization." My suggestion was substantially accepted in the draft adopted by the conference.

The subject of nationality has come to be recognized not only as a proper but as a necessary subject for international action. The policy of some states to use their legislative control over nationality as a political weapon against their own minorities has greatly increased the number of stateless persons throughout the world. Before the passage of the Cable Act, I remember calling attention in public addresses to the necessity of taking account of foreign law and legislation so as not to create more problems than benefits for women by our own legislation. Efforts were made to have these amendments introduced into the bill, but we were told, as even disinterested lobby-ists so frequently are, that if any changes were desired there would be a danger of not having the bill passed at all.

A few years after the Stockholm Conference I was invited by the Conference on Immigration Policy to speak on "Legal Aspects of Naturalization." I drew attention to these efforts and told a story. Japanese businessmen in Japan have always had much trouble with the English language, especially when they try to put up signs on shop windows and stores to draw in customers. One of these signs for a dressmaker's shop situated above the street floor read as follows: "Ladies executed upstairs according to their own design." The Cable Act was designed to *benefit* the status of women, but very frequently it acted as a boomerang.

The whole question of nationality and naturalization is today, as it was thirty years ago, complicated not only by the introduction of a separate status for married women but also because each nation seeks to legislate without giving consideration to what other nations may do. "If we came from another planet and were told about the organization of nations, each within a certain definite territory, yet with the very greatest freedom of movement from one to another in peace times (at least as between the free nations of the world) it would shock us to know that there was no *international* arrangement for determining where the various individuals really belonged. . . . I say it would shock one to know that the regulation was made by each of the nations themselves individually and not by any agree-ment."

Speaking before the Conference on Immigration Policy in Febru-ary, 1927, I showed the necessity of making compromises. I said that if we were willing to withdraw our claim to the *jus sanguinis* in cer-tain cases, so as to determine citizenship by parentage in certain foreign countries like France which does not recognize the American citizenship of a child born here of French parents, it would be pos-sible to arrive at a basis of agreement that would avoid conflict.

After I had finished my discussion, a gentleman was recognized who arose and said, "I am Exhibit No. 1." He was Professor George

Raffalowich. "I am an American citizen by choice, born in France of a French mother and a partly Russian and partly Dalmatian father. I took the British nationality for a certain time, so that I have really four nationalities. Personally, this weighs very lightly on my shoulders, as I manage to go back and forth to Europe without any disturbance. . . . I served in the French Army, but not during all the reserve period. I served in the American Army instead. My son was born in Boston of an American mother. He is supposed to serve in the French Army."

In the course of the discussion, I recounted a case from my own practice during World War I, illustrating problems involving life and liberty arising from situations of this character during wartime. Shortly after the United States entered World War I, a young Swiss citizen came to my office looking pale and frightened. Before the war broke out in Europe, he was employed in New York and had declared his intention of becoming an American citizen. He was called back to Switzerland for neutrality service in the Army, and afterward was allowed to come to New York again on a furlough. He was then drafted under our Selective Service Law. He refused to accept service in our army because he was still subject to neutrality service in Switzerland, and was in danger of severe punishment should he return to Switzerland at a later date. He was taken to Camp Upton and was threatened with most serious consequences if he refused to take the oath of allegiance. The officer—jestingly perhaps—told him he would be shot. The chairman of his draft board happened to be Julius Henry Cohen, whom I knew and with whom I arranged a brief postponement of "execution at dawn." Afterward I argued the case at considerable length before the draft board, presenting a brief both on the liability of declarants under the Draft Statute and also on the interpretation of our treaty with Switzerland granting certain exemptions from military service. Our own statutes on the automatic loss of nationality under certain circumstances also entered into the argument. The whole matter was brought to the attention of the Adjutant General in Washington, and the order of induction was revoked.

3. *Williamstown Institute of Politics*

The Institute of Politics was organized in 1921, under the auspices of the faculty of Williams College and under grants from John D. Rockefeller, Jr., and Bernard Baruch, as a forum for the discussion of politics in the widest sense of the term, both national and international. It sought principally to deal with the various elements entering into our relations with the nations of the world, these elements being not only legal, but financial, social, economic, diplomatic, and others of practical interest. The business of the institute was conducted by conference leaders at round tables dealing with the various assigned topics. In addition, prominent leaders from foreign countries were invited to speak at the plenary sessions of the institute and at the open meetings. The month of August was usually selected because the buildings of the college were available as dormitories during that month.

I was invited to lead a round table in August, 1924, on "The Conflict of Laws and International Trade." Before World War I it was thought that differences in the legislation of the various countries had little if any influence on the course of good relations. However, the application of the law of different countries to the same dispute and the preference given to local rather than to foreign law in a given case often cause severe disruption of smooth trade relations and therefore of international good will. Before World War I a French jurist, M. Aubry, said, "In spite of the arbitrary or fantastic solutions which the conflicts of laws may have received, they have never provoked even the slightest frown upon the brow of a diplomat." It was precisely this misconception that I determined to dispel, as far as I could, in the round table at Williamstown.

In addition to the conflicts of private law, I pointed out divergences of a quasi-public character which were causes of ill feeling. One of these is the restriction against the holding of land by aliens which exists under the laws of many of our States. On the other side of the ledger, I referred to discriminations by foreign countries of a similar nature, such as the Mexican laws which limit the rights of foreigners in the ownership of land, waters, and mines. Many countries strictly limit the holding of shares in local companies by foreigners.

Dr. Harry A. Garfield, president of Williams College, took an active part in the discussions of the Institute, and was a most generous host to guests of honor and to the conference leaders. Once a week the conference leaders were invited to dinner at his home to meet guests of honor. I recall an amusing incident. As we were waiting to be seated around the dinner table, a lady guest began to chat with me and I soon observed that she was mistaking me for our host, Dr. Garfield. There was a fine portrait painting of his father, former President James A. Garfield, hanging above the mantelpiece. I quickly informed her that I was not Dr. Garfield but that, curiously enough, I could accept the portrait as an excellent likeness of my own father. I remember my father telling me that he had sometimes been taken for General Garfield, later to become the President. Dr. Harry Garfield and I were about the same height and build and we were both wearing the type of clothing adopted for wear at the Institute. There was something in the expression of the eyes in that portrait which aroused many memories.

One of the subjects which we dealt with at my round table was the dislocation to international trade caused by the divergence in the laws of various countries relating to negotiable instruments, that is, bills, notes, and checks. I called attention to the work being done under the auspices of the League of Nations embodied in a report recommending the adoption by all countries of a uniform code upon this subject. Some years later, a uniform code was elaborated into a multilateral treaty adopted by a large number of nations. The United States is not a party to the convention, doubtless owing to the fact that the subject matter is within the powers reserved to the separate states.

Another vital subject which we discussed was a system of international commercial arbitration in order to prevent the loss of time and money in litigating disputes arising out of international trade not only because of the divergence in trade laws of different countries but also because of the difficulty of conducting litigations in court at long distances from the place where the witnesses were available. Great progress has since been made along these lines, especially through the International Chamber of Commerce and the American Arbitration Association by improving arbitration procedure.

I said: "In doing this, they are accomplishing what the Governments themselves have failed to do, namely, to coördinate the laws of the different countries and cause a selection in advance by the contracting parties, of the law which shall apply to the transaction. Thus the United States Chamber of Commerce has entered into agreement with the Argentine Chamber of Commerce for the arbitration of disputes of a certain character between their members. . . . The Economic Committee of the League of Nations reported that it deemed the system of commercial arbitration of essential importance and recommended that when two parties of different nationalities agree to refer disputes to arbitration, an action brought by either party in any country other than that agreed upon as the place of arbitration, should be stayed by the court of the country in which it is brought. The American Bar Association has submitted a draft treaty providing that an award in case of commercial arbitration in one country shall be enforceable in the other."

Where distinct progress has since been made, it is gratifying to look back for more than a quarter of a century to the discussion of problems in their early phases. On the other hand, some other subjects dealt with at my round table were upon issues which have today become more acute than ever. One of the burdens upon international trade was then, and is now, that of double or even multiple taxation upon the same source of revenue in more than one country. Wars make countries rapacious in respect to their tax policies. I compared conditions after World War I with taxation policies following the Napoleonic Wars. The burdens of taxation lead to impoverishment, especially where a person has been "guilty" of carrying on trade or making investments in foreign countries, and where inheritance taxes approach the confiscatory stage. A decedent in an example which I gave had been a resident of Wisconsin. As a result of his carrying on business in other States, the inheritance taxes imposed upon his estate amounted to 130 per cent. I remarked that taxation should not become a ransom. The international significance of double and multiple taxation is sometimes forgotten. In one of the sessions I remarked, "Keep people from becoming angry and you will avoid friction leading to war."

Two years later I was again invited to conduct a round table at the Institute of Politics. This time my subject was "The Diversity of Legislation Relating to Nationality." Here again the lack of coordination tends toward international friction. The significance of this topic in world affairs lies in the fact that each country has the right to determine what class of persons should be considered citizens. There is no law of nations which controls, and therefore each nation adopts its own system. No difficulty is encountered so long as the various nations adopt systems which are alike or similar. The fact is, however, that many of them do not coordinate with others. Thus, some countries, like our own and Great Britain, predominantly recognize nationality by birth upon the territory. Countries of the Continent of Europe recognize parentage as the principal rule. It is clear that both principles cannot work together if followed rigorously. A person born in the United States of persons who are citizens of a country recognizing citizenship by blood acquires double nationality. Fortunately, some nations yield to one another in part so as to permit the individual to choose, but this is by no means universal. On the other hand, the rule of nationality by parentage leaves many persons stateless. Illegitimates, foundlings, and children of parents who in turn have lost their nationality for one reason or another are persons without a country. Statutes like our own which require nationals to register with foreign consuls abroad after an absence of a certain period are fruitful causes of leaving persons without any nationality. They fail to register and yet do not take steps to acquire a new nationality. These problems have increased since the two world wars owing to the break-up of empires into smaller states.

The significance of nationality is greater in Europe than in the United States at least in one respect; namely, that private rights in trade and business and in family life are often governed by national law even when the citizen resides abroad. This is true today although there is some tendency to change it. I called it to the attention of my round table at the Institute of Politics. It is difficult for Americans to visualize the rule, although we have one striking and expensive example in our own law. The obligation to pay taxes on income from whatever source derived follows the American national wherever he may be domiciled. This double liability is alone a warning to the individual not to indulge in the luxury of retaining more than one nationality. Some relief has been granted in recent years through treaties with a number of countries designed to avoid double taxation.

In the General Conference of Public Opinion in World Affairs conducted at the Institute of Politics by Arthur S. Draper, editor of the New York *Herald Tribune*, I was asked to speak on the influence of members of the Bar on public opinion. I said:

"In a democracy like ours, with a written Constitution, and a system of government divided between Federal and State, it is but natural that men trained in the law should have an important part in the conduct of public affairs, and be influential in moulding public opinion. Lord Bryce and other trained observers have referred to the dependence upon trained legal minds in the working of a system like our own. It is therefore not to be wondered at that from the beginning, lawyers took a prominent, some say even a disproportionate, part in the conduct of public affairs. This has continued even to the present day where the members of our legislatures are mostly lawyers. Curiously enough, however, the influence which they, as a class, have upon public opinion is small in proportion to the part they take as individuals. Even in the election of judges, where their advice and opinion might be considered to be most acceptable, it has been proven that a choice endorsed by the lawyers is often repudiated at the polls.

"Public opinion is dividing itself more or less according to the bloc system. We have the farmers' group, the labor group, the industrial and financial groups. The Bar of the country has also become more self-conscious and proposes to take a more active part in moulding public opinion on legal questions. The growth in the number and power of Bar Associations is one manifestation; the cry for incorporation of the Bar, whether it succeeds or not, is another. . . . The task of the Bar is to refrain from abstruse terminology in the presence of the average citizen. Scientists in other fields have succeeded in popularizing the high points of science, and the lawyer, who should be a scientist in his own way, must learn to simplify the legal problems affecting the country so as to extend and fortify the influence which rightly belongs to him in a government of laws and not of men."

Continuing to speak on the influence of public opinion on international relations, I took this subject up again from a different angle a few days later. I spoke of the responsibility which was borne by members of the press in emphasizing the sensational incidents of international life. An untoward occurrence could be magnified out of all proportion so as to stir up ill feeling in the public mind. The press of our own country, as well as abroad, is frequently guilty of doing so, often with no other purpose than to make their newspapers "interesting." In countries where the press is controlled by government or rigorously censored, it is difficult to convince the reading public that the press is free to publish interpretations and opinions in conflict with the official view. This is a source of danger to peaceful relations today as it was then. My discussion was noticed in some of the newspapers of our Latin American neighbors, and Leo S. Rowe, director-general of the Pan American Union wrote a note to me enclosing a clipping from an Argentine newspaper in order to show that these round-table discussions were being followed there.

At this session of the Institute of Politics, there occurred a curious incident involving a practical application of international law. At one of the round-table conferences at which Mr. Nicholas Politis was taking part, he was served with a summons to appear before a Massachusetts court sitting at Salem in a controversy over funds belonging to the Greek Orthodox Church in Peabody. Mr. Politis, a distinguished Greek lawyer and publicist, was at this time Greek

Conference Leaders of the Williamstown Institute of Politics, 1926. President Harry A. Garfield in center, the author at extreme left.

ambassador to France. He had been invited to deliver a series of lectures at the Institute, and he had come to the United States specially for that purpose, intending to return immediately. He was very much disturbed by the interruption, especially because it dealt with matters affecting the finances of the Greek Church during a period when he was prime minister. At first Mr. Politis relied upon his alleged immunity as a diplomatic official. On this question Dr. Garfield called me into conference, together with Philip Marshall Brown, formerly a professor at Princeton University. We had to advise Mr. Politis that he was not strictly on the business of his diplomatic mission, nor was he in transit in connection with his mission. An application had already been made before the judge at Salem to punish him for contempt. However, things were finally arranged by long-distance telephone, and he agreed to appear within a few days so as not to interfere with his lectures.

I attended the Institute for a number of years after this, taking partial responsibility for round tables. The experience was always valuable as well as delightful because it gave the opportunity for a meeting of the minds with leaders of thought all over the world. Perhaps the spirit of the Institute can be best reflected, when reviewed *vingt ans après*, by quoting the lines with a Hiawatha setting published in the newspapers in the early days of the Institute and ascribed to C. Schofield, who, I believe, was a student at Williams College:

The Political Institute

> Where the purple mountains cluster,
> Where the Mohawk Trail winds upward,
> In the shadow of old Greylock
> Nestles here a peaceful campus—
> Lies a campus of green velvet
> Dotted o'er with stately elm trees,
> Pines and birch and noble wigwams—
> Wigwams for the great white tribesmen
> Who have gathered from the Southland,
> From the Northland and the Westland,

With their squaws bedecked with wampum,
Gathered here to seek the answers
To the riddle of the Nations,
To bring order out of chaos
Which has been since the beginning.

Mighty Braves there are aplenty—
Admirals, Reporters, Statesmen—
Warriors all with arrows ready—
Arrows ready in their quivers,
Feathered from the wings of learning,
To be sped at the Round Tables—
The Round Tables—fields of battle—
When they mount their steeds of rhetoric
And ride forward into conflict.

There are chiefs from far-off countries—
Ministers and Counts and Canons,
Mighty Knights with tongues of silver
Who from hunting-grounds far distant
Came across the big sea water,
Came to smoke with us the peace pipe,
Each one fain to help his people
With a little propaganda,
And a Big White Chief is with us—
He the great wild Turkey Tamer—
Man of prowess, man of wisdom,
He whose tales of the wild tribesmen
Of the lands in which he sojourned
Sends the shivers down our backbones,
While the nearness of his presence
Makes us shine as by reflection.

There are squaws who would be warriors,
Delving into books of learning
While their pretty strings of wampum
Get all mixed up in the pages.
Other squaws, content with squawdom,

Silent sit and weave their blankets—
Weaving threads of thought and wonder,
Listening to the tales of valor
Of their braves—or brainy sisters—
Through the trails they cannot follow.

When the purple mists of evening,
When the twilight shadows gather,
Hastily we leave our suppers,
Hustle we from out the Commons
Where the "Little Alice" wonders,
Where the chocolate sauce is melting,
Hasten we across the greensward
To the stately hall of Chapin,
There to hear the nightly pow wow—
Pow wow of the mighty war dance
With the thunder of the tom-toms
That goes echoing down the ages.

Where the gentle Canon, pleading,
Brings the teardrops to our eyelids,
And the able Count exhorting
Makes us fear we are pro-German
Till we don't know where we are at,
While the brace of "sirs" would have us
Join the hunting-ground with their one,
Make one big and happy prairie,
Chase our bison herds together,
Bring our tribes into a union
Under rule of their great chieftain.

Thus we dream and see our visions
In this green and peaceful valley,
Blowing bubbles jewel-colored—
All about a League of Nations,
Bubbles gleaming, floating, bursting,
Melting in the misty background,
Where the purple mountains cluster,

And the Mohawk Trail winds upward,
In the shadow of old Greylock.

In the book of recollections of Dr. Harry A. Garfield, entitled *Lost Visions* and published after his death by Mrs. Garfield, he relates that the idea of the Institute of Politics came to him suddenly, as though by the inspiration of a vision. Quite apart from whatever influence the Institute exerted over a period of some ten or fifteen years, it must be said to the lasting credit of Dr. Garfield that the idea took root. Similar institutes were established at the University of Virginia, at Colgate University, and elsewhere throughout the country. The good that men do is fortunately not always interred with their bones, but lives after them. I think it fair to say that the Institute introduced a new idea for the molding of public opinion, both nationally and internationally, on the highest level and on the basis of truth and fact.

4. *The Hague Academy of International Law*

The Academy of International Law was established with the support of the Carnegie Endowment for International Peace in 1923. Andrew Carnegie had already subscribed funds for the building of the Peace Palace at The Hague, and it was natural that the seat of the Academy should be placed at the Peace Palace. I was invited to deliver a course of lectures in the regular curriculum of the Academy during the summer of 1925, the assigned subject being "Les effets de commerce en droit international" (Negotiable Instruments in International Law). At this time all the lectures in course had to be delivered in the French language, and the seminars, which were conducted by the professor allowing free discussion with his students, were also in French. This rule has been changed somewhat in recent years because of the difficulty of many of the teachers in conducting their courses entirely in French. I confess that it was not entirely easy for me to do so, but I was told that my pronunciation was excellent, and perhaps because of that, errors in grammar or syntax were forgiven.

I remember seeing the president of the Curatorium, Professor Charles Lyon-Caen, sitting in on one of my lectures. He did so to observe at firsthand how the system of education was being carried out. It was with considerable trepidation that I observed him sitting there, because he had been one of my teachers at the Law School in Paris twenty years earlier, and he was known to be a rigorous critic, allowing the chips to fall where they might. I was very much relieved to hear at secondhand that he found my delivery satisfactory. He had sharply criticized an English-speaking colleague because of his inadequate French pronunciation, although I knew him to be much more fluent in French than many of us. Some of the teachers from countries outside the English-speaking group also had difficulties, and this gave rise to a remark which was made at one of the dinners given by the Curatorium to the teachers and students. A member of the Curatorium in a welcoming speech said that it was well understood that at the Academy, French was being spoken in all languages!

The Academy constitutes a center of advanced studies in international law both public and private, as well as in connected sciences of administration, economics, and finance so far as they relate to international affairs. Accordingly, the students consist of advanced scholars in law and political science, some of them already occupying positions of authority in various branches of government in their home states. The students of my group in 1925 were of various national origins, mostly from countries of the Continent of Europe. Because of the subject matter, they were advanced students in the field of public or private international law or of banking practice.

My lectures endeavored to outline the unification which had taken place in the adoption of the Uniform Negotiable Instruments Law which had been adopted in nearly all of the forty-eight States, in comparison with the proposed unification being undertaken under the auspices of the Inter-American High Commission for all the countries of the Americas, and also in comparison with the laws of the countries of Continental Europe.

Without going into technical details, it is sufficient to recall that I laid stress upon the desirability of greater uniformity in commercial law generally, between the principal commercial countries of the world, for which the unification of the laws governing bills, notes, and checks would constitute an important beginning. Diplomatic conferences at The Hague had already been held with this in view in 1910 and 1912. Under the auspices of the League of Nations, the movement gradually attained momentum, culminating some five years after my lectures in the signing of two important conventions at Geneva, one relating to bills and notes and the other to checks.

Three years later, in 1928, I was again invited to deliver a series of lectures in course at the Academy, this time on "La Conception du droit international privé d'après la doctrine et la pratique aux États-Unis" (Theory and Practice of Private International Law in the United States). This was, of course, a subject with which I had had long familiarity through my teaching at Columbia Law School. However, the presentation of principles by a course of lectures differs widely from methods used under the Case System. The former has certain distinct advantages, for it allows the teacher to enlarge upon his subject by a comprehensive exposé of its history. Accordingly, at The Hague I endeavored to show the origin of the conflict of laws under our dual system of government, and how the system was developed by the early writers such as Livermore, Kent, and Story. It is often forgotten that the conflict of laws is one branch of law which was developed in the United States before it reached any degree of maturity in England.

Looking back upon the subject from the point of view of the middle of the twentieth century, we can say with greater force today than we did a quarter of a century earlier: "The immense expansion of American commercial and financial transactions has drawn attention to a great number of problems of private international law. In order to accomplish desirable progress in support of this expansion, it is necessary that these problems should receive a solution which meets the demands of international justice. In a period where economic considerations play a role more and more important in the relations between peoples and states, the principles of private international law will have greater and greater significance in the maintenance of peace."

The Academy of International Law represents an influence that is not to be undervalued in the maintenance of better understanding and of good will between advanced students coming from many countries. This was an element well recognized from the very beginning by James Brown Scott, one of the principal founders of the Academy, and by his associates on the Curatorium. Dr. E. N. van Kleffens, who acted as secretary-general for many years, later becoming foreign minister of The Netherlands and ambassador of his country to the United States, exercised great influence in making the various national groups better acquainted with one another. I believed then, and still believe, that institutions like the Academy of International Law at The Hague are not sufficiently appreciated by the general public for the work they are doing in creating relationships of lasting value between advanced scholars in international law and diplomacy. These men and women are sure to be leaders of public opinion, if not of actual administration, in their own countries. Where, then, could be found a force more potent for the maintenance of peace than one established on the basis of friendships and fairer law for mutually advantageous trade relations between the countries of the world.

VIII

Pathways of Judicial Settlement

1. *Organization of a Permanent Court*

The idea and ideal of substituting law for war may be traced far back in the history of civilized society. It is, indeed, what may be called a "current illusion" (to use a phrase of John Bassett Moore) to believe that the idea accomplished its first fruition in our own times. On the contrary, various forms of arbitral procedure between peoples and nations have been resorted to not only in ancient times but also in the Middle Ages and in the Renaissance period. The new idea for which our own times may justly claim credit, so far as practical effectuation is concerned, is the creation of a *permanent* tribunal for the settlement of international disputes by judicial processes.

The Joint Conference of the Inter-Allied Associations for a League of Nations, whose work I have already referred to, recommended in its Paris Protocol of January, 1919, the creation of "an International Court of Justice charged with the duty of deciding all justiciable disputes, and to assure the execution of its decisions by all appropriate international sanctions, diplomatic, juridical, economic, and, if necessary, military." One may be permitted to take a pride in having assisted in the preparation of this draft even though we are still a long way from its realization. Curiously enough, the Protocol actually anticipated the title which the tribunal at The Hague now possesses, although the original Court bore a different name. The proposed Court was not created at the Paris Peace Conference. The Covenant contented itself with a provision (Article 14) that the Council shall formulate, and submit to the members of the League for adoption, plans for the establishment of a Permanent Court of International Justice. It is regrettable that the steps taken for the creation of the Court were not made independently of the League. As the United States did not ratify the Covenant, its adherence to the Court Statute was inextricably bound up with all the parliamentary and political differences involved in our ratification of the Treaty of Versailles. This might have been avoided if the creation of the Court had been independent of the setting up of the League.

When the Court was constituted and the first bench of judges was elected, I was delighted that John Bassett Moore was among those chosen. Two other judges, André Weiss of France and Max Huber of Switzerland, were also jurists with whom I had studied in law-school days. The first and opening session of the Permanent Court of International Justice, as it was called originally, took place at the Peace Palace in The Hague on February 15, 1922. Some months later, when Judge Moore returned to the United States, he surprised me with a photograph of this historic occasion, accompanying it with a letter to me in his own handwriting dated May 20, 1922, saying, "With this, I am sending an original autographed picture of the Permanent Court of International Justice as it appeared at the formal opening—something that few persons in the world will possess." The photograph was indeed autographed by every member of the Court who took part in the opening session. Needless to say, I was deeply touched by this evidence of Judge Moore's thoughtfulness and friendship, and I was determined to respond to it by taking a special interest in the work of the Court.

The first case to be submitted to the Court for judgment was that of the British merchant ship *Wimbledon*, which came before the

Court for argument in July, 1923. I attended some of the sessions of the argument. Sir Cecil Hurst appeared for Great Britain, Professor Basdevant for France, and Herr Schiffer for Germany. The ship had been chartered by a French company and carried a cargo of munitions consigned to the Polish naval base at Danzig. It was refused passage through the Kiel Canal by the German authorities because of the neutrality orders issued by Germany in connection with the Russo-Polish War. The Treaty of Versailles (Article 380) provided that the Kiel Canal was to be open to the vessels of commerce and of war of all nations at peace with Germany. The Court held that a neutrality order issued by an individual state could not prevail over the affirmative terms of the treaty. The dissenting opinion by Judges Anzilotti and Huber maintained that the treaty was subject to the same obligations which the neutral state (Germany) would have in respect of internal navigable waters of international concern. The argument of the case was conducted with great dignity, and although the issue at stake was not a matter of peace or war, it was of sufficient importance with reference to the navigation of the Kiel Canal and similar waterways to demonstrate that the Court could serve its high function in the maintenance of peace. I am pleased at the thought that I had been privileged to attend at the argument of the first case to come before the first permanent court for the judicial settlement of international disputes.

One argument presented by Germany is worth mentioning because it arose from a concept which is widely maintained even today in debates in our own Congress. Counsel for Germany argued that the interpretation claimed by Great Britain and its allies would compel Germany to surrender some of its rights of sovereignty. To this the Court replied that *any* convention creating an obligation places a restriction upon the exercise of the sovereign right of the state in the sense that it requires it to be exercised in a certain way, and the Court held that "the right of entering into international engagements is an attribute of state sovereignty."

2. *Lectures on the World Court at the University of Pennsylvania*

Some years after being present at the first case, I was invited by Dean Micheles of the University of Pennsylvania Law School to become an auxiliary lecturer upon the jurisprudence of the World Court. I entered upon my duties in the autumn of 1926, and continued throughout the administration of Deans Micheles and Herbert F. Goodrich. The latter named has become United States Circuit Court Judge for the Eastern District of Pennsylvania.

I believe that my course was the first to be given anywhere dealing comprehensively with the work of the World Court. My classes were unusually large, reaching to about 150 students of both sexes. The hour was so arranged that students of all the three years of the curriculum could attend. With the approval of the dean, I did not restrict myself to the lecture method but engaged in open discussion with members of the class, encouraging debate upon various topics. I was gratified with the large attendance and the interest shown in a course for which no direct credits were given.

As more cases came before the Court, I was surprised to observe a certain diffidence in exercising its jurisdiction where it was the plain intent of the parties to refer disputes to the Court. Perhaps this is attributable to political conditions in what is still a nationalistic world.

After I had been conducting classes on the jurisprudence of the World Court for some four years, there had accumulated a body of decisions of some sixteen judgments and seventeen advisory opinions. I thought it would be interesting to make a survey of how far American legal precedents and the practice of the United States in the interpretation of treaties had played a role in the jurisprudence of the Court. I did this in an article published in the *University of Pennsylvania Law Review* for November, 1930. There was then and there is now no body of international law having a definite scope or content approved throughout the world. Accordingly, the law to be applied by the World Court is to be found in no particular statute or code and in no particular system of the world. Chief Justice Hughes once remarked, after he had served as one of the Judges of the World Court, "If you were to wait for an international court until you could get a satisfactory body of international law, the only time that such a court would function would be in the millennium and most people may doubt whether at such a time it would be necessary."

In the Wimbledon Case to which I have already referred, the Court took account of the view which the United States had taken of its rights and liabilities under the Hay-Pauncefote Treaty and under the treaty with Panama with reference to passage through the Panama Canal in time of war. This was in order to draw an analogy with passage through the Kiel Canal. In effect, the Court adopted the practice of the United States as evidence of "the general opinion according to which, when an artificial waterway connecting two open seas has been permanently dedicated to the use of the whole world, such waterway is assimilated to natural straits in the sense that even the passage of a belligerent man-of-war does not compromise the neutrality of the sovereign State under whose jurisdiction the waters in question lie."

In the Mavrommatis Case, brought by Greece against Great Britain for damages suffered by a Greek subject under the Mandate for Palestine, Judge Moore, who dissented from the opinion of the Court on the first submission of the case, did so largely upon the authority of the Supreme Court of the United States in cases in which its jurisdiction did not affirmatively appear from the record.

References to American authorities were made also in the celebrated Lotus Case, brought by France against Turkey. The French steamship *Lotus* was in collision with a Turkish steamship on the high seas, an accident that resulted in the death of passengers and crew members aboard the latter vessel. Officers of the French vessel were prosecuted criminally before a Turkish court. The French Government maintained that the Turkish court had no jurisdiction to punish for an alleged crime committed by persons on board a foreign vessel on the high seas. American authorities, particularly the well known Cutting Case, were cited by Judge Moore in support of this claim in his closely reasoned dissenting opinion. The Court was evenly divided, but the French contention was not upheld by reason of the deciding vote of the Presiding Judge.

My survey was intended to show that there was no substance in the allegation that the Court was applying "League law," but that precedents of the United States were given consideration on the basis of complete equality whenever pertinent to the issue.

⁓ IX ⁓

Pathways of Professional Interchange

1. Warsaw Conference of 1928

The meeting of the International Law Association at Warsaw in the summer of 1928 presented an opportunity of becoming acquainted with a country that, though it had been under Russian domination, had nevertheless maintained its own cultural independence. Although I had never been able to visit any part of the Russian Empire, I had long wanted to visit Poland because of its unique history, which partook of the cultures of both the East and the West. I had met Polish jurists in Europe and found many of them highly cultured and well grounded in the principles of public and private international law. I knew of their struggle to improve and consolidate the various old provincial and territorial laws they had inherited so as to consolidate the body of their law into a system favorable to more intimate relations with the family of nations.

We had a strong representation from the American Branch, and I was pleased to be elected by the Executive Council of the association as national representative of the United States for the conference. I took part in some of the discussions, but I fear that my ceremonial duties tempted me away too often from the business of the conference. I am sure that my time was not wasted, however. I had an interesting interview with President Ignacy Mościcki of the Polish Republic, in which he expressed the hope that Poland might make a real contribution to the promotion of better international relations. He said that he had had a visit some time before from Chief Judge Robert von Moschzisker of the Supreme Court of Pennsylvania, who was of Polish origin and that, indeed, they found that they were distantly related. Marshal Jósef Pilsudski was elected honorary president of the conference but was unable to attend because of illness. I found Professor Zygmunt Cybichowski, president of the conference, a person of extraordinary legal ability, and one known for his liberal views. He was basely assassinated by the Nazis during World War II. In his inaugural address he pointed out how Poland was deprived for over a hundred years of the power of regulating her own activities. He said that, having recovered her freedom, Poland, with a population of thirty million inhabitants, with a fertile soil and large natural resources, wished to consecrate as much energy as possible for the development of prosperous international relations.

Our Polish hosts were unusually hospitable. They opened some of the fine old aristocratic mansions of Warsaw for receptions to be given in our honor. I remember especially one evening reception held in the lovely Lazienki Palace, with its large lagoon and ancient courtyards beautifully illuminated. A fine symphony orchestra gave a concert of classical music in the open air. This palace was completely destroyed in World War II. A special performance of the celebrated Warsaw ballet was also given at the Opera House, with appropriate music by the great Polish composer Frederic Chopin. To attend a performance of Chopin's polonaises and mazurkas in his native land was an unforgettable experience.

The conference was not without real contributions to international law. A Draft Code on the Rules of War in Occupied Territory was presented and approved. The draft represented in the main the work of Hugh H. L. Bellot, the secretary-general of the association. Unfortunately, this was to be his final contribution. I was seated with him and a small group of members in the lounge of the Europa Hotel, discussing the work of the conference, which had then been in session three days. Dr. Bellot was quite cheerful, and said that he wished to retire early for he had much work on the following day.

He died in his sleep during the night. In his honor these Rules of War were given the title "The Bellot Regulations."

This was also to be the last conference attended by another old English friend, Lord Phillimore, who passed away in March of the following year. At the Warsaw Conference Lord Phillimore was, as usual, one of the most active members. Lord Phillimore represented the ideal protagonist of conciliation and compromise. Without these, agreement among nations would be impossible. In commenting on his death, Mr. Elihu Root, who had been his principal collaborator in framing the Statute of the Permanent Court of International Justice, remarked: "His services were invaluable. His serene and lovable character created in the committee room an atmosphere of kindly consideration favorable to agreement. His superior intelligence, trained by long judicial experience, at once informed and clarified our thought." I had a feeling of deep personal loss in the passing of these two jurists, Bellot and Phillimore, with whom it had been my privilege to work over a long period of years.

While in Warsaw, I was able to meet personnally the claimants in an action which had been pending in my office for some time. It involved the performance of contracts payable in Russian rubles, which had become practically valueless after the Russian Revolution. My clients were the heirs of Henri Marconi, a cousin of the famous radio scientist. He had settled in Warsaw long prior to World War I and had taken out a large amount of life insurance with a New York life-insurance company through its general agent in St. Petersburg. The policies were written in the Polish language but payable in Russian rubles, for Poland was, of course, a province of the Russian Empire at the time. There were a large number of policies of a similar nature, written for residents of Poland and of other parts of the Russian Empire, upon which actions had been brought and which were pending in New York courts. Curiously enough, the general agent of the company in St. Petersburg was also a policyholder, and his counsel was the most energetic in prosecuting claims for him and other holders. In order to save expense, and for other reasons, he organized a group of policyholders so that their respective counsels could join forces as far as possible. He also was the first to carry forward the litigation for his own client on the difficult question of the standard of value to be placed upon the currency in which the policies were payable. I had had some successful results with regard to the valuation of the depreciated German mark in the settlement of legacies made payable in marks by wills executed prior to the war. In the case of wills, however, the question of the intent of the testator is a material element. Intent could not very well be implied in a contract expressly made payable in a foreign currency.

The counsel for the general agent of the company succeeded in scoring some notable victories in the early stage of the proceedings by which he sought to recover the surrender value of the policies in dollars. This gave him, or perhaps his client, a feeling of assurance and a desire to "go it alone" without the necessity of further consultation with the other members of the group. He then gave notice of withdrawing from all further cooperation. In doing so, he was completely within his rights, but I was considerably nettled because he had had the benefit of our experience and counsel up to that time. Furthermore, his client would have been a valuable witness, perhaps an essential one, in any testimony concerning the circumstances under which the policies had been written. I was fully aware of the dangers which lay ahead, and welcomed the opportunity of meeting personally in Warsaw the various members of the Marconi family interested in the policies, to whom I explained the situation. Fortunately, the other members of the group of counsel continued to cooperate loyally, and, except for policyholders resident in the Soviet Union, we were able to effectuate a very favorable rate-of-exchange value for the ruble, to the satisfaction of my clients in Warsaw. Some years later the case of the group represented by counsel of the general agent was decided by the New York Court of Appeals. It was held that the plaintiffs could only recover if they could show that, by the law of Soviet Russia, preexisting obligations were to be paid ruble for ruble in the new chervonetz gold note. The court said, "The ruble which they could recover is valueless." (Dougherty *v.* Equitable Life Assurance Society, (1934) 266 N.Y., at p. 100). Even in private practice, "Peace hath her victories, no less renown'd than war."

The Warsaw Conference gave us the opportunity of seeing what might soon have been a *Polonia restituta*, in the sense of modern Polish patriots, had not a tragic fate brought disaster to the whole of Europe. We saw Warsaw at a time when factional strife had grown less acute and the rights of minorities were beginning to receive recognition. All this was soon to disappear, and World War II saw widespread carnage and massacre, together with the destruction of the physical remains of Poland's past glories.

2. *Visit of the Foreign Bars to New York in 1930*

In the summer of 1928, when we were meeting at Warsaw, the members of the American and Canadian Bars were being lavishly entertained in the British Isles by their brethren there. I was unable to take any part because I was busy not only with the meeting at Warsaw but also with lectures at the Hague Academy. An invitation for a return visit to take place in the summer and autumn of 1930 went out from the American Bar Association to the British, French, Irish, and Scotch Bars. The International Law Association, which had not met in the United States since 1907, decided to hold its next conference in New York in connection with the visit of so many of its members responding to the invitation of the American Bar. This placed a heavy but agreeable responsibility upon the American branch of the International Law Association.

With the authority of the American Branch I called upon John W. Davis, our former ambassador to Great Britain, and asked whether he would accept election as president of the American Branch in view of the forthcoming visit of so many distinguished members of the British Bar with whom he was personally acquainted. He graciously consented with the understanding that the executive burdens would be largely carried by the other officers. I was at that time first vice-president. By selecting a very active committee of arrangements to act in cooperation with committees of the local Bar associations of New York, we were thus able to carry out an extensive program for entertaining our foreign guests. Besides an inaugural reception by the Association of the Bar, there was a banquet by the six Bar associations of the City of New York, presided over by Mr. Davis, a trip up the Hudson combined with a motor trip through Harriman State Park and a review of cadets at West Point, a formal reception by Mayor James J. Walker at City Hall, and a reception by the Chamber of Commerce of the State of New York. There was also a convocation at Columbia University at which the honorary degree of LL.D. was conferred on four delegates: Baron Tomlin of Ash, Sir Frederick Pollock, Professor Pierre Arminjon of France, and Dr. Walter Simons of Germany. A delightful garden party was given by Clarence H. Mackay at his magnificent country estate at Roslyn, Long Island, with a classical concert outdoors performed by the Philharmonic Society of New York. Samuel Untermyer received the party at his home Greystone, near Yonkers, which had formerly been the home of Samuel J. Tilden. I remember a curious incident in connection with the latter visit. It had been arranged that the party should be conveyed by bus from the Algonquin Hotel immediately following the luncheon given there by the American Foreign Law Association. The principal speaker was Sir Frederick Pollock, then in his eighties, who entertained us with a description of his duties as Admiralty Judge of the Cinque Ports, a very ancient English office. As the institution had a long history, Sir Frederick became forgetful of the passage of time in the present, and I was advised there was danger of arriving too late for the reception at Greystone. Several of the members of the committee seemed equally aware of the impasse and, at what seemed an appropriate period, initiated tremendous applause which brought the address to a close without discourtesy to our distinguished guest.

The Bar of the City of Philadelphia did not wish to be outdone in hospitality, and with the cooperation of Mayor Harry Mackey a special train for the trip was arranged and a resplendent reception was given by the mayor in the City Hall or Public Building. It fell to me to introduce our guests to the mayor and city fathers by a brief address in which I referred to the fact that it was to my native city of Philadelphia that I was bringing this distinguished gathering. Mayor Mackey, who seemed to have been better instructed than I had thought, in his speech of welcome took occasion to say that he was proud that Mr. Kuhn came from the City of Brotherly Love but that he had not proved very loyal to it since he had left it at the age of four and it had taken him a long time to come back and again identify himself! At least the mayor proved willing to slay the fatted calf for the prodigal son. The party was given a banquet and taken through Independence Hall and other historic buildings and then for a trip round the port on the Delaware River.

On the serious side of the conference in New York, I presided over a discussion on the legalization of foreign documents and the adoption of a more simplified procedure for their certification. We also discussed the effect of war on contracts. There was a lack of agreement as to whether war should dissolve all contracts between the citizens of belligerent countries, subject to specific exceptions, or whether the general rule should be that contracts should not be dissolved except in certain cases. Edwin Borchard of Yale presided over the discussion of a Draft Convention on the rights and duties of belligerents with regard to neutral property at sea, and Oscar Houston presided over a section dealing with sales contracts containing the c.i.f. clause. The conference adopted a resolution recording its satisfaction at the adoption of the so-called Kellogg-Briand Pact, and recommended that further measures be taken for adding to its practical effectiveness. Dr. Walter Simons, one of the delegates, was former acting president of the German Reich (on the death of Friedrich Ebert) and former Chief Justice of the Supreme Court of the Reich. He expressed sympathy with the Pact but recognized that there were barriers to be overcome. He believed that if the nations of the Continent were to survive commercially and economically, a Pan European agreement was necessary. He favored a project of a "United States of Europe," and believed that all German statesmen with foresight must subscribe to the general thesis of Pan Europeanism. He said, "I look forward to its inevitable accomplishment by the year 1940." In this respect his insight may have been prophetic, except that he allowed too little time for the fruition of his ideas.

The Kellogg Pact was then the only international plan for peace to which the United States was officially committed. The administration in Washington was centering its hopes upon it instead of upon the League. It was natural that proposals for making it effective should have attracted the cooperation of the American members. A number of plans were proposed by delegates. Wyndham Bewes of England proposed a supplementary agreement pledging the signatory powers to refrain from affording any aid, comfort, or support to a nation using nonpacific means in violation of the Pact. I offered a proposal that in the event of a violation of the Pact, the adoption of a policy of nonintercourse with the violating country should not be deemed a violation of neutrality. Judge Thorvald Boye of the Supreme Court of Norway proposed that a violator of the Pact should be denied all right of visit-and-search of neutral merchant vessels on the high seas. These proposals led to a very active general discussion showing complete lack of agreement; accordingly, it was determined to allow the whole question to be taken up at the next conference of the association.

3. *Correcting the Record*

It was in connection with preparations for the visit of the British and French Bars that I was able to correct an erroneous impression that was being circulated concerning the official policy of Charles Evans Hughes. I first became acquainted with him when he was Secretary of State and at the same time president of the American Society of International Law. Mr. Elihu Root had also served in the same capacity when he was Secretary of State.

Early in 1930, I had occasion to write to Mr. Hughes about the preparations for the visit of the foreign Bars in his capacity as chairman of the Special Committee of the American Bar Association. At one of the meetings held in New York in January, 1930, Mr. Hughes called me aside and said that he was much annoyed at the unfair attacks then being made against him as a supposed enemy of the League of Nations. He said that he found it inappropriate for him to make a direct reply but that someone who knew the facts ought to defend his position. I said that I quite agreed and would endeavor to have a suitable reply appear in the newspapers. Accordingly, I wrote a letter to the New York *Times* which appeared in its issue of January 24, 1930:

> The statement of Professor John H. Latané reported in your columns today, that the American Society of International Law had adopted the official attitude of its President, Mr. Hughes, and ignored the existence of the League of Nations, must not go unchallenged. It is unfair not only to the Society, of which I have been an active member since its foundation, but especially to Mr. Hughes, who as a Judge of the World Court cannot very well enter into private controversy upon such matters.
>
> The fact is that in 1925, attending his first meeting as President of the Society, Mr. Hughes said: "It should be apparent that the controversy over the Covenant of the League of Nations involved no hostility in international conferences," and he went on to favor our collaboration with the League "in the promotion of humanitarian measures" and "the development of new and improved rules upon particular matters to which we have direct relations," but also publicly recommended the admission of Germany to the League.
>
> At the 1926 meeting he referred to the League question as "an old controversy," saying that the United States would have joined in the Covenant had it not contained certain commitments which could not be accepted "as requiring its action in unknown contingencies and in relation to controversies to which it might not be directly related."
>
> Professor Latané, for whom I have had great respect, seems to have been carried away by emotional excitement of the moment when he thus unjustly attacked one of our leading statesmen and jurists. Mr. Hughes, both in and out of office, has constantly urged that "we must continue the search for all practicable methods of settling existing disputes, of preventing the development of grievances, of ending estrangement."

Mr. Hughes wrote to me on January 30, 1930, "I greatly appreciate your kindness in writing to The Times." He was appointed Chief Justice of the Supreme Court of the United States on February 3, 1930. It is a cause of satisfaction to me to have found recent corroboration of my conclusion that Mr. Hughes had favored the League. In the authoritative biography written by Merlo J. Pusey and published in 1952, the author relates that in a personal interview with Mr. Hughes in 1946 he said he had continued to press for early consideration of our adherence to the Covenant, with reservations, after his appointment as Secretary of State. He was prevented from doing so by Senators Brandegee, Johnson, Borah, and others, who threatened to retaliate by blocking administration measures if adherence to the League was pressed.

$$\text{\textdbend} \quad X \quad \text{\textdbend}$$

Pathways in Legislation

1. *The Harvard Research in International Law*

At the time of the New York Conference of 1930, a considerable part of the activity of jurists in the field of international law revolved around codification. A great impetus to this movement had been given as early as 1924, when the Assembly of the League of Nations adopted a resolution requesting the Council to convene a committee of experts representing the main forms of civilization and the principal legal systems of the world. This committee was to prepare a list of subjects of international law, public and private, which would seem most desirable and realizable to meet "the legislative needs of international relations." The committee promptly entered upon its duties, and as a result of its work through the years official representatives of forty-eight nations met at Geneva in March and April, 1930, to try to reach agreement on three selected subjects for codification. These subjects were Nationality, Responsibility of States, and Territorial Waters.

The codification of the law relating to any subject, even those having no political connotations, is a task requiring careful preparation. Ordinarily, such preparation goes on in the departments and ministries of government having to do with legislative or diplomatic drafting. The officials of government, no matter how competent, frequently have neither the time nor the inclination to conduct research upon the subject in hand, beyond their own domestic jurisdictions. Accordingly, the action of the Harvard Law School faculty in organizing a "research in international law" for the preparation of draft conventions on the subjects recommended by the League of Nations Committee was both wise and timely. Manley O. Hudson, professor of international law at Harvard, who afterward became Judge of the World Court, had long been a member of the staff of the Secretariat of the League of Nations at Geneva. The idea doubtless originated with him; at least he became its director and, throughout the years, remained its chief activator.

I was invited to serve on the Advisory Committee of the Research, and I took an active part in its work from its first session at Cambridge, Massachusetts, in January, 1928, until its last session in 1949. The committee was made up of a selected group not only of teachers of international law and related subjects but also of practitioners of the Bar, Federal judges, and officials of the State Department. The actual work of drafting was done by a *rapporteur* assigned to a particular draft, working with a group of advisers selected for the draft. Over the years I worked as an adviser with Richard W. Flournoy, of the State Department, on the draft on Nationality; with Philip C. Jessup, who was rapporteur on Competence of Courts in Regard to Foreign States; with Edwin D. Dickinson (afterward dean of the Law School of the University of Pennsylvania), rapporteur on Jurisdiction with Respect to Crimes; and with James Grafton Rogers of Yale and A. H. Feller (afterward Assistant Secretary-General of the United Nations in charge of the Legal Department), as rapporteurs on Judicial Assistance; with Jessup on Rights and Duties of Neutral States in Naval and Aerial War, and with Jessup as rapporteur on Rights and Duties of States in Case of Aggression.

The procedure of the Research followed largely the method of the American Institute of Law, which had drafted the restatements of the various branches of the common law as developed and applied in the various States of the Union. The latter work was also a codification, with this important difference that it was not intended to have the force of law. The drafts of the Research were usually for the purpose of elaborating an instrument which could form the text of a multilateral convention. The draft presented by a rapporteur and his advisers was submitted to a plenary session of the Research for final adoption after lengthy and detailed discussion. A unique feature of the Research was that each draft was accompanied by an elaborate survey of the laws of many countries of the world, whether derived from legislation or jurisprudence, together with any treaties or conventions, bilateral or multilateral, affecting the particular subject of the draft. These surveys had immediate and continuing authority and were recognized as such no matter what ultimately was to be the fate of the particular drafts.

I have mentioned that Elihu Root believed that the real test of whether an idea had any value for legislative purposes could come only after reducing it to writing in technical legal phraseology. That was the task which the Reseach sought to perform, and the analytical and critical mind of the director, Judge Hudson, never allowed the discussion, often bitterly controversial, to drift very far from this ideal.

The results of the Research were published in detail from time to time with the cooperation and assistance of the Carnegie Endowment for International Peace and the American Society of International Law, with George A. Finch as the liaison.

2. *The Kellogg-Briand Pact*

We have mentioned that the Warsaw Conference recorded its satisfaction at the signing of the Kellogg-Briand Pact and recommended that further measures be taken for making it more practically efficacious. Its official title was Treaty for the Renunciation of War. It was signed at Paris, August 27, 1928, only a few days before our conference asked that the proposal be made more than a mere pious wish. For years this point of piety plus ineffectiveness was doomed to plague all those persons, official as well as unofficial, who sincerely wished to see our country play a worthy part toward securing future peace. Our adherence to the Covenant of the League was getting to be more and more improbable, and yet the Republican administration under the initiative of Secretary of State Kellogg was endeavoring to put something before the world by way of a multilateral agreement which might represent a step toward this goal. Unfortunately, membership in the League had by this time become a partisan issue.

The Pact consisted of a solemn declaration that the nations of the world "condemn recourse to war for the solution of international controversies, and renounce it as an instrument of national policy in their relations with one another." They also agreed that the settlement or solution of all disputes or conflicts of whatever nature or of whatever origin they may be, which may arise among them, "shall never be sought except by pacific means." The Pact in itself provided no sanctions or means for enforcement. There was no specific reference of disputes to the World Court or to any other tribunal. If there were a violation by one nation, could other nations take sides in favor of the innocent nation and determine for themselves the question of guilt or innocence? In other words, in case of war would the usual rules of neutrality apply? The committee which was appointed as a result of the Warsaw Resolution recognized that the Pact was intended to "outlaw" war, so that a violator would be an offender against the law of nations. The signature of practically all the nations of the world would really have accomplished this end if it had been uniformly interpreted in this sense. Within the five years following the signing of the Pact, there came about a veritable Babel of interpretation, both within and without the League, some jurists maintaining that as a result of the Covenant and of the Pact the nations of the world had intended to abolish the old international legal rules of neutrality, at least as they were understood and applied prior to 1914. Another group denied that either of these agreements had made any change in the underlying laws of war. This controversy flared up intensely at the meeting of the American Society of International Law at Washington, in April, 1933. The controversy centered around an able paper presented by Philip C. Jessup. He maintained that the laws of neutrality had not been eliminated, but he preferred to speak of belligerents and abstainers instead of belligerents and neutrals. He did not answer the question whether the United States as a nonmember of the League would insist on its traditional neutral rights if the members of the League were acting in common against a covenant-breaker. Charles Warren, formerly Assistant Attorney General, believed that while the old rules persisted in form it was no longer possible to retain strict impartiality in application. Clyde Eagleton, professor at New York University, believed that by making war illegal under the Kellogg Pact and the Covenant, we had eliminated the obligation of neutrality against the violator under the right of self-help which an otherwise neutral nation could apply in its conduct toward a violator. Edwin Borchard of Yale was the most extreme antagonist toward this view. His opposition was characterized by his ridicule of the idea that a state could pick out an "aggressor," and he even opposed the use of the word "aggression" as a term in international law.

I was far from wanting to be a "Daniel come to judgement" in this melee of opinion on what was destined to be one of the most critical problems of our foreign policy for many years to come. Perhaps I had the spirit of the schoolboy who, seeing a good fight, did not want to be left on the side lines. My position was that the question was not merely whether neutrality had disappeared in international law or in fact. I said:

"Those who so learnedly and so eloquently argue here in favor of neutrality and of the right of states to hold apart from any conflict at all times are not so much interested in the development of the law of neutrality as they are interested in opposing proposals for world organization. Now, we have not perfected any world organization at the present time either in the League, or through the Kellogg Pact, or through any other machinery. We may be in the process of so doing. It is imperfect. We are still in the twilight stage. . . . I think that not to be 'off with the old' until you are 'on with the new' is a doctrine which holds just as well in law as it does in love. . . ." I then quoted from a statement which had been made only recently by Mr. Borchard, in which he said: "To prevent the natural development of strong and responsible states by supporting the chaotic, the weak and the disintegrating, is sorry service to peace and stability." To this attack I replied: "Well, sir, you have the thing unmasked. We are not to support weak states. We are to allow them to be overcome by the aggressor if the aggressor is strong enough, and let us stand on the side lines and see the weak nation crushed, no matter how unjustly and unfairly, in order—Lord save the mark—to preserve the peace of the world."

As we look back to the crucial year of 1933, when this discussion took place, the year in which Hitler assumed power in Germany, and as we compare the doctrine of neutrality then prevailing with the world situation of the present day, in the Far East and in Europe, we find that in the course of less than two decades the term "aggression" has become a key word in international relations and in international law. The determination of whether a nation has by its conduct become an aggressor lies at the very root of the foreign policy of all peace-loving nations. The Charter of the United Nations and other multilateral and bilateral agreements have in effect made the obligation of neutrality to depend upon nonaggression by the state which demands neutrality from another state.

It may be interesting to see how this idea of freedom from aggression began to take root in our own legislative and foreign policy. It did not come about suddenly and, indeed, some of the steps taken about this period were designed to take us directly away from this idea. My own pathways in international law required me to take a definite stand although I held no public office. It was rather because of the many opportunities which came to me for influencing public opinion. In 1935 the New York County Lawyers Association, the largest local Bar association in the United States, determined to create a standing committee on international law. I was invited to become its first chairman. I had already served for a number of years on the committees on international law in other Bar associations. This committee, however, was different because it did not make its report directly to the body of the association; according to the rules, any report must first be submitted to the board of directors or to the president for approval. This meant that reports on any important subject would be subjected to criticism and debate before reaching a stated meeting and before they could be presented to official bodies as representing the will of the association. Accordingly, reports were prepared with considerable care.

Our first report related to the so-called Neutrality Act of August 31, 1935, adopted at the time of the Italo-Ethiopian conflict, under which Congress directed the imposition of an embargo on arms, ammunition, and "implements of war" to any belligerents. We pointed out that the Act was not clear concerning whether it was intended to prevent shipment of all articles which could be considered contraband. We said that Congress should grant some discretionary powers to the Executive to restrict or control, in whole or in part, trade in what might be called secondary articles of warfare. We also called attention to the question of giving some meaning to the Kellogg Pact. We quoted the statement of Norman Davis at the General Disarmament Conference of May, 1933, in which he said that the policy of the United States was to refrain from any action tending to defeat the collective efforts taken by other states in conference where a nation has been guilty of a breach of peace in violation of its international obligations. We called attention to the fact that we could take a timely step with reference to the pending conflict even though we were not members of the League of Nations. The endeavor to apply economic sanctions against Italy in order to restrain the aggressive policy of Mussolini failed miserably. The committee had at least placed itself on record against the defects of our own legislation in this respect. Its report was approved.

The committee was again obliged to take up the question in 1938, after amendments had been made in the previous year to the Neutrality Act. The amendments did give the Executive a certain amount of discretion, but, unfortunately, it was provided that once an embargo was declared it must apply equally to all belligerents irrespective of the guilt or innocence of the party in having started hostilities. This worked most inequitably upon weaker states who lacked the means of providing the highly technical equipment required for defense in modern warfare. We said:

"It is sufficient to point out that the legislation precludes the President to act, by way of embargo, upon any moral question involved in the particular armed conflict. The President, charged with the duty and responsibility for the conduct of our foreign relations, is thus prevented from making use of an important diplomatic resource common to other nations. The knowledge that the President has thus been deprived of discretion places him at a distinct disadvantage in dealing with a belligerent charged with violation of the rights of the United States under the recognized principles of international law."

3. *Neutrality Legislation*

At the time of which we are speaking, the Secretary of State, Cordell Hull, had in effect already classed Japan as an aggressor. In his statement of October 6, 1937, on the Far Eastern crisis, he said that the United States has been forced to the conclusion that the action of Japan in China was inconsistent with the principles which should govern the relationship between nations and was contrary to the Nine-Power Treaty.

As a result of this statement, I felt that we were justified in recommending that the inflexible provisions of the Act be amended so as to leave the time and scope of their applications to the discretion of the Executive. "It may be difficult to arrive at a satisfactory distinction in advance between aggressive and defensive warfare, but no nation should place limitations upon its power to act upon the breach of a treaty obligation entered into with it by another nation; and yet, under the present legislation, a treaty-breaking belligerent may be dealt with upon the same terms as one which has observed its treaty obligations with the United States. An embargo declared equally against both might work to the advantage of the treaty-breaking belligerent. A neutral should not thus tie itself in advance to go beyond the duties recognized by international law." This is what we said and what I firmly believed to be the only realistic attitude in view of the new threats to the peace of the world which were appearing both in Europe and in the Far East. Our report had, however, by no means plain sailing before the board of directors of the Bar association. Robert C. Morris, its president, informed me that there was a lively debate with arguments both pro and con but that finally the report was approved. It was afterward sent to the President, to the Senate, to the House of Representatives, and to the Secretary of State. My colleagues on the committee were Frederic R. Coudert, Allen W. Dulles, Phanor J. Eder, Mansfield Ferry, Edward Goodell, Allen R. Memhard, Eustace Seligman, and Dorothy Straus.

It should be remembered that what we were speaking of was not neutrality in its technical sense, which means the status of a nation not taking part in a war between two or more other states or belligerents. We were speaking really of the *policy* of neutrality, which means a course of conduct to prevent a nation from becoming embroiled in some present or future war. The subject was therefore not strictly juridical, but one of diplomacy and foreign policy. Indeed, the adoption of an embargo was a relinquishment of certain neutral rights which we had traditionally maintained. It was plain that the equal exercise of the embargo was playing straight into the hands of strong and aggressive elements both in Europe and in Asia, because shipments of materials such as oil and scrap iron were reaching Japan and Germany in large quantity from the United States. The situation was probably as unsatisfactory to President Roosevelt as it was to the majority of the people, but Congress was allowed to adjourn without bringing the issue to a head. When the war broke out in Europe in September, 1939, urgent demands for repeal could no longer be neglected. To my astonishment, the position was taken by certain distinguished international lawyers that it would constitute a violation of international law for the Congress of the United States to change its legislation during time of war by the repeal of the arms embargo for the purpose of helping the enemies of Germany and Japan. The New York *Herald Tribune* asked a number of jurists connected with the Harvard Research to express themselves upon the question. I did so vigorously in its issue of October 26, 1939, to the effect that practice does not support any obligation to refrain from changes in domestic law during wartime which might indirectly affect the interests of one or other of the belligerents. The Research had held that a neutral state had the right to adopt new measures for the purpose of better safeguarding its rights and interests as a neutral if the ordinary and recognized rules of neutral status were not violated. At all events, a special session of Congress had finally been called after regrettable delay.

In the meantime the American Bar Association, a national body, through its section on International and Comparative Law had taken up the subject, and a prompt report was requested from the Subcommittee on Law Protecting Americans and their Property in Foreign Countries and on the High Seas. I was a member of the committee, and we reported that we were of the opinion "that action to avail of rights open to neutrals under generally accepted international procedure, if taken because of considerations of domestic welfare, involves no violation of legal neutrality, even though the action occurs after the outbreak of hostilities, and would not give rise to valid claims for the indemnification of belligerents who might be injured thereby." This was accompanied by a full memorandum of facts and points. On October 26th, Senator James M. Mead of New York rose in the Senate and said that he desired to have this report, which he called an "illuminating document," inserted in the Record, naming members of the Subcommittee who had prepared the report, who, besides myself, included James W. Ryan, chairman; John Foster Dulles and Major General Allen W. Gullion, Judge Advocate General of the Army.

The Neutrality Act was finally passed, on November 4, 1939, along lines which we had been recommending for nearly two years. It did not change the laws of neutral status, but it undoubtedly took a bold step with reference to what, in happier times, might have been considered a departure from correct neutral policy. It may perhaps sound a little banal to say that times change and we change with them. It certainly is not in the cause of national safety nor even of world peace to continue to follow policies which had developed under a wholly different state of international society. Indeed, the relentless progress of the new attitude gained momentum after World War II not only through the Charter of the United Nations but also by reason of the imbalance of power left by the war. As late as April 2, 1951, President Auriol of France declared before the Congress of the United States that "neutralism" was a barbarous name for an attitude foreign to the French soul. "They know that isolation is death. They know that neutrality, whether declared, armed or disarmed, has protected neither Belgium, the Netherlands, Norway nor Denmark, and that an aggressor would never stop at a frontier post, even should it be surmounted with a dove holding the branch of an olive tree."

4. *Comparing National Systems of Private International Law*

War exercises a nationalistic influence on international jurisprudence. When a dispute arises between two or more states, each party relies upon its own interpretation of international law to justify its conduct or its rights with reference to the dispute. No codified system exists, although, as we have seen, the attempts to codify at least portions of such a system were accelerated after World War I. In the main, however, the tremendous number and the acrimonious character of the disputes resulting from the war led to interpretations which departed from previously conceived norms. Treatises on the public phases of international law tended more and more to rest upon *national* interpretations of what was once discussed as a universal system. Thus, Charles Cheney Hyde's comprehensive work published in 1922 dealt with international war "chiefly as interpreted and applied by the United States."

The same influence was observed to be happening in other fields of international jurisprudence where the rights and obligations of private individuals were involved and not the relations of states. The freedom of movement of persons and property between the various countries of the world, which characterized modern life almost everywhere until the most recent period, brought with it many disputes as to whether the local law or some foreign law was applicable to transactions which did not take place in any one territory or jurisdiction. The branch of legal science which regulates these problems is referred to in most countries as Private International Law or the Conflict of Laws. Until a comparatively recent period it was theoretically regarded as constituting a universal or uniform system. After World War I it began to be recognized by competent authorities that the attempt to deal with the complicated and difficult situations which the war had produced, required giving up the fictitious concept of a universal system of principles for the choice of law.

I have already mentioned that in 1928 I had been invited by the Academy of International Law at The Hague to deliver a course on the Conception of Private International Law in Theory and Practice in the United States, thus recognizing the national character of the system. It occurred to me then that a comparison of our own system with the systems which had grown up in the countries of continental Europe and in the countries of Latin America, and even a comparison with the rules recognized in British courts, would be a worth-while study. Accordingly, in the years following these lectures I took as much time as possible from my practice and other duties to present in a critical manner and within reasonable compass the legislation and jurisprudence of common-law jurisdictions relating to private international law in parallel comparison with the other principal systems of the Western World. The book was published by Macmillan's in 1937 under the title *Comparative Commentaries on Private International Law or Conflict of Laws.*

The comparative method was made more timely not only because of the Restatement but also because the Code of Private International Law popularly knowns as the "Bustamante Code" had recently been adopted in the form of a treaty by some fifteen Latin American countries. Its principal draftsman was the eminent Cuban jurist Dr. Antonio Sánchez de Bustamante y Sirvén. I accepted the provisions of that Code as being characteristic of the law of Latin

American countries, although its specific provisions did not prevail in all.

I have referred to the principles of the conflict of laws as having a national character. As a matter of fact, in the United States there was not even uniformity as between the separate States because of the reserved sovereignty residing in each State jurisdiction. When the Restatement of the common law of the American States was undertaken by the American Law Institute in the early twenties, the first subject to receive consideration was the conflict of laws. The complete Restatement of the Law of Conflict of Laws was promulgated in 1934 after a decade of research and discussion. This was not strictly speaking a codification, for it had no legislative sanction, but the courts of the various States have generally tried to apply its principles. As we now had an approach to national uniformity, I considered it timely to examine the principles recognized in foreign countries in comparison with the Restatement. Even assuming that private international law rests upon a national basis, the practitioner must know the rules of conflict in foreign jurisdictions as well as in his own, because upon these rules may depend the choice of the forum and the application of the law. I did not attempt to present the foreign systems with completeness because to attempt to do so would have made the book encyclopedic in character; neither did I attempt to give all the various academic theories prevailing in the various European countries. This was done many years later by the distinguished German jurist Ernst Rabel. It is a method appreciated more in continental Europe than in the United States, where at least the practitioner and the judge lay far greater stress upon decisions of the courts and, of course, upon legislative provisions, than upon the opinions of the most learned jurisconsults.

Wars and rumors of war have not prevented countries of the Continent of Europe from holding diplomatic conferences at more or less regular intervals for the codification of certain fields of private international law. Some of the multilateral conventions which have been drafted and signed at these conferences have received ratification of a sufficient number of countries to give them binding force.

The process of codification has now taken on a much more ambitious character and deals with a number of subjects which extend beyond the field of conflicts of law into the field of public law. In October, 1951, a diplomatic conference held at The Hague was attended by delegates from sixteen nations of Western Europe, including Great Britain. In addition to drafts of various conventions, the Conference added two most signficant *voeux* indicating the direction which the conferences are likely to take in the future. The first of these was that the Netherlands Government should be charged with the task of concluding an agreement of mutual cooperation between the Council of Europe and the Conference under which the Council should refer to the Conference all matters relating to the unification of private international law and that both bodies should work together to obtain adherence to the draft conventions with such modifications as may be made by the Council and agreed to by the Conference.

In commenting editorially upon this action in the *American Journal of International Law* for July, 1952, I said: "It is indeed significant that the participating nations recognized the importance of establishing a permanent relationship with the Council of Europe. The accomplishment of a closer political and economic integration of the free nations of Europe is not dependent upon mere good will alone but upon the progressive development of appropriate international administrative and judicial institutions.

I have already pointed out some of the problems which I encountered in my practice when a judgment obtained in the court of a foreign country was sought to be given recognition in the court of one of our States without going over the whole controversy again from the beginning (see Chapter IV, 3). A similar problem exists when we seek to execute an American judgment in a foreign court. In 1945 a governmental commission was appointed in France to prepare a revision of the French Civil Code, or Code Napoléon. Experiences of World War II have made France much less liberal toward foreign judgments than she once was. Now it is proposed that no foreign judgment be executed in France except on condition of reciprocity. A list of states is to be published by joint order of the ministers of justice and foreign affairs showing the countries which grant reciprocity. When the proposal was considered in February, 1950, the late Professor J. P. Niboyet, an able jurist, fell into the egregious error of stating that the United States does not execute foreign judgments. He misjudged our law because it is different from the French procedure of "*exequatur*." Dr. Kurt H. Nadelmann, in the *Harvard Law Review* (May, 1952), appropriately suggests that, if adopted, the proposal would constitute a reprisal against American judgments. At all events, here is a striking example of the need for comparative-law studies.

The French jurist Édouard Lambert would not have fallen into this error. He made many valuable contributions to a better understanding of foreign law to promote good international relations. I was invited to contribute to a volume published in his honor on his seventieth birthday. My contribution to this collection dealt with "The Function of the Comparative Method."

It is gratifying to any writer to see practical significance given to his ideas over the passage of time, ideas which were originally merely philosophic in character. My contribution in honor of M. Lambert was originally written in French but appeared in English in the *Tulane Law Review* for April, 1939. I did not at that time intentionally combat the great virtues and benefits claimed by the ideology of the Soviet state. However, since the passage of time has made these pretensions more relevant to our own welfare and security, the comment which I then made has present application and bears repetition:

"The tendency of human life upon this planet during recorded history has been toward the development of aggregations of individuals living together as organized units. Families and tribes evolve into peoples and nations. It has been supposed by one school of thought that a general similarity in the conditions of individuals of like class, occupation, or economic conditions was tending toward a horizontal stratification of different classes of society, leading toward international solidarity between such classes. Could such a state of society be realized, it would represent the corporate idea in an universal application. If such a state of society would suffice to accomplish the results claimed for it by its advocates, it would assume the existence of ethnic as well as physical and moral characteristics in the inhabitants of the globe *contrary to those hitherto observed."*

Paul Reinsch, a publicist learned in the way of life on three continents, once said that it is impossible to dispense with the *psychic.* Indeed, psychic unity often survives the loss of national sovereignty. Accordingly, I said:

"We see then that even under the sway of an empire theoretically all-powerful and universal, conditions of practical life demanded recognition for the diversification of tradition, custom and law among aggregations of peoples. The importance of this is often lost sight of by reason of the fact that sovereignty has become coincident with territorial jurisdiction and is regarded to be the source of all law. But although sovereignty may constitute the ultimate sanction of all law, it cannot by a mere act of will, change custom, which is a fact. Our purpose is merely to point out that law is as much a part of human life and characteristics as language, manners, or moral standards. It is affected by all of these and in turn reacts strongly upon them. No conqueror, no matter how ruthless, can change the customs and habits of a people by mere fiat. He may exterminate them, but so long as their community life exists, so also will there remain a certain residue of legal identity which is just as likely to modify the law of the conqueror as to be modified by it. This was the experience of the Roman law. During the period of the most complete dominance of the Roman state, the Roman system was most powerfully influenced by servient peoples. . . . It was precisely this adaptability and tolerance of the Roman legal system toward servient systems which gave to it its final cosmopolitan character. Being itself largely the product of foreign law, it was found to be sufficiently elastic to be 'received' in turn by the peoples and nations who had, in the march of history, succeeded to the Roman dominance."

My purpose in all this was to point out that it would be a false ideal to expect uniformity of law in the civilized nations of the world so long as there are ethnic and psychic differences. Family and personal laws are most deeply affected by these influences. On the other hand, commercial law rests upon like foundations in most countries. Banking and finance are international. Bills of exchange, promissory notes, checks, stocks and bonds circulate throughout the world. Corporations, partnerships, and other group forms are carried on in the various commercial jurisdictions under different systems of legislation, but their fundamental characteristics are sufficiently alike to permit of international commercial transactions without undue friction. In the fields where ethnic differences or folkways play little part, there is chance of uniformity, but here again differences in economic policies tend to create legislative controls which often constitute divisive influences between nations which politically and psychologically are friendly. Members of the Bar can play a worthy role in overcoming such barriers. The movement toward international judicial cooperation, which is still in its infancy, represents a promising field in the direction of integrating the processes of national systems of law.

Latin American jurists have often shown their good will along these lines. As recently as 1951, the official Inter-American Juridical Committee made a report on the possibility of an approach to Anglo-American principles by changes in the Code of Private International Law accepted by fifteen Latin American countries. The committee, referring to an earlier comment of mine, found the task almost impossible. In analyzing the latest report, I recommended that *specific* topics should be undertaken, such as those with respect to proof of foreign law and taking of testimony in a foreign jurisdiction. There are other hopeful fields. *Moderata durant.*

5. *The American Foreign Law Association*

Interest in comparative-law studies and research was not new in countries of Europe. For example, the Société de Législation Comparée of France issued its valuable *Bulletin* as far back as 1869. Similar societies supporting periodicals devoted to comparative law had also been established in Great Britain. We have already referred to the Comparative Law Bureau of the American Bar Association and its excellent work in stimulating interest in this country in foreign law and legislation. However, the comparison of legal systems is usually thought of as an academic study related to the philosophy of law. Prior to 1925 it had never occurred to any larger group that the knowledge of foreign law and legislation as such was of direct interest and benefit to the American practitioner. The publications of the Comparative Law Bureau of the American Bar Association opened up new mines of valuable material which practitioners having anything to do with foreign business found to be valuable. Our participation in a European war brought new contacts with European business and European clients.

A group of practitioners situated mainly in New York and Philadelphia determined in 1925 to organize an association specially devoted to the needs and interests of practitioners in foreign law. The original impetus came, I think, from G. Evans Hubbard of New York. He formed an organizing committee of whom some of the members were W. W. Smithers of Philadelphia, Charles B. Fernald, Judge Otto M. Schoenrich, Phanor J. Eder, Edward Schuster, and myself. I became president in 1941 and served for two years.

The association was at first modest in its activities and aims. It met from time to time at luncheons at the Lawyers Club and engaged in postprandial discussions among the members upon some announced subject of foreign law. I remember engaging in a symposium with Mr. Smithers and Mr. Fernald on November 21, 1927, on "The Effect of French Divorce Decrees in the United States." We were dealing mostly with litigations with which each of us had had some direct contact. There was no unnecessary reference to either jurisprudence or literature, and we dealt with the stark facts of life in the twentieth century. For example, it was quite new to most of us to have a graphic description of the proceedings known as *concilia-*

tion, required by French law, initiated by a *sommation de réintégrer,* or demand for reinstatement of the conjugal life, followed by the final declaration of the bailiff announcing that "response was made by Monsieur that he did not understand the insistence of his wife, that he refused absolutely to live again with her, that his decision was irrevocable." As both parties to this particular divorce were American citizens, the proceedings described also included the manner in which a French tribunal applies the national law of the spouses not only to determine whether a divorce can be granted or a separation only, but also to weigh the grounds for the divorce or separation. These discussions constituted a sort of legal clinic of operations in which, although no blood was spilled, there were undoubtedly ample substitutes in the form of tears shed by at least one of the original contestants.

The part of the discussion to which I was asked to give attention was the effect of the French decree of divorce or separation in the State in which the spouses had been domiciled. This question was a difficult one then, and we are still far from certainty even today as to what recognition will be given in any particular case.

Earlier in the same year, we had the benefit of having light thrown upon the converse question of "The Effects in France of Foreign Judgments" discussed by a French *avocat*, Dr. Pierre Mariotte.

In the early years our group was comparatively small. Later, the impact of totalitarian régimes in a number of European countries brought to our shores a large number of refugee lawyers who sought contacts with their brethren of the Bar in this country but who, because of not being admitted to practice, were unable to join the local Bar associations. Under our liberal rules they were enabled to become associate members of the American Foreign Law Association, and brought to our work the benefit of their rich experience and wide learning gained in practice in their country of origin.

Nothing succeeds like success, and the association now has successful branches established in a number of other cities in the United States. A close liaison is also maintained with the Société de Législation Comparée of Paris, the Instituto de Derecho Comparado of Mexico, the Instituto de Dereito Comparado of Brazil, and the Institute of Comparative Law of the University of Upsala, Sweden. The field of comparative law is now one of the activities of UNESCO for which an international committee has been organized. The American Foreign Law Association has been recognized as its official representative for the United States. The association now sponsors the *American Journal of Comparative Law,* the first publication of its kind in the United States.

⁓ XI ⁓

Pathways in the Shadow of

World War II

1. *The Lytton Report on the Manchurian Crisis*

It is believed by many competent observers that World War II began, not at the time of the march of the German legions into Poland in 1939, but at the time of the military events of September 18–19, 1931, by which Mukden was seized by Japan and, later, a large part of Manchuria was added to the zone of military occupation. This is particularly true with regard to the participation of the United States in the war, because the attack on our fleet at Pearl Harbor was conditioned by the American reaction to Japanese aggression begun by the overt acts at Mukden.

At the invitation of the editor in chief of the *American Journal of International Law*, I undertook to make a study of what was then called the Manchurian Crisis, on the basis of the facts disclosed by the so-called Lytton Report. My comment appeared in the January, 1933, issue. I believed that many of the problems analyzed by the report must be taken into account both today and in the future in respect to our Far Eastern foreign policy.

It will be remembered that the Commission of Inquiry which prepared the report was selected by the Council of the League of Nations. The proceedings were initiated by the Chinese Government under the provisions of the Covenant which declared that "any war or threat of war, whether immediately affecting any of the members of the League or not" was "a matter of concern to the whole League." The Chinese Government was insistent that it was necessary to take immediate steps "to prevent the further development of a situation endangering the peace of nations." The commission selected by the Council was made up entirely of neutrals consisting of nationals of France, Germany, Great Britain, Italy, and the United States, who in turn elected the Earl of Lytton to be chairman.

Reliance on the importance of the Lytton Report was justified because of the long visit of the committee to the devastated area and to other parts of Manchuria, China, and Japan. I have always considered the report to be a model of neutral observation and recommendation. Its thoroughness was enhanced because it went back both to the Sino-Japanese War of 1894–1895 and to the Russo-Japanese War ten years later, both of which were fought to a great extent on Manchurian territory. The commission found that the military operations of Japan at Mukden could not be regarded as measures of legitimate self-defense. On the other hand, the report showed the aggravating nature of the Chinese boycott in Manchuria as far back as 1893 through a body which the commission considered to be the progenitor of the Kuomintang. In my analysis of the Lytton Report, I said:

"International jurists will some day be obliged to take a much more sophisticated attitude toward the boycott than is taken at the present time, especially when the boycott has assumed the character of an instrument of national policy. The tendency of so many writers to classify it among the peaceful means of settling disputes will have to undergo modification and qualification. The Japanese merchants interviewed by the commission insisted that the boycott as practiced in China was an act of aggression against which Japanese military measures were a retaliation, and though it did not confirm this view, the commission refused to sustain the contention of its Chinese assessor that the boycott was pursued, generally speaking, in a legitimate manner.

"The question whether, conversely, the boycott is a legitimate weapon of defense against military aggression by a stronger country, especially where arbitration has not been resorted to, raises a question of a much wider character which the commission does not answer. It regards the question whether the organized application of the boycott to a particular country, is consistent with friendly relations, or in conformity with treaty obligations, to be a problem of international law, and expresses the hope that, in the interest of all states, this problem should be considered at an early date and regulated by international agreement."

The task of the commission was rendered difficult by the fact that Soviet Russia, the owner of the Chinese Eastern Railway and possessing a long frontier line to the north and northeast, was not a member of the League. I maintained then that any settlement which ignored its interests, or indeed that of other nations entitled to trade in Manchuria, could not be permanent. Now the situation is reversed and Soviet Russia is in possession of Manchuria, but no permanent settlement will endure without taking account of the interests of reconstructed Japan or of other nations entitled to trade there. Some day we must come back to the recommendation of the Lytton Commission that the maintenance of a real Open Door is in the true national interests of China and Soviet Russia.

For a settlement on the basis of peace in the Far East, the recommendations which were thus emphasized in 1934 must some day be considered, chief among which were that a solution from which the parties interested would not derive economic benefit would not in the long run serve the cause of peace; any agreement should lay down the respective rights, interests, and responsibilities of China and of Soviet Russia in Manchuria. Because of its peculiar history and geographic location, it cannot be allocated to the full sovereignty either of China or of Russia. The Lytton Commission recommended that the control over Manchuria should be modified so as to secure a large measure of autonomy consistent with the sovereignty and administrative integrity of China. This is just as important to peace in the Far East today as it was at the time of the Lytton Report. I recognized then, as I do now, that these proposals may be a counsel of perfection, but any settlement which is to be effected should be permanent and not one of immediate expediency. Korea was not then the problem which it has since become, but when it is settled the status of Manchuria will be found inextricably involved with it.

2. *The London Economic Conference of 1933*

The Lytton Report laid emphasis on the importance of corrective measures of an economic character to be taken in Asia. At the same time the dangerous economic situation prevailing in Europe had become more menacing. My comment on the Lytton Report appeared in January, 1933. In June of that year, I submitted an analysis of the financial and economic situation in Europe and its explosive possibilities. A World Economic Conference was called to meet in London in that month. This served to focus attention upon the fact that many of the causes of the crisis in trade and finance were international and that the steps necessary for cure did not lie entirely within the control of any individual state. I pointed out that the crisis could not be dealt with adequately if nations separately continued to exercise control powers, although permitted to do so under international law.

It is not new to students of international affairs that economic conditions are as important for the maintenance of peace as are political understandings. The trouble is that, like campaign oratory, everybody talks about economic strains but no effective action is taken before it is too late. So many of the conditions which existed five years after World War I still continue to be a danger. An analysis of these conditions may serve in the public interest.

Any analysis of world economic conditions just prior to the London Economic Conference of 1933 might appear to be more suitable for a financial chronicle. However, there were so many questions involving sovereign rights and treaty law that I undertook to make such an analysis in the *American Journal of International Law* (July, 1933):

"Dealing specifically with questions of finance, every state may, and in fact does fix the ratios of gold, silver, or other commodities used in its monetary standard. For a long time prior to the great war, the purchasing power of gold remained relatively stable, though having variations due to certain natural causes. A rise in the output of gold, especially through the development of new sources of supply in the Alaskan and the South African gold fields, was largely responsible for the rise in the prices of primary commodities during the two decades preceding the outbreak of the war. The dislocation of international monetary stability did not make itself completely felt until the shortage of goods consumed by the war had been made good. Increased productivity by new means and sources of production supplied the new demands with an increasing momentum, and not only caught up with the normal requirements of world trade, but soon far exceeded such requirements. World stocks of primary materials, agricultural and industrial, are reported to have been double in 1932 what they were in 1925. Aggravating the situation were the endeavors made in many countries to restrain the disastrous fall in prices by the erection of tariff and other trade barriers so as to keep commodities out of competition with domestic producers, while at the same time restricting the outflow of gold through exchange regulations. Many governments, including our own, have laid an embargo more or less complete on the exportation of gold. All these measures are strictly within the sovereign legislative powers of every independent nation, though they manifestly may cause great injustice and indeed sometimes extreme injury and hardship to other nations."

The influence of world debts and reparations upon international financial problems must be taken to be an element of world politics, although frequently treated as though it were only an economic problem. The Lausanne Conference of June and July, 1932, at which I was present as an observer, laid the foundation for the London Economic Conference of one year later. The participating nations had called upon the League to convoke a world conference which should decide "upon the measures to solve the other economic and financial difficulties which are responsible for, or may prolong, the present world crisis." It is not generally understood how greatly the gold standard or any other standard of monetary exchange affects the international relations of states. I said then, as I say now, that whatever may be the other factors entering into a world economic crisis, it is plain that the restoration of stability depends upon the establishment of an international monetary system under which national currency would rest upon some common basis. Without such a basis the value of national currencies can be expressed only relatively in comparison with the values of each of the others. "So long as the gold standard was maintained, such a common basis existed, but with the surrender by all but a very few nations of the attempt effectively to maintain a gold standard without restriction of one kind or another, an international common basis no longer exists. In order to remedy these conditions, nations sometimes resort to bilateral treaties dealing with specific restrictions."

If it had been possible to revert to the gold standard, or if it were possible to do so at the present time, it would have been, and would be, an easy way out of many international financial difficulties. The preparatory commission of the London Conference originally favored this solution. However, it was soon recognized that the restoration and the continued effective functioning of the gold standard in international commerce required the fulfillment of a number of conditions which could not be carried out by any international agreement without supplementary action by nations acting separately. After World War II efforts were made to meet a similar situation through the creation of two international agencies, the International Monetary Fund and the International Bank for Reconstruction and Development. I had occasion to comment on these in 1945 at a symposium, "Money and the Law," held under the auspices of the New York University School of Law and the Economists' National Committee on Monetary Policy—but of this more later. Now we are back in 1933. It is sufficient to say that in my analysis for the London Conference, I said, "It is probably impossible to maintain permanently an international monetary system except on the basis of an international economic system sustained by cooperation within the fields admittedly within the autonomy of the individual nations."

Nations are as free to conduct economic wars upon each other even in times of peace as they formerly were to initiate political wars. However, there is such a thing as economic aggression, as well as political aggression. Some day the United Nations may have to take measures to combat economic aggression, for it may easily lead to physical aggression. The experience of recent times shows that such "wars" are often fully as disastrous to internal economy as to the "enemy" without. As to the London Conference of 1933, I expressed the hope that the nations acting separately would be willing to make sacrifices in view of the threat of a common peril, and I concluded my analysis by quoting the words of the Preparatory Commission: "In the movement toward economic reconciliation, the Armistice was signed at Lausanne; the London Conference must draft the Treaty of Peace."

Notwithstanding all the high hopes entertained both at home and abroad for the relief of world economic tensions, the London Conference resulted in a fiasco. It is not profitable to review the reasons except to say that President Roosevelt's fear of disturbing domestic prices resulted in his message of July 3, 1933, to the American delegation, wherein he said, "The world will not long be lulled by the specious fallacy of achieving a temporary and probably an artificial stability in foreign exchange on the part of a few large countries only." Many volumes have been written by the experts, but the fact is undisputed that the failure of the London Conference was followed by Europe's progressive fall into a slough of despond. From the point of view of present-day problems, one whose interest lies in world cooperation by international agreement cannot fail to sense the irony of what the President then said: "Let me be frank in saying that the United States seeks the kind of dollar which a generation hence will have the same purchasing and debt-paying power as the dollar value we hope to attain in the near future." We are still seeking that kind of dollar. Intervening events may have made the dream impossible, but one experience should be drawn; namely, that first things come first and that no crisis such as confronted the world in 1933 should be left to drift because a permanent settlement was not presently possible. It is regrettable that Mr. Hull's advice had not been followed. "Every nation" he said, "must supplement its domestic program with a basic international economic program of remedies for business recovery." Among these he mentioned the reduction of trade barriers, the stabilization of exchanges and currencies and monetary standardization. The fact is that there were too many jealousies within our own camp, and too many imponderables working against taking these steps. For all of this the world later suffered grievously.

3. *The Paris Conference of the Institute, 1934*

The Institut du Droit International was founded in the historic city of Ghent in 1873, the same year in which the Association for the Reform and Codification of the Law of Nations (now known as the International Law Association) was organized at Brussels. Both societies were the result of earnest and well planned steps taken by leading members of the Bar in the countries of Europe to establish a better international organization with some hope of preventing further disastrous wars. In this movement, David Dudley Field of New York had played a prominent part. As early as 1866, he attended group meetings abroad, especially in the British Isles, at which he expounded his ideas for the codification of the unwritten and fragmentary system which theoretically united the family of nations, within the bonds of law. Later, in 1873, this movement eventuated in the founding of these two associations, both of which have continued with expanding influence down to our own day. The Institute is strictly an academy devoted mainly to the scientific and academic study of problems of international law both public and private. Its founders consisted of a small group among whom were Pasquale Mancini of Rome, Tobias M. C. Asser of Amsterdam, J. C. Bluntschli of Switzerland, Carlos Calvo of the Argentine, David Dudley Field of New York, and G. Rolin-Jaequemyns of Belgium.

At Cambridge, England, in 1931, I was elected an associate member of the Institute, being elected a full member in 1947 at Brussels. I was of course highly gratified at this honor. Membership is strictly limited to sixty members and sixty associates. There is a limitation of a certain fixed quota for different countries which varies somewhat from time to time. Each of the two great organizations founded in 1873 and devoted to international law have their special functions, with the Institute governed under more rigid controls over the work of its committees between sessions and the International Law Association more inclined to venture into the maritime and commercial field with a view to unification rather than codification. Both organizations have their particular role to play and both are of equal importance in promoting a more constructive system of laws between peoples and nations than the human race has achieved up to the present time.

The first session of the Institute which I attended was at Oslo, Norway, in 1932. I took some part in the discussions but confess that I did so with considerable diffidence because all proceedings were conducted in French, the traditional language of European diplomacy. My senior American colleagues, Frederic Coudert and Philip Marshall Brown, assured me that all American members were inclined to restrict their discussion because they felt at a disadvantage in debating against foreign colleagues to whom French was either a native language or a second language acquired in childhood. Later this rule was altered, so that now discussions may be either in French or in English. If in English, a translation follows.

The Institute was to have met at Madrid in September, 1934, under the biennial rule. I had made my plans to attend. Our colleague, James Brown Scott, then vice president of the Institute, proceeded to Madrid a few days in advance of the meeting. When he arrived, violent hostilities were raging in the streets because of the civil war. The session was finally canceled. By great effort the officers were able to arrange a transfer of the meeting to the Palais Royal in

Paris. The inaugural session was held on October 15, with Charles Lyon-Caen presiding.

We arrived in Paris about ten days before the meeting. On October 9th, as we returned late in the evening from a visit to a friend, we noticed a strange hush in the usually noisy boulevards. At our hotel we were informed of the assassination of King Alexander of Yugoslavia and M. Louis Barthou, French Minister of Foreign Affairs, while the former was making an official visit to France.

Political conditions in Europe in 1934 bore certain parallels to what they are in the mid-century. Fascism and nazism were then menacing, and what we are pleased to call "the free world" was then, as now, endeavoring to unite in defense. M. Barthou, who was an active member of the Institute, had made a number of fruitful visits as French Foreign Minister to various European capitals in the work of stabilizing European peace. The visit of King Alexander was part of this movement. Investigations carried on in France and elsewhere indicated that the crime was committed as part of a political plot in order to further designs by Hungary to recover districts made part of Yugoslavia and which were formerly part of Hungary. There may have been other more sinister purposes, because support of the conspiracy was also traced to fascist sources in Italy. Political tension between Hungary and Yugoslavia became intensified, and Yugoslavia invoked Article XI of the Covenant before the Council of the League of Nations, specifically accusing Hungary of complicity in the crime. Czechoslovakia and Romania joined in the complaint, alleging danger to "the general conditions upon which the peace of Central Europe depends."

I was deeply shocked at the abominable crime because it not only took the life of the king but that of an innocent scholar and statesman who had devoted his life to the maintenance of peace through law. I undertook to inquire into legal questions affecting plots organized abroad with government support. It was plain then, as it has become more menacing now, that the world is confronted with a new type of subversion with foreign support, a breach of peace largely uncontrolled by any pertinent international regulation.

In the *American Journal of International Law* for January, 1935, I emphasized that the complaint of the three governments, though sharp in tone, did not ask for any special measures, which might have been done under the Covenant. The peace of nations has often been endangered by assassinations and other terroristic acts committed by individuals closely associated with political groups acting with the connivance or knowledge of a foreign government. The Soviet Government has been accused of fomenting disorder abroad through the Third International. The assassination of Chancellor Dolfuss was attributed by Austria to activities of the German National Socialist party.

"The extent to which a government is responsible for preventing or repressing subversive or revolutionary activity by persons or groups within its territory directed against the peace and order of a foreign state is not well settled in international law. It has been said that even treason is not an international crime. Certainly the lack of any general agreement and practice upon the subject represents one of the lacunae which one would least expect to find. An international community of states, wherein each was insistent upon the maintenance of its own sovereignty and wherein the equality of each was recognized as axiomatic, would be likely to develop a mutual obligation to suppress subversive acts directed against a friendly foreign nation." This is not entirely a new principle, but it has been forgotten in our day and to renew it has come to be of vital interest. Vattel, the eminent Swiss jurist of the eighteenth century, maintained that if a sovereign who has power to see that his subjects act in a just manner permits them to injure a foreign nation, either by an act directed against a state itself or its citizens, he does no less a wrong than if he injured that state himself.

I pointed out that some states had assumed to punish unauthorized acts by private persons tending to draw the local state into complications with a foreign government, and I referred to legislation in France, Germany, and Italy. I emphasized that legislation in Great Britain and the United States was silent except with regard to an obligation under the laws of neutrality in relation to an actual or impending civil war. Political plots are made punishable in Great Britain and in the United States so far as they are directed against foreign governments, but only if such acts amount to making the national territory a base for a military or naval expedition against a friendly state. The complaint of Yugoslavia related to a state of facts which would not be covered by political plots to carry out a military or naval expedition. It related to a situation which more nearly approaches the type of subversion with which we have become only too familiar in the mid-century, and it is for that reason that I refer to my discussion of the assassination of King Alexander. The complaint specifically alleged that "the assassination was organized and executed with the participation of those terrorist elements which had taken refuge in Hungary and which have continued to enjoy the same connivance in that country as previously, and it is only thanks to this connivance that the odious Marseille outrage could have been perpetrated."

In dealing with subversion organized or encouraged by a foreign state, one must retain an impartial viewpoint. I was struck by the remarkable resemblance of the accusation to that brought *against* Serbia after the assassination of the Archduke Francis Ferdinand and his wife at Sarajevo. It was then asserted in the German White Book that the plot was planned and promoted in Belgrade with the cooperation of Serbian officials, with the ultimate object of bringing about a separation of the southwestern region of the Austro-Hungarian Monarchy and to unite it with Serbia. In 1914 it was impossible to have the issue brought out in the open, for there was no League of Nations. In 1934 the fact that such a forum existed at least postponed the conflict. In my appraisal of the situation I drew attention to this favorable factor, as well as to other factors not so favorable. Nationalism had increased since World War I; indeed, some had maintained that it had been overstimulated by the principle of "self determination." Acting under Article X of the Covenant, a resolution was unanimously adopted by the Council on December 10, 1934, presented by Anthony Eden, Lord Privy Seal, which, besides insisting that all those responsible for the "odious crime" should be punished, declared that it is the duty of every state "neither to encourage nor tolerate on its territory any terroristic activity with a political purpose," and that every state must do all in its power to prevent and repress acts of this nature and must for this purpose lend its assistance to governments which request it. The Council called upon Hungary to take at once appropriate punitive action in the case of its officials whose culpability may have been established, and it set up a committee of experts to study the question with a view to drawing up a preliminary draft convention to assure the repression of conspiracies or crimes committed with political and terrorist purpose.

Since these events occurred, the course of history has enhanced the importance of setting up some machinery on the international level. The United Nations General Assembly, by resolution of September 9, 1948, invited the International Law Commission to consider whether it was desirable and possible to establish an international judicial organ for the punishment of the crime of genocide and of other crimes to be defined by international convention. The proposal for setting up a court of this character is of long standing and has been the subject of discussion from time to time before unofficial bodies such as the Inter-Parliamentary Union, the International Association of Penal Law, the International Law Association, and others. The International Law Commission, through its Committee on International Criminal Jurisdiction, discussed certain basic principles for setting up such a court at its session at Geneva in August, 1951, on the basis of which Professor Vespasien Pella of Romania presented a carefully documented opinion at the request of the Secretariat of the United Nations. Professor Pella expressed the conviction that if a permanent international criminal court had been in existence, some of the principal offenders tried at Nuremberg and Tokyo would never have committed the criminal acts in question.

Plans for the setting up of any international jurisdiction always require a long period of discussion and even controversy before they are realized. This will undoubtedly be true with reference to the setting up of an international criminal court. Objections to such jurisdiction usually proceed from countries where judicial administration conforms to strict constitutional control in the interest of individual rights. Possibly an optional system restricted to crimes which may fairly be regarded as directed against the peace and security of the international community may form the basis for a beginning.

My own conviction at the time of the assassination of King Alexander was that no real progress toward cooperation and peace can be expected if conspiracies may be concocted, yea, encouraged, with the knowledge or participation of one government against the peace and order of another. This should not impede groups of persons displaced or exiled because of political reasons from the exercise of rights of free speech and cooperation in a psychological campaign for the restoration or maintenance of free government.

The Paris Conference of the Institute was associated with signs of trends which were forboding both from fascist and communist directions. On the voyage over from New York I met Alexander Troyanovsky, Soviet ambassador in Washington. I was introduced to him by Elisha Friedman, economist, who had lately visited Russia under the Intourist system, and had written widely on Soviet economy. Mr. Troyanovsky was quite amiable but unusually inquisitive. He wanted to know the mission that was taking me to Europe. When I replied that I was going to attend a conference on international law, he laughed and asked what practical value could possibly come out of such a meeting. I happened to have a copy of the agenda in my pocket, and I read to him some of the subjects coming up for discussion. When I came to the subject of "Diplomatic Immunities of Persons Exercising International Functions," his expression suddenly changed and he remarked that he never realized that international law concerned itself with anything quite so practical. Mr. Troyanovsky was not a lawyer, and his conversation reflected the Soviet emphasis on administrative power, without judicial control as understood in the United States. Curiously enough, his remark reminded me of a story told about John Hay by Charles Noble

Gregory. After his term of office as Secretary of State had come to an end, Mr. Hay continued to reside in Washington. He asked my friend one day where he had been the night before. When Dean Gregory said that he had been at a meeting devoted to international law, Mr. Hay remarked, "Oh, I see, you have been sitting up with the dead!"

The sessions at Paris were overshadowed not only by the event at Marseille but also by the manifest coolness shown by many of the delegates toward the German members. Hitler had been in power over a year. Some of the German members were already living in exile, and this attitude, of course, did not apply to them. Karl Strupp, a brilliant teacher and writer on international law, was living in France, and later met a tragic end by his own hand prior to the German occupation. Dr. Walther Simons, whom I had known at Heidelberg in 1912 and also at the Williamstown Institute of Politics, looked careworn. He was said by some to have been a Nazi, but I felt that if so it must have been under duress. I could not bring myself to believe that one who had resigned as Chief Justice of the Reichsgericht, the Imperial Supreme Court, because of governmental interference with his judicial functions, could possibly have accepted a complete tyranny except under pressure. He had been, only a few years earlier, the honored guest of the American Bar Association at its meeting in Memphis.

4. *Secretary of State Cordell Hull's Declaration of Principles*

The shadows of discord began to lengthen perceptibly in the years following the assassination of King Alexander. Though the United States Government attempted to stem the tide toward war in perfect good faith, it found itself in an embarrassing position, diplomatically speaking, because it was not a member of the League of Nations and had not even become a member of the Permanent Court at The Hague, nor had it contributed to the expenses of the Court, although an American national had been elected by the members of the League as one of the judges. The Kellogg-Briand Pact of

1928 had been only mildly effective and, indeed, had never received any sanction whatever in the judicial sense until after World War II, through the decisions of the Military Tribunal under the Nuremberg Charter.

We have now reached 1937, at which time Cordell Hull was Secretary of State. A new step was necessary, which, like many others, had to be taken outside the international organizations set up by the peace-loving nations of the world after World War I. Accordingly, Secretary Hull issued an official pronouncement on July 16, 1937, setting forth the position of the United States "in regard to international problems and situations with respect to which this country feels deep concern." This was communicated to all foreign governments with the request for an expression of opinion upon the principles enunciated. When the replies were received and published by the Department of State, I undertook (January, 1938) to analyze the replies for the *American Journal of International Law*. These replies gave a deep insight into the diplomacy, open or concealed, of the various countries in the year preceding the outbreak of World War II. Curiously enough, I found the reply memorandum of some of the smaller countries to be particularly important, demonstrating what I had long believed and frequently advocated; namely, greater opportunity for participation by the smaller nations in the affairs of the world. I pointed out that Portugal had issued a mild reproof against the attitude of the great Powers; it warned against the "abstract and generalizing tendency of jurists," and cited as causes for failure the insufficient study of the causes of world unrest and the desire to find a single formula for the solution of international problems.

I quoted from the memorandum as follows: "Everyone desires peace, everyone proclaims the sanctity of treaties and the faithful compliance therewith, everyone desires that there be less difficulties in international trade, and everyone wishes to have the burden of armaments removed or lightened. Difficulties begin only when it is sought to pass from the field of intentions into that of action. . . ." I praised the insight of the memorandum in pointing out that interference in the internal affairs of other nations is now carried on by a new technique in the form of revolutionary agitation and that in the Soviet Union mysticism has been adopted to gain political and economic ends from within.

The Latin American nations for the most part gave categorical approval to Secretary Hull's excellent principles, but some of them coupled this approval with the hope that the declarations might have an influence in settling particular conflicts in which they were interested. European countries like Bulgaria and Hungary considered the principles from the point of view of modifying treaty provisions growing out of World War I. Hungary made the direct accusation that the states which had benefited at her expense after World War I had sabotaged the portions of the Peace Treaty which were favorable to her, and Hungary also claimed that upon principle it had already regained a free hand because of the "fiasco of the Disarmament Conference."

In my analysis I pointed out similarities in the tone of the replies received from Italy, Japan, and the Soviet Union, in that each of these governments expressed approval of the general principles of the declaration but laid particular emphasis on disarmament. The reply of Soviet Russia was in the form of a personal communication from Mr. Litvinov to Mr. Hull, clothed in a degree of politeness that has long since passed out of Soviet usage. It contained a proposal for "a permanent peace conference within the framework of which the cooperative efforts mentioned in Mr. Hull's statement could be exerted." At the other end of the political spectrum, the Spanish Republic replied that it had never deviated from the course indicated in its own Constitution of 1931, which renounced war as an instrument of national policy. The Spanish note pointed to a complete coincidence both in doctrine and in practice with the principles defended by Mr. Hull.

In this analysis of the policies of foreign governments immediately prior to World War II, the most astonishing replies, in some respects, were those received from the Union of South Africa and from the Dominion of Canada. While not couched in identic terms, both replies called attention to the necessity for studying barriers and rigidities, both economic and political, tending to deny peoples or nations equality of opportunity or treatment. While both gave approval to Mr. Hull's principles, each of these countries within the British Commonwealth pointed out the necessity of examining the *status quo* as established by the peace treaties in order to anticipate and forestall revolutionary and catastrophic events.

In summing up my analysis, I wondered whether the statement of principles in Mr. Hull's declaration was timely in the light of apparently irreconcilable differences both in Europe and in the Far East. I would not dwell upon the analysis of the replies received by Mr. Hull in the year preceding World War II were it not that I believe that these considerations are of even greater importance to us at the present time. I said: "In drawing conclusions from the observations taken as a whole, three points may be emphasized. First, that there was a manifest solidarity of the nations of the Western Hemisphere in specific acceptance of the principles. Second, that the problem of intervention in international law has become complicated by the fact that the respective dominant political parties of certain countries assume to extend their sphere of action beyond the territory of their own state, thus engendering a conflict of ideologies without being guilty of intervention in the hitherto accepted sense. Third, that too much reliance must not be placed upon the acceptance of general principles and that the actual and factual elements of international differences must be explored to their foundations if any real contribution is to be made to the maintenance of international peace."

Our interest in Secretary Hull's declaration of principles and the replies received from the Powers is not merely one of diplomatic history. It bears upon present-day situations. The event showed that contestants who have cast the die of armed intervention, or who are determined to seek their purposes in more subtle ways by boring from within, are not likely to give serious consideration to the most sincere appeals to reason, if not concretely connected in some way with a solution of their claims. We may say that they insist upon an applied rather than upon a pure science of diplomacy. Many will urge that when the blood is up, it is futile to expect any sincere conformity to a declaration of general principles. We are living in an age of evident resurgence of Machiavellian methods of statecraft. When an effort was made to apply the declared principles at the conference held at Brussels under the Nine-Power Treaty, the late Edwin L. James of the New York *Times* remarked that "moral suasion is impotent in the world today, even when it is American." Secretary Hull announced that he was well satisfied with "the solidarity of attitude and aspiration" revealed by the replies of the foreign governments. They had their value even though this solidarity was unable to avert World War II. A reaffirmation of the moral and spiritual values in international relations is never to be regarded lightly, even though practical diplomacy must know how to evaluate the sincerity of declared principles in the light of deeds.

5. *The Outbreak of World War II*

Fast-moving events in the international arena were destined to prove only too soon that the fine phrases used in the interchange of notes between the United States and the various nations of the world were in large measure mere window dressing.

The Institut de Droit International had planned to hold its biennial session in Neuchâtel, Switzerland, in the first week of September, 1939. We crossed the Atlantic the latter part of August and went direct to Geneva. The events occurring in Poland, in Austria, and in the Far East were more and more menacing, and it seemed as though war was not far off. While waiting to learn whether the conference would be held, we spent our time visiting the truly remarkable collection of old masters, from the Prado Palace and from other royal museums, sent by the Spanish Government to Switzerland for protection from the dangers of civil strife. Visitors from many lands came to see this assemblage of priceless art. We were soon rudely interrupted in our escapist occupations by a call from Professor André Mercier of the University of Lausanne, who informed me that the conference would not be held in view of the invasion of Poland by the German armies and the ensuing declarations of war.

For the second time I found myself in Switzerland when it could be properly described as "a neutral island entirely surrounded by war." I had learned in 1914 that to remain for any extended period would mean an indefinite interruption of plans. Accordingly, we left Switzerland for France the very next day. I knew that Paris would be in a disturbed state owing not only to mobilization but also to the converging upon that point of American and other tourists. Accordingly, we stayed at Vichy, of all places, because of its central location. There I found my friend Judge Megalos Caloyanni of Greece, formerly Judge of the Mixed Courts of Egypt. My wife was acquainted with Madame Caloyanni, who was of French origin. We spent about a week together discussing the legal and political implications of the war, while I sought information of the possibilities of a quick return home. I determined to return through Holland, if at all possible. We left for Paris, where I found all travel offices so besieged by tourists that it was quite impossible to enter. I learned, however, that a Dutch ship, ordinarily sailing to the East Indies, had been chartered for returning Americans through the aid of the American Embassy. It was impossible to arrange accommodations, but I succeeded in getting seats on the special train from Paris to Amsterdam, from which port the ship was scheduled to sail. Leaving the train at Rotterdam, I was soon in touch with the officials of the Holland Line and arranged passage home on board the S.S. *Statendam,* which sailed five days after our arrival.

I had a curious feeling of insecurity during this waiting period. I felt that Holland, particularly its ports, was not safe against German attack. This contrasted with the feeling of the Dutch population generally, who had close racial and economic ties with the Germans and who, as neutrals with an impeccable respect for the precepts of international law, had escaped molestation in World War I. Unfortunately, and tragically, this was not to be, because on May 14, 1941, Rotterdam was bombed by the Nazis, and thousands of innocent human beings lost their lives.

I recount these incidents of our escape from the conditions of this sudden outbreak of aggressive warfare not because of their interest or novelty. The experiences of many others of my acquaintance were more exciting. However, they represented a personal contact with the wanton disrespect for international law manifested from the very beginning by the German armed forces. When the good ship *Statendam* left port, we were aware that the British passenger vessel *Athenia* had already been sunk at sea, either by a submarine or by a mine, with great loss of life. The use of the submarine without the preliminary obligation of visit and search toward an unarmed merchant vessel had been strongly condemned by neutrals in World War I. It was certainly one of the basic causes for the entry of the United States into that struggle. By 1939, however, the employment of the submarine as a commerce destroyer had become common practice and, in a sense, tolerated, provided only that passengers and crew be permitted to reach a place of safety before the sinking of the vessel. So too, the planting of mines in the open seas, even within a designated belligerent zone, was strongly condemned. The sinking of the *Athenia* convinced at least one student of international law that these elemental human rules of warfare were going to be violated from the very beginning.

When we reached the North Sea and the Channel, we were carefully briefed to remain below decks as much as possible, since no lights would be permitted on the ship. We moved around cautiously, for the most part with life preservers strung across our shoulders. We soon sighted submarines, or at least their periscopes, close to our vessel, but they proved to be British. After leaving England, rules were somewhat relaxed, but when we were two days out of port we sighted several lifeboats filled with the crew of the British freight steamer *Winkleigh* on a voyage from Seattle, Washington, which had been sunk some two days earlier, after the crew had taken to the lifeboats. Anyone who has witnessed the cruelty of abandoning passengers or crew to open lifeboats in midocean, many to die a death of slow torture, will be imbued, as I was, with the realization of how far the human race has descended, in a comparatively short period of history, from the observation of the former humane rules in mitigation of the cruelty of warfare to the present-day callousness toward the suffering of noncombatants. *Facilis descensus Averni!*

Because of these experiences, with their attendant psychological influences, there was published over my name shortly after our safe arrival in New York an editorial in the *American Journal of International Law* for October, 1939, relating to the inhumanities of war practices considered to be permitted by the laws of war. I took as my point of departure an address that former President Hoover had made a few months earlier before the Christian Endeavor Societies. The significance of his statement was his insistence that there is a bond of connection between ascribing a contraband character to food shipments in time of war and the adoption of such ruthless methods of warfare as the bombing of civilian populations from the air and the sinking of ships at sea without visit and search. I said:

"It is only the deluded who think that soldiers, munition workers, or government officials ever starve. These categories of the population were not short of food in blockaded Germany during the World War. It was the ordinary civilian population, the women and children, who suffered most. Mr. Hoover insists that the real purpose of a food blockade is, under modern war strategy, to break down the morale and resistance of the civil population, which, in turn, reacts upon the conscripts at the front. Its final purpose is to make the enemy people supplicate its own government for peace. Indiscriminate land warfare by aerial bombardment of civilian population behind the front, just as, indeed, indiscriminate sea warfare by submarines, is thus viewed as mere reprisal."

My purpose was to explore two interesting proposals of Mr. Hoover, (1) that shipment of food supplies should be in full cargoes under the management and jurisdiction of a commission of neutral nations and (2) that neutral observers should be continuously in session within every belligerent country to determine the facts of any attacks upon civilians from the air. These proposals had a deep humanitarian purpose. They seem visionary today, and yet Mr. Hoover, writing in 1951, expressed his belief that the starvation of civilian populations in belligerent countries, especially after the armistice of 1918, but before intercourse had been resumed, was one of the main influences which brought about the chain of events leading to World War II. From the point of view of international law and practice, I said in 1939, and, of course, I would have to repeat it today, that it would be almost impossible to have commissions of this nature clothed with sufficient freedom of action to obtain the necessary evidence within belligerent territory. "The delay of neutral commissions in ascertaining and reporting facts constituting violations of law or breaches of treaty even in peace time is well known." I called attention in 1939 to the ineffective activities of the so-called Non-Intervention Committee in Spain of then recent memory, but today the examples could be multiplied by reference to the United Nations committees sent to observe the hostilities in Greece and in Korea.

I concluded my editorial of October, 1939, with a somewhat Cassandra-like prophecy: "The slight consideration given to the protection of women and children in the undeclared wars of recent years has led to a certain spirit of despair and defeatism in the matter of enforcement of the laws of war. Neither in Spain nor in China could the ruthless employment of aerial means of warfare be predicated upon prior measures taken against the food supply by opposing forces. In Poland, no such claim has been asserted. The problem is no longer merely one of amelioration of the laws of war, but of the preservation of civilization as we have known it. The real hope lies in the force of neutral opinion, and to make this effective when the auspicious moment arrives, there should be left no ambiguities in respect to the restrictions which are to constitute the law."

When I arrived home, I soon found that the position of the United States as a neutral was again uppermost in the minds of many persons in official Washington as well as throughout the country. Germany's attack upon Poland and the indications already given of disrespect of the rights of neutrals and noncombatants were beginning to make the Neutrality Statute unpopular. I have already referred to the report of the Committee on International Law of the

New York County Lawyers of which I was chairman, which took a strong stand in opposition to the enactment of the Neutrality Act of 1937. Legislation was already pending in Congress for the amendment of the statute. The question was raised as to the rights of a neutral nation to change its rules of neutrality after the outbreak of war. Senator Mead of New York was particularly interested in the international legal aspect, and requested an advisory report from the American Bar Committee on Law Protecting Americans and Their Property in Foreign Countries and on the High Seas, of which I was a member. The committee met promptly, and after a careful consideration of law and precedent we reported "that action to avail of rights open to neutrals under generally accepted international procedure, if taken because of considerations of domestic welfare, involves no violation of legal neutrality, even though the action occurs after the outbreak of hostilities, and would not give rise to valid claims for the indemnification of belligerents who might be injured thereby." The report was signed by the chairman, James W. Ryan, and by the other members, John Foster Dulles, Major General Allen W. Gullion, Robert T. Swaine, Ralph N. Carson, Thomas W. Palmer, and myself. It was presented to the Senate by Senator Mead on October 26, 1939, and published in the *Congressional Record.*

The necessity for bringing our report to the attention of Congress was due to the fact that some American jurists of high standing believed that the United States could not repeal the arms embargo without violating our neutrality. There appeared in the New York *Herald Tribune* of October 25, 1939, an article entitled "An Exercise in International Law," setting forth a poll of opinion on the subject conducted by this newspaper and taken from thirteen specialists, of which I was one, throughout the United States. As the editorial comment of the newspaper seemed to point to some doubt about the result, I wrote a letter to the editor which was published on the following day, in which I said:

May I suggest that your editorial comment seems to draw conclusions of wide differences among experts not warranted by the poll.

Only three of thirteen believed repeal of the arms embargo to be a violation of our neutral obligations, a small minority indeed, especially as two of the three are closely associated on the same law faculty, and the one not voting was assistant to one of these two when the draft-convention was prepared.

May I also add a consideration which seems to have been completely neglected. The three dissidents agree in laying emphasis on the motive with which the repeal of the embargo is undertaken and assume that as it cannot be with a view to aiding Germany, it must of necessity be with a view to aiding France and Great Britain. It seems to be entirely overlooked that the motive may not be either of these, but to promote our own national interests. The war was not of our making but its economic consequences bear heavily upon us. Our shipping is to be swept off the wide zone of belligerent seas. If the Congress determines that the arms embargo would bring such further contraction as to threaten economic disaster, is it not acting with perfectly legal motives in the light of international law, if it decides to repeal or amend the act in order to preserve our own internal welfare and vital interests?

In this connection I recall a remark made by Governor Dewey of New York at the annual meeting of the same Bar association in September, 1951. He said that it is always good to do the right thing even though it be late. It was indeed very late. As early as January 18, 1938, I submitted a report as chairman of the Committee on International Law of the New York County Lawyers Association in which we said: "We have already called attention to the fact that under the present legislation, no discretion is permitted in the application of an embargo so as to apply to one belligerent and not to another. This is again a matter of policy which the Committee does not assume to consider upon the merits. It is sufficient to point out that the legislation precludes the President to act, by way of embargo, upon any moral question involved in the particular armed conflict. The President, charged with the duty and responsibility for the conduct of our foreign relations, is thus prevented from making use of an important diplomatic resource common to other nations. The knowledge that the President has thus been deprived of discretion places him at a distinct disadvantage in dealing with a belligerent charged with violation of the rights of the United States under the recognized principles of international law." It was not until September 21, 1939, that Secretary Hull made the following public statement: "In advocating repeal of the embargo provisions of the so-called Neutrality Act, we are endeavoring to return to a more rational position and one that is more in keeping with real neutrality under international law." The new Neutrality Act, correcting the conditions to which we had called attention over a period of two years, went into effect November 4, 1939.

In consequence of my returning home from Europe through a neutral country, the Netherlands, my attention was drawn to the new dangers to neutrals and the status of neutrality by the enormous advance which air navigation had made since the close of World War I. I have already said that I had experienced a feeling of insecurity while remaining in Rotterdam. In November, 1939, a German military plane was brought down by pursuit planes of the Dutch forces; other occurrences of the same kind were also reported. In the same month it was reported from London that the Nazi leader was considering a plan to shorten the flying distance between German air bases and British seaports by claiming that jurisdiction over territorial waters is limited to a three-mile zone and that therefore jurisdiction over the airspace should be limited to the distance above the earth's surface at which antiaircraft guns are effective (New York *Times*, November 24, 1939). I therefore felt it appropriate to call attention, by writing an editorial in the *American Journal of International Law* (January, 1940), to what I believed to be the correct rule of international law. I said that it is well to realize at the outset the serious threat which the whole structure of neutral rights and duties in warfare would sustain if there were any vertical limits whatever to the control by neutrals of the airspace over their territory. "It is plain that once a limit were set, the burden would be upon the neutral to prove that any aircraft shot down or compelled to alight was below such vertical limit. All neutrals, especially the weaker ones within the line of combat, would find themselves powerless to protect either their neutrality or the safety of life and property

within their domain." In World War I the British Government was
at first not inclined to recognize the existence of a sovereignty of the
air. However, as early as 1911, at a meeting of the Institute of International Law, it was the British jurist Professor T. E. Holland of
Oxford who opposed the idea of free passage. Holland deeply re-
gretted that science had made aerial flight possible at all. Perhaps he
was right. The course which civilization is to take from this time
forth will have to decide. As with so many other new scientific discoveries, a right path may lead to the City of Light, the wrong, to the
Valley of Destruction.

In 1940 I said: "The technical advances made in the art of flying
and the increasingly deadly character of bombs and other weapons
carried aboard aircraft in war, have made impossible the recognition
of any vertical limit to the sovereignty of the subjacent state. The
force of gravity, omnipresent and relentless, makes any vertical limit
to sovereignty over the air-space impossible in time of war." Unfortunately, this reaffirmation of the laws of warfare was followed only
too soon by the bombing of Rotterdam and the direct violation of
the neutrality of the Low Countries. It was still a long way thence
to the Nuremberg Military Tribunal. The mills of the gods grind
slowly but they grind exceeding fine.

The aggravated violations of the rules of land warfare committed
by our enemies in World War II, almost from the beginning, were
such as to sicken the heart of any individual of fair mind and
humane emotions. I remember a certain colleague, now passed on,
who was accustomed to refer to opinions on international law with
which he disagreed as being "emotional." Lawyers as a class are
trained to keep their emotions well under control. I have never interpreted this to mean that we should be impervious to reaction against
human suffering and willful cruelty. I confess that I "emoted"
violently when I learned that civilian hostages were being executed
in France by German military authorities during February and
March, 1942. The United States War Department issued a com-
muniqué based upon information received from General Mac-
Arthur that the Japanese authorities were using similar tactics.

As a result, I made a study of the customs of war relating to hostages and published the results in the April, 1942, number of the *Journal.* I found that the term "hostages" in connection with military action against noncombatants was of comparatively recent origin. Originally it represented a kind of human pledge by one belligerent to another to ensure the performance of an agreement. Thus, after the peace of Aix-la-Chapelle in 1748, two British peers, Lord Sussex and Lord Cathcart, remained on parole at Paris until the Cape Breton Colony was restored to France. "If we admit the right of a belligerent to take hostages to insure the good behavior of the civil population, it does not follow that a belligerent has a right to execute the hostages without proof of their personal responsibility for the acts complained of; otherwise the use of the term becomes merely a ruse to mask an ugly act. Even the Romans, who were not particularly celebrated for their consideration toward the inhabitants of occupied enemy territory, recognized the obligation to connect the hostage with the reprehensible act. It is recounted that Scipio in his invasion of Spain had seized hostages taken from the domains of certain Spanish princes. He declared that he would hold the princes themselves responsible for revolts and would not avenge himself upon innocent hostages."

The United States in its instructions for armies in the field defines a hostage as a person accepted as a pledge for the fulfillment of an agreement concluded between belligerents. If accepted, he must be treated like a prisoner of war. We had come a long way from these ancient and humane conceptions of hostages, and I recounted some of the extreme usages during World War I. "International criminal jurisdiction for the punishment of war crimes has been often discussed but never carried to the degree of practicable acceptance. The futile efforts made in this direction at the Paris Peace Conference and in certain Articles of the Treaty of Versailles will be remembered. Even as late as December, 1921, Mr. Elihu Root favored the idea of a general agreement upon an international criminal code under which individuals such as submarine commanders could be held personally responsible for illegal acts and could be brought to trial in any country of the world. He felt that the Peace Conference had missed a great opportunity by failing to establish this procedure. In this connection it is to be noted that when once set up, such procedure will not attempt to indict or punish nations or communities, but the individuals responsible for giving the illegal orders or for their execution." Fortunately, these predictions were verified in the procedure adopted by the Nuremberg Military Tribunal, but it will require the existence and successful enforcement of such a system over some period of time before deterrent effects can be expected upon forces operating under ruthless military discipline.

My comments on the law of hostages were quoted with approval by recent writers who have gone much more comprehensively into the field, such as the Dutch jurist van Nispen tot Sevenaer, whose work *La Prise d'otages* appeared in 1949. The punishment of war crimes is closely allied with the question of whether there should be some *permanent* tribunal having jurisdiction. The UN General Assembly, on September 8, 1948, invited the International Law Commission to explore this question. Later the Secretariat requested an advisory opinion from Professor Vespasien Pella, formerly of Romania but residing in the United States. In the draft submitted with his memorandum, the jurisdiction would be primarily applicable to the crime of genocide, but it would also cover the execution of hostages and other war crimes provided such crimes were defined by treaty and the Assembly of the UN would consent to a reference to the Court. The conduct of forces opposed to the UN in Korea and the allegations against Soviet Russia with reference to the treatment of prisoners of war make this subject one of immediate interest and appeal to those pursuing the pathways of international law.

6. *Inter-American Cooperation*

A few months after I had made these studies in the laws of war and neutrality, I was appointed one of the delegates to attend the Eighth American Scientific Congress which was held in Washington in May, 1940, under the auspices of the Pan American Union. This permitted me to devote some attention to pleasanter and more constructive topics. I had been a delegate to the Second American Scientific Congress which met in Washington in December, 1915. It is curious that both congresses met after war had broken out in Europe but before any American nation had been drawn into the conflict. In both instances it was pleasant to feel that one could, as a North, Central, or South American, dwell together in unity and in cooperative effort with his fellow Americans throughout the Hemisphere. This did not prevent any of us from realizing fully the dangers of having the conflict spread to American shores and of having a close cooperation between all American nations for their common defense. I recalled the remark of Elihu Root at the earlier congress: "We desire no benefits which are not the benefits rendered by honorable equals to each other." Dr. James Brown Scott, who was director of the section of the Congress devoted to International Law, voiced the feeling of many of us when he said, "Many young people look pessimistically at the current scene, their eyes disillusioned, their hearts sick at the sight of half the world in the throes of war." These congresses were not devoted merely to the social sciences but to every important branch of human knowledge. The wide dissemination of the efforts of such congresses in the preservation of the treasures of civilization, especially in time of threatened danger to peace, itself constitutes a morale builder of no mean importance.

At the Congress of 1915, the subject assigned to me was the question of the codification of international law. At the Congress of 1940, the subject assigned to me was "The Scope of Private International Law in Latin American Countries Compared with the Conflict of Laws in the United States." The problem of whether to codify or not to codify, as well as the scope of such codification, is still with us at the present day. The United Nations has created an International Law Commission which meets at regular intervals at Geneva. I mention this in passing to remind us that the subject is not one of mere academic interest.

In my address before the Second Scientific Congress I expressed my views on codification. In the intervening period I had the opportunity of testing those views. I was confirmed in my opinion in 1940, and I firmly believe today that it is the correct approach. I said:

"The desirability of immediate codification of international law depends upon whether, in the particular branch, agencies for its enforcement already exist, or whether its interpretation in the last analysis lies only in the sovereign will of the individual nations. Where the latter is the case, as, for instance, in respect of the laws of warfare, codification should be undertaken only hand in hand with the organization of international agencies with authoritative power. The nature of law is generally dependent upon the organic character of institutions. Codification in the field mentioned, in order to be permanently effective, must receive its direction and character from the structure and *modus agendi* of the agencies intended to enforce it.

In those branches of international law which do not concern the rights and duties of nations *qua* sovereigns, no international agency or forum is essential to its obligatory character. Accordingly, codification may proceed there without danger of political *arrières pensées* either in elaboration or in construction. Codification combines uniformity with certainty and is particularly desirable, therefore, in the regulation of peaceful commerce between nations and in the coordination of the national systems of justice. It promotes the advent of an international basis of civilized society."

The subject assigned to me belonged, of course, to the second category, and therefore lends itself to possible codification. Judge Herbert F. Goodrich, Circuit Judge of the United States Court of Appeals, approved this view in his Benjamin N. Cardozo Lecture delivered before the Association of the Bar of New York on May 4, 1950, when he said that conflict of laws is a field in which certainty is almost the only criterion on which to judge whether a given rule is good law and where rest is preferable to motion. He ascribed this view also to Judge Cardozo, who had been active with the group engaged upon the Conflict of Laws Restatement. I had been a member of this group, and I mention it here because it was the first subject undertaken for restatement by the American Law Institute. The Restatement, while not strictly a codification, comes as near to codification as we can expect in a federal state such as ours, where the central government is one of limited powers and the reserve of sovereignty is in the States.

Returning to my address before the Eighth American Scientific Congress (published in the *Proceedings*, Volume X), I endeavored to explain this more fully.

"Although not having the authority of a statute, the Restatement is nevertheless a codification elaborated under the auspices of leading members of the Bench and Bar on a national scale. It has already been widely accepted in the application of its rules by the courts. It is characterized by the great care given to the rules which seek to determine the competence of particular courts to hear and determine particular issues of law. Ordinarily this would belong to the *public* law of the state and would be so considered in countries of Latin America. That these numerous articles and provisions should be contained in a codification relating to the conflict of laws is due to the historical development of a federal system originating with thirteen independent States, loosely organized by Articles of Confederation, afterwards united more strongly by a Constitution which nevertheless reserves all rights to the States which are not granted to the central government. As the separate States will retain their sovereignty in matters of private law, a careful definition of conflicts of jurisdiction is necessary, both between the separate States and between the Federal government and the State governments. While this is characteristic of a federal system like that of the United States, it is also true that the same reservations of power are found in Latin-American federal systems, such as in Argentina, Brazil, Colombia, Mexico and Venezuela. In these countries, however, the codification of civil and commercial law has *national* force, having existed in some measure even before the adoption of the respective constitutions. On the other hand, procedural law still remains provincial or state, although differences are not as widespread on matters of procedure as between some of the States of the United States. It thus follows that the scope of jurisdictional questions within the sphere of private international law is not so wide in Latin-American countries as in the United States."

As we view the scene today, one sometimes hears the view expressed that the problems of private international law have little, if any, bearing upon the relations of states. This view is expressed more frequently by persons whose interests are academic and have had little, if any, experience in the practice of law. I had occasion to point this out before the Scientific Congress of 1940, because the scope of private international law in Latin-American countries extends to subjects, which in the United States are considered to be part of public law. Thus the status of persons in many countries of Latin America, as of Europe, is determined by national law and not by the law of the domicile. Accordingly, the rules and laws governing citizenship determine the private rights and obligations of an individual as well as his allegiance to the state. Private international law thus concerns itself also with law and legislation relating to the acquisition and loss of nationality. Indeed, I made a suggestion which I believe to have significance at the present time and also for the future. I recommended that legal science might be advanced if the subject of nationality and citizenship, as well as the rules which determine the domicile of individuals, should be segregated into an independent field separate from private international law or the conflict of laws. "The nationality of certain persons or the domicile of certain persons is a preliminary question which may determine the choice of law in a particular case, but the rules which determine nationality and the rules which determine domicile are not in themselves rules relating to the choice of law."

The Latin American Code of Private International Law, or "Bustamante Code," has been adopted by treaty by a substantial majority, if not by all, of the countries of Latin America. It deals with another subject, extradition, which is well within the field of general international law. I pointed out that a reason for the difference in approach may be explained in part by the fact that in the United States the punishment of crime is almost exclusively governed by territorial law, whereas elsewhere a wider jurisdiction to punish for crimes committed abroad is recognized. With us, extradition is considered to be a question strictly of interstate or international public law. So far as it is international, it rests upon regulation by treaty.

A few years before this congress, I had occasion to draw attention to a curious lacuna caused precisely by the fact that under the law of the United States extradition rests upon treaty. Two native-born American citizens were charged with the commission of crimes in France. After they had fled to the United States, the French Government requested their extradition under our Treaty of 1909 with France in which the alleged crime was one for which extradition could be sought. On the other hand, the treaty also provided as follows: "Neither of the contracting parties shall be bound to deliver up its own citizens or subjects under the stipulations of this convention." When the accused were arrested under a preliminary warrant, they sued out writs of *habeas corpus* challenging the power of the President to surrender them to France. This was upheld by the Supreme Court of the United States (Valentine *v*. United States *ex rel*. Neidecker, 299 U.S. 5 [1936]). Without criticizing the opinion of the court on strictly legal grounds, I called attention to the regrettable situation left by this case. If the crime charged had been murder, the result would have been the same on principle, and yet no jurisdiction of the United States would have been competent to try the prisoners because the basis of jurisdiction under our law is that the crime must be committed within the territory of the state. It was contended that the phrase "bound to deliver up" still left open a discretion to extradite voluntarily. However, the United States had, in 1899, already negotiated a new extradition treaty with Mexico expressly granting discretionary power. The Court concluded from this that if discretionary power had been intended, it would have been included in the later treaty.

In my analysis of this regrettable situation, I maintained (*American Journal of International Law*, July, 1937) that the most direct method of cure would be a general statute empowering the President, in his discretion, to extradite American citizens charged with crimes committed abroad wherever an extradition treaty provides for extradition of citizens of the foreign state and wherever the evidence of criminality is such as to justify the arrest of such person for trial if the crime had been committed where the accused shall be found. This would grant discretionary power without the necessity of renegotiating a large number of treaties. I closed my analysis as follows:

"It is not to be expected that Congress will attempt to grant jurisdiction to punish nationals for crimes committed abroad, even though the question were free from serious constitutional difficulties. But we must choose between the two alternatives which the late Professor Louis Renault was wont to express succinctly in the command: 'Extradite or punish!' A government which has not lodged with any of its appropriate organs the power to do either, bears a heavy moral responsibility."

Judge John Bassett Moore wrote to me, on December 31, 1936, that he quite subscribed to Renault's saying, but added: "This sentiment has not generally prevailed in the United States. There has been a popular prejudice against extradition which, curiously enough, has not been manifested in matters of immigration."

$\rightsquigarrow$ XII $\leftsquigarrow$

Pathways in Postwar Problems

1. *International Protection of the Individual Against the State*

The beginning of the New Year of 1941 was not exactly an auspicious time to speak of world peace, and yet I could not resist the urge to do so. If it be wise in time of peace to prepare for war, it is equally appropriate in time of war to prepare for peace. This seemed especially true because we had not yet entered the conflict. During the period of the participation of the United States in World War I, certain preparatory studies for peace were undertaken to which I have previously referred. The studies made prior to 1919 laid particular emphasis upon the geographic, ethnic, and political elements underlying the fixing of boundaries. In an editorial in the January, 1941, number of the *American Journal of International Law*, I insisted that if enduring peace was to follow the conflict then raging, a much wider basis should be sought. I said, "It will be nothing less than the creation of a moral order for international justice, both political and economic, and the establishment of conditions of a proper balance between order and liberty throughout the world." This problem is still to be solved.

A Commission to Study the Organization of Peace had already been constituted under the auspices of certain unofficial associations long interested in the field and under the able chairmanship of Dr. James T. Shotwell of Columbia University. The commission had already issued a preliminary report, and I made this the basis of my comments on the organization of peace. The report recognized that peace is not obtainable by the mere renunciation of war and that the modern world differs from the ancient in that the peoples composing it are not ignorant of science, though many of them are still indifferently instructed in the political idea of liberty. The report of this commission appeared at about the same time as that of a group called the International Consultative Group, which had been meeting in Geneva, Switzerland, and I undertook to compare the solutions recommended by each. The American group was strongly in favor of federation, at least in Europe; the Geneva group envisaged some sort of limitation of sovereign power without federation. I pointed out that what had emerged from both groups was a realization that a threat to peace anywhere creates a danger to the entire international community, and I quoted what M. Briand once said, anticipating Mr. Willkie at a later date: "There is not one peace for America, one peace for Europe and another for Asia, but one peace for the entire world."

It also was made manifest by the work of both these unofficial groups that the protection of the rights of man which our own Declaration of Independence had declared to be unalienable was destined to play an important if not a preponderating role in the peace settlement, whenever it should be consummated. This was due to the shocking violations that had already occurred of the essential rights of human beings practiced not only against those with enemy status but also against minorities, political, racial, religous, who would otherwise have been entitled to the protection of their own government. In the month in which my analysis appeared, President Roosevelt made mention of the four essential human freedoms to which he looked forward as the foundations of a future world. His use of the word "freedom" as applied to certain of his aspirations was destined to cause considerable ambiguity in later years, but none could misunderstand the general trend of his thought at the time. From the point of view of international law, the question raised by the march of events and by this message was that of the extent to which any nation enjoying sovereignty in the family of nations could violate every principle of humanity and justice against the inhabitants of its own territory, whether citizen, alien, or stateless, and yet be able to defend itself upon a supposed legal principle of having unlimited powers in its domestic affairs.

This then was the issue of the conflict on its ideologic side. One of my colleagues, Philip Marshall Brown, formerly of Princeton University, expressed it in precise terms. "The very menace of the totalitarian concept would seem to indicate the main direction to be taken in the renovation of international law. Its emphasis must be on the rights of individuals and of democracies. We need to remind ourselves constantly that the primary object of law is the protection of the rights of individuals, and that the law of nations, as conceived by Grotius, was concerned with peoples rather than with sovereigns."

As a minority group which had suffered the most by the advent of the totalitarian régime in Germany, the Jews of the United States had organized various committees to make a study of the protection of human rights. I was asked to become a member of the Committee on Peace Problems of the American Jewish Committee. I attended meetings of the committee from time to time and was consulted by its very able staff of young lawyers active in its Overseas Department. This question had been considered under different circumstances after World War I. I reminded the committee of the symposium that had been held before the Judaean Society in January, 1926, on the treaties with the new states created after World War I, which were designed to protect the racial, religious, and linguistic minorities of those states. The speakers were Louis Marshall, a leader of the New York Bar, Professor Manley O. Hudson, afterward Judge of the World Court, and myself. Mr. Marshall explained how these treaties came to be elaborated and how the violation of minority rights was made an obligation "of international concern" and placed under the guarantee of the League of Nations. Professor Hudson had the task of explaining the legal processes for enforcing the guarantee and the role that the World Court might play. He pointed out that a minority problem may be an international problem because the peace of the world may be threatened by the unrest of people within a particular state, and also that it may lead others outside the country to organize an expedition to free their brethren inside that country.

My part in this symposium expressed strong dissatisfaction with the way things had been going in execution of minority rights under the treaties, notwithstanding the high humanitarian purpose with which they had been conceived. It is a curious phenomenon of human nature that groups of individuals who have been persecuted are frequently callous of the rights of other minorities when they have become a dominant majority. The Puritans of New England represent an example in our own history; otherwise Roger Williams would never have left the Massachusetts Bay Colony. The wrongs that had been visited upon Poland over the centuries ought to have been an assurance that when she had regained her independence after World War I, she would be scrupulously fair to her own minorities. However, before the end of 1923, two advisory opinions had been requested of the Court on complaint of the German Government in behalf of minorities in territories annexed to Poland after the war. Suppose, however, the complaining minority does not have the protection of a particular State. Suppose the group is racial or religious, like the Jews or the Armenians. It would have no chance for a hearing on the merits unless a member of the Council espoused the cause. Members of the Council represented nations, and ordinarily no nation wishes to interpose in a dispute between another friendly nation and its subjects. I pointed out the essential weakness of this procedure was that the question of hearing a minority petition was entirely political, even though the determination of the controversy, if it ever were heard, would be judicial.

I have related the discussion because I brought it to the attention of the Committee on Peace Problems at an early date so that this error should not be made again and that a broader basis should be found for the enforcement of human rights.

When the committee had its final meeting prior to the San Francisco Peace Conference of 1945, intensive studies had been made upon the question of enforcement. As is well known, recommendations were made for the elaboration of an International Bill of the Rights of Man. Later the specialized agencies of the United Nations elaborated a Declaration and a Covenant, both of which have given rise to much controversy and need not be discussed here. One does not wish to be captious with regard to any movement that is based upon humanitarian principles and that is struggling to advance the cause of human freedom everywhere. As a lawyer, I believe it to be unfortunate that the drafting of such clauses, especially when they are to be embodied in a multilateral treaty, is often entrusted to committees which have insufficient juridical expertness and experience. The use of the phrase "fundamental freedoms" applied to such matters as "freedom from want" or "freedom from fear" is confusing and has already led to much misapprehension. In like manner the classification of social and economic advantages as "rights" is likewise confusing. These are matters which cannot yet be accurately defined in juridical terms, nor is there agreement as to the extent to which such advantages can be guaranteed by the international community.

Quite a different problem is presented by the ruthless extermination of peoples and races as practiced by the Axis Powers in World War II. In 1944 a record of these abominable practices was presented with great ability by Raphael Lemkin, a Polish lawyer who had found refuge in this country. He published a work under the auspices of the Carnegie Endowment for International Peace under the title *Axis Rule in Occupied Europe*. I was determined to bring this work of research to the attention of as wide an audience as possible. I wrote an extensive review of it in the April, 1945, number of the *Journal*. I said:

"Not a pleasant record, this book, of how a tyranny under the guise of law engulfed substantially an entire continent. The collection and presentation of the most important laws, decrees, and proclamations of the occupying forces, country by country, in excellent English translation, constitute a veritable *tour de force*. The part of the book containing these texts is source-material of inestimable value in the making of plans for restoration and reparation, as well as for the practitioner and the historian. The author feels that such evidence is especially necessary for the Anglo-American reader, who, with his innate respect for human rights and human personality, may be inclined to believe that the Axis regime could not possibly have been as cruel and ruthless as has been described.

"One of the most original and important chapters of the book is entitled 'Genocide.' This is a term coined by the author to denote an ancient practice in its modern manifestation. It does not mean immediate destruction of a nation or of an ethnic or religious group but rather a coordinated plan of different actions aiming at the destruction of essential foundations of the life of national groups, with the aim of annihilating the groups themselves. The aim and purpose of genocide laws are readily discernible from the texts. It is astonishing to observe how widely they were resorted to not only against the Slavic peoples of Eastern and Central Europe but also in countries like The Netherlands and Norway. They are the very antithesis of the fundamental principle of international law that warfare is directed against governments and armed forces and not against civil populations."

The book, with its inestimable source material, received wide attention both here and abroad, from individuals and from groups determined that there should be an international deterrent of some kind to prevent a repetition of what had occurred. Soon proposals were brought for action by the organs of the United Nations. Unfortunately, these proposals were contemporaneous with activity for the protection of fundamental human rights generally. Fear was expressed in certain sections and among certain groups in the United States that there was danger of infringing upon the reserved sovereignty of the States of the Union through the acceptance of guarantees contained in treaties which, by our Constitution, would become the supreme law of the land. It was and still remains of the utmost importance to separate guarantees for the enjoyment of fundamental human rights from the establishment of an effective sanction against the mass murder of minority populations. Accordingly, I attempted to make the distinction clear in an editorial published in the July, 1949, number of the *American Journal of International Law*:

"The assumption is sometimes made that the Convention on the Prevention and Punishment of Genocide is in some way connected with the proposed Covenant and Declaration on Human Rights. Indeed, it has been asserted that it presents for consideration many of the same basic questions. Objection has been made to the Declaration of Human Rights on the ground that it would impose by treaty, legislation reserved to Congress or to the separate States and that this also applies to the Genocide Convention. We believe that this is an erroneous identification which has probably arisen because both conventions were approved during the same session of the General Assembly held in Paris in December, 1948.

"The crime of genocide comes within the category of offenses described in Article 6 (*c*) of the Charter of the International Military Tribunal as 'crimes against humanity,' or to use the more precise phraseology employed by the General Assembly, 'offenses against the peace and security of mankind.' The convention should not be classified as one for the protection of human rights, but for the preservation of international peace. Its purposes are objective, not subjective. Genocide was described by the General Assembly on December 11, 1948, as 'a crime under international law, contrary to the spirit and aims of the United Nations and condemned by the civilized world.' Under Article I, the Contracting Parties 'confirm that genocide, whether committed in time of peace or in time of war, is a crime under international law which they undertake to prevent and to punish.' It is defined as meaning any of a number of acts committed with intent to destroy, in whole or in part, a national, ethnic, racial or religious group, as such. Persons committing genocide or attempting or conspiring to commit genocide shall be punishable 'whether they are constitutionally responsible rulers, public officials or private individuals' (Arts. II-IV). The convention would require national legislation, to give it effect, because persons charged with genocide are to be tried by a competent tribunal of the state in which the act was committed, and the parties agree to grant extradition in accordance with existing laws and treaties without the crime being considered 'political' under the usual rules relating to extradition (Arts. V-VII).

"The convention contemplates that a permanent international penal tribunal may be set up later by special agreement. This was suggested as early as September, 1947, by the representatives of the United States to the Secretary General of the United Nations. The convention does not provide for such a tribunal nor is any nation bound to accept its jurisdiction. Of course, if it is created, it may have concurrent jurisdiction with respect to those Contracting Parties who have accepted it. On the other hand, the convention provides that any dispute relating to the interpretations, application, or fulfillment of the terms of the convention shall be submitted to the International Court of Justice at the request of any of the parties in the dispute.

"The International Military Tribunal at Nuremberg followed the rule that criminal acts committed by an accused prior to the declaration of war could not be considered a means of executing a conspiracy against the peace of the world unless it was directly connected with the plan for making war. However, it recognized that many criminal acts committed after the declaration of war presented the double character of war crimes and crimes against humanity. The Tribunal thus recognized a category of crimes against humanity without defining such crimes and without distinguishing them from war crimes in the strict sense. This applies particularly to genocide. After the close of the war, the conscience of the world was shaken by confirmation, theretofore deemed incredible, of the enormous scope of the mass exterminations carried out on racial, religious and political grounds by the Hitler regime. It became necessary to give a name to and define this abominable crime and to make it punishable whether committed in peace or in war.

"There is nothing new in thus recognizing by multilateral treaty certain offenses which would often go unpunished if left to the jurisdiction of any one nation. Thus piracy derives its internationally illegal character from the will of the international society. That society, by common understanding, reflected in the practice of states generally, yields to each of its members jurisdiction to penalize any individuals who, regardless of their nationality, commit certain acts within certain places. . . . National authorization of the commission of piratical acts could not free them from their internationally illegal aspect.

"To a limited extent, the slave trade, the traffic in women and the opium traffic have likewise been placed under international cognizance by special agreement. All these offenses are considered to be matters of international concern.

"At the annual meeting of the American Society of International Law on April 19, 1907, Mr. Elihu Root, President of the Society, who was at that time Secretary of State, said: 'It is, of course, conceivable that, under pretense of exercising the treaty-making power, the President and Senate might attempt to make provisions regarding matters which are not proper subjects of international agreement, and which would be only a colorable—not a real—exercise of the treaty-making power; but so far as the real exercise of the power goes, there can be no question of State rights, because the Constitution itself, in the most explicit terms, has precluded the existence of any such question.'

"The distinction made under the rules regulating the Nuremberg Tribunal between genocide committed in time of war and the same crime committed by a nation against its own subjects in time of peace is understandable in view of the conditions under which the Tribunal was to operate. Fundamentally, the distinction is an artificial one. Mass extermination of populations in war or in peace with intent to destroy national, ethnic, or religious groups, constitutes an offense of international concern and a serious threat to the maintenance of peace. Even before the conscience of mankind had reached its present state of awareness, mass exterminations were recognized as creating a spirit of vengeance continuing for generations and even for centuries both within the state and in other states where related groups seek action to revenge the crime. One has only to think of events like the massacre of Saint Bartholomew's Night and others committed in periods between religious wars, the Armenian massacres and those of our own day, to realize that genocide is a threatening danger to peace and the source of international wars and civil hostilities.

"It should be remembered that notwithstanding the reference of the General Assembly to genocide as an international crime, the nations of the world do not yet consist of a society of individuals all subject to the authority of a definite legal order. The world may well be progressing toward that end, but it is a gradual process. Even with respect to piracy, all that the customary or conventional law assumes to do is to establish an extraordinary jurisdiction and fix the duties of the several states *inter se*, leaving to each state the decision how, through its own law, it will exercise its rights and powers. So with respect to genocide, the effective establishment of a special rule of jurisdiction requires international cooperation in order to pursue those charged with genocide beyond the borders of a single state in exchange for reciprocal powers granted to the other parties. Only the treaty-making power can accomplish this result. From the very nature of our Government, the treaty-making power must reside centrally or nowhere. State rights cannot be an obstacle to the participation of the United States in a genocide convention, otherwise the power of the nation would be prevented from acting effectively to combat this threat to the peace and security of all nations and the establishment of a civilized standard of international life."

I believe that if the Declaration of Human Rights and the Covenant which was designed to put it in effect had been more modest in their scope and had not embraced also economic and social so-called "rights," the Genocide Convention would not have aroused serious opposition. The two subjects were confused with each other in the minds of the public. Many lawyers who were heartily in favor of a genocide convention were quite justifiably alarmed at the somewhat irresponsible nature of undertakings for the enforcement of human rights without due regard for the excellent separation of State power from Federal power in our own Constitution.

Another related subject which became a target of opposition upon similar grounds was the proposed permanent International Criminal Court. In the report to the President on June 7, 1945, Justice Robert H. Jackson, as chief counsel for the United States in the prosecution of Axis war criminals, remarked that we are put under a heavy responsibility to see that our behavior "will direct the world's thought toward a firmer enforcement of the laws of international conduct, so as to make war less attractive to those who have governments and the destinies of peoples in their power." In February, 1947, President Truman submitted to the Congress his first report on the activities of the United Nations, in which he strongly approved the action of the Assembly with respect to genocide, and said, "We cannot have lasting peace unless a genuine system of world law is established and enforced."

I am usually apprehensive of such ambitious phrases as "world law" without specific juristic definition. Accordingly, I felt that it would be worth while to analyze how far the world could safely advance the cause of world order under law. In my editorial comment in the *Journal* for April, 1947, I said that the phrase "world law" was not to be taken too literally. The great advance in international jurisprudence of the postwar period is the recognition of the principle that certain behavior of individuals violates the common conscience of mankind. I pointed out that the various instruments which set up the Military Tribunal at Nuremberg were made necessary because there was no jurisdiction able to punish war crimes and crimes against humanity. The failure to establish the necessary basis for such jurisdiction between the two world wars had been characterized as a lamentable error of foresight by the statesmen of the world. Judge Megalos Caloyanni, with whom I had spent some interesting days at Vichy at the outbreak of World War II, had pleaded, as early as 1931, in his lectures before the Academy of International Law, that there should be permanent penal jurisdiction for international crimes because repressive law and sanctions have always been necessary in order to protect every collective society, great or small.

I remarked that in my opinion the plans for an international jurisdiction for the punishment of international crimes foundered after World War I because of the too ambitious nature of the various projects. Various bodies, including the Committee of Jurists which drafted the statute for the Permanent Court of International Justice at the request of the League of Nations, had also recommended the establishment of an international criminal court. The Inter-Parliamentary Union adopted a draft at its Washington conference in 1925. The problem was therefore not a new one. I had grave doubts that even after World War II we could expect the setting up of a permanent court of this character. However, I signalized two events which made direct evolutionary progress in this direction. The first is the fact that the procedure of the Nuremburg Tribunal gave satisfaction to the Allied participants (even to the Soviet representative), as measured by the various standards of their systems of jurisprudence. The other influence is the realization by a large majority of the United Nations that all methods of mass destruction should be controlled by law. "If the violation of agreements not to use nuclear energy except for peaceful pursuits can be controlled by law through sanctions operating against individuals as well as against states, a road will have been opened for the establishment of international penal jurisdiction generally." The imperative need for protection against the new forces of mass destruction, atomic and others, may eventually lead the way to some form of international penal jurisdiction.

Another influence has come from the large number of simulated trials in certain countries where American citizens have been charged with espionage and other offenses under procedure violative of the basic principles of justice. The report presented to the New York Association of the Bar in October, 1951, dealing with the case of William N. Oatis, chief of the Associated Press Bureau at Prague, correctly points out that any statute for an International Criminal Court such as that prepared by the Committee of the General Assembly of the United Nations at Geneva in August, 1951, should set forth the explicit rights of the accused, representing a standard of justice in accordance with existing concepts of a fair trial.

The idea of an international court of criminal justice is being studied by a number of groups of jurists here and abroad. Its jurisdiction would be limited but its power should eventually extend beyond the trial of offenders charged with crimes of an international character such as genocide. It should also be empowered to examine on complaint of a member state whether the trial of one of its nationals in another state has not conformed to that minimum standard of justice required by all civilized nations. Doubtless this is an achievement to be looked for only in the future, and perhaps only after an evolutionary process under more limited jurisdiction. The Vogeler and Oatis cases both aroused public opinion in the United States to the need for a corrective against simulated trials beyond the remedies of diplomatic action.

2. *International Monetary Cooperation*

Among the many subjects which the Allied Powers were discussing shortly before the end of World War II was the setting up of two international agencies, the International Monetary Fund and the International Bank for Reconstruction and Development, which were to be charged with the function of promoting permanent monetary cooperation between the nations. Draft conventions for this purpose had been elaborated by representatives of forty-three friendly nations meeting at Bretton Woods, New Hampshire, in July, 1944. On January 15, 1945, the Law School of New York University and the Economists' National Committee on Monetary Policy conducted a symposium for the study of these proposals both from the economic and from the legal angles. As Chief Judge Arthur T. Vanderbilt, then dean of the Law School, expressed it, "The day has long since passed when the economist and the lawyer could afford to regard each other as foreigners."

I was invited to participate in the proceedings of this Institute on Money and the Law, and I dealt with the Bretton Woods recommendations in the light of international law. It did not require a very long memory to recall how the disequilibrium (to use an economist's term) caused by reparation payments without adequate international cooperation soon brought on a serious degeneration in political relations between the Allied and Associated Powers and, indeed, throughout the world after World War I. The Bretton Woods Conference sought to avoid this error by devising a practical scheme for exchange stability. I pointed out that the legal structure for effecting these objects might conceivably have been accomplished by multilateral accord for establishing parities and granting credits, followed by frequent consultation. This was suggested by the French experts. However, postwar peace plans now envisaged various autonomous international agencies with special functions, such as the Food and Agricultural Organization, the International Air Administration, and others.

In discussing the legal status of the Fund and the Bank respectively, the feature which principally raised doubt in my mind was the extent to which sovereign immunity was extended to these specialized agencies. I maintained that while I was not opposed to protecting the property of both the Fund and the Bank from local restrictions and from local fiscal charges, their immunities should not be enlarged to the extent of placing these institutions outside the competent jurisdiction of domestic courts as to transactions with private individuals and commercial banks. It is true that the Bank was made subject to judicial process wherever it has an office or has guaranteed securities. The Fund, however, enjoys absolute immunity. I said: "It is quite understandable that the ordinary transactions of the Fund will be with its own members and not otherwise. On the other hand, the Fund is not prohibited from dealing outside the circle of its members. Thus, the Fund may be called upon to replenish its holdings of scarce currencies and for this purpose it is provided that the Fund may 'borrow such currency' from some other source than the state of issue, either within or outside the territory of the member, provided it has the approval of the member.

Accordingly, legal disputes may arise which may not be entirely a family dispute within the Fund."

How, then, were these disputes to be decided, especially in view of the fact that the smooth working of these institutions has political as well as economic significance? There is indeed a procedure for arbitration, but it is limited to "any question of interpretation of the provisions" of the agreements. This I found to be inadequate, and I still believe that it may some day give rise to serious difficulty. Disputes will inevitably arise which are not mere interpretations. "They are rather questions of the conduct of officials of the Fund or of the Bank toward member-states or on the part of the member-states toward the Fund or the Bank. The furnishing of credits in the way of foreign exchange or of scarce currencies, the guarantee and placement of loans are inevitably tied up with the maintenance of certain standards of domestic economy. Where is the conduct of a member [government] respecting its domestic economy to be judged with reference to undertakings with the Fund or the Bank?"

As I look back upon what I then contended, I believe that I correctly anticipated difficulties of the present time and of the immediate future, when, to use the vernacular, the going will be tough. As inflation creeps over us, more and more demands will be made upon these institutions for scarce currencies, and there will be more careless conduct of domestic economies, violating undertakings with these institutions. The local courts will not be competent because of the well known rule of international law granting immunity not only to states but to their instrumentalities or agencies. In my opinion this principle is being increasingly applied with alarming implications, because states, even those which would resent being characterized as not democratic, are engaging in private business under corporate forms and then insisting upon complete exemption from judicial process when sued in foreign courts.

I called attention to the meager provisions for arbitration of disputes compared with the carefully drafted provisions of the Bank for International Settlements after World War I. There the convention actually set up an arbitral tribunal instead of a mere agreement to arbitrate disputes. The tribunal was competent to settle disputes between the governments themselves, or between the Bank and any government, with reference to interpretation or application of the entire plan then referred to as the "New Plan," with a final reference to the Permanent Court of International Justice. I said then, and it will remain true for some time to come, that we are living in a period of economic strain and that one or another of the parties to these international financial agencies may at some time default upon some of their undertakings. Governments come and go; states remain, but new governments may have different fiscal policies. I expressed my opinion that there was a lack of enforcement provisions. It was intended that the Economic and Social Council of the United Nations should have supervision over the specialized agencies. Later in the year, the adoption of the Charter of the United Nations took place, and provisions of this kind were actually realized in Chapter X of the Charter, but the function of the Economic and Social Council was limited to receiving reports from the specialized agencies and communicating its observations to the General Assembly or to the Security Council upon its request. I concluded my critique by expressing the hope that the Fund and the Bank would not be allowed to develop in a vacuum, but saying that there should repose somewhere a responsibility to some organ of the United Nations or, as I then expressed it, of the "International Authority." "As they are to be created by international legislation, their economic and political future will depend upon integration with the general structure of international coöperation."

My address was published in full in the New York *Financial and Commercial Chronicle*. The proceedings of the symposium were published as a separate supplement of the *New York University Law Quarterly Review*. I had accepted the invitation with considerable diffidence, but I am now more than ever convinced that it will be part of the education of every lawyer, if he intends to devote his attention to matters of international concern, to be well grounded in the fundamental principles of international finance.

3. *Socialization of Property in Its International Aspects*

International friction does not arise ordinarily from differences in the forms of property. On the other hand, the ownership and control of all forms of property and industry in whole or in part by socialist and communist governments has been the source of serious international tension at the mid-century. The taking over from private ownership of property and industry has come to be called the "nationalization" of property, and will have our attention later. Here we wish to discuss the principle of international law granting immunity to a sovereign government from the ordinary jurisdiction exercised by the judicial or other authorities of another sovereign government. The usual consequence of government ownership of an industry is the operation by government officials of the industry taken over. So long as the operation remains within the territory of the state, no international problem is likely to arise. However, under modern conditions of life, the activities of important industries are international in character, and when transactions are undertaken in a foreign country the operating government seeks to enjoy comparable power and advantages abroad with those it enjoys at home.

Perhaps it was somewhat quixotic on my part, but I unsheathed my sword against the inequities of this situation as early as 1934. An American company had supplied coal to the Swedish State Railway System, whose operations were conducted in the name of a Swedish corporation. Not until an action in a United States court for breach of contract had resulted in a judgment in favor of the American corporation was there any direct intervention on the part of the Swedish Government. Only then did the Swedish minister present a certificate to the court that the Railway System was in reality an organic part of the Swedish Government. Under instruction from our own Department of Justice, the United States Attorney filed a "suggestion" with the court that the claim of immunity was to be treated as a matter of comity between the United States Government and the Swedish Government. A settlement was later effected through diplomatic channels, but, as so frequently happens in such cases, for an amount far below the amount of the judgment.

This case, known as the Dexter and Carpenter Case, was analyzed by me from the point of view of international relations as well as of international law (*Journal,* January, 1934). Among other things, I said: "The extension of governmental activity into the field of private business has been proceeding at a rapid pace during the past two decades. The extreme application of this trend is, of course, to be found in the communistic state, but fascist states have also absorbed many economic activities formerly left in private hands. Even democratic governments are drifting in the same direction, not as a political end in itself but in execution of various plans of social and economic welfare." I called attention to the necessity of regulating by international agreement the competence of courts in regard to foreign states not only with reference to immunity from suit and judgment but also with reference to immunity from execution against property. Very little has been attempted up to the present time in that direction, although the United States, one of the few large industrial nations which have refrained from nationalization of industry, has the greatest interest in arriving at international agreement.

The extension of sovereign immunity to government-owned commercial corporations is a question which seems to plague us more and more as commercial activities of modern governments tend to expand. I analyzed the situation again in the *American Journal of International Law* for October, 1945, as a result of the decision of the New York Court of Appeals in the United States of Mexico *v.* Schmuck (1944, 293 N.Y. 264). A Mexican corporation called Petroleos Mexicanos was organized for the purpose of conducting business in petroleum not only in Mexico but abroad. Its assets consisted in part of properties expropriated by Mexico from various oil enterprises owned by American and other nationals. The Mexican company was owned by the Mexican Government, although its business was not at all confined to government functions. When the Mexican company was sued in a New York court by an American company on a contract for materials purchased, the Mexican Government claimed immunity for the company although the contract provided that any dispute should be determined by New York and/or United States laws. Here again the Department of Justice supported the claim through a "suggestion of immunity" presented to the court. The Court of Appeals sustained the claim. Waiving aside any question of the company having waived its immunity, I said:

"It is of the greatest consequence, however, to draw attention to certain repercussions likely to follow the expansion of the principle from its origin as the immunity enjoyed by a sovereign prince, then extended also to the person of certain state functionaries, then to the property in possession of the sovereign, and now finally to a corporation endowed with fictional personality and engaged in commercial pursuits. We recognize the importance of not embarrassing the political department of government in the conduct of foreign relations. We have grave doubt, however, whether the surrender of the judicial function to examine the law and the facts upon which such immunity is predicated will result in the improvement of international relations. On the contrary, it tends toward a policy of perpetual appeasement which may lead to widespread abuse. It lays a burden upon the executive which, in a constitutional democracy, should be more readily borne by the courts through regular judicial processes.

"The question whether sovereign immunity should be extended to agents of foreign states engaged in commercial transactions will mount in importance with the nationalization of industry. In some countries all export and import is already completely in the hands of government. In others, even in hitherto so-called 'capitalistic' countries, certain industries are coming into control and operation by the state. The problem in the United States is, therefore, not a mere question of jurisprudence, Federal or State, but one of high policy as well. In departing from its previously expressed policy the State Department may, we believe, have unwittingly admitted a Trojan horse and taken a step which may lead to serious consequences. The courts have indeed surrendered to the place where power lies.

"It would be interesting to learn whether the Department acts upon a mere *ex parte* application for immunity after process against the foreign corporation has been instituted, or whether the plaintiff in the court proceedings is given an opportunity to be heard. Otherwise, the plaintiff has been deprived of his right without his day in court, by action which the court now declares to be final. Again, is the action taken by the Department to be affected by the momentary diplomatic relations existing between the United States and the particular foreign nation? Would the action have been the same in the case mentioned, if the foreign state had been Argentina or Spain instead of Mexico?

"All these questions are rendered even more perplexing when we contemplate the new economic conditions resulting from the widespread ruin of the war. Cartels may disappear but in their place will come huge corporations for commercial business created and owned by foreign governments. Under the new immunity rule, these will be free from process in our courts while native citizens and domestic corporations doing business with such corporations within our own borders will enjoy no such immunity at home or abroad. As there are no international tribunals to which such citizens and corporations may have access, they will be obliged to seek redress before the courts of the particular foreign state, although the transactions occurred within the United States. The threat to free enterprise which all of this implies is only too obvious."

Curiously enough, the Supreme Court of the United States had no hesitation in limiting the claim of sovereign immunity on the part of one of the States of the Union, New York, when the Federal Government sought to recover taxes assessed on the sale of mineral waters taken from Saratoga Springs. The Supreme Court said: "If a state chooses to go into the business of buying and selling commodities, its right to do so may be conceded so far as the Federal Constitution is concerned; but the exercise of the right is not the performance of a governmental function . . . when a state enters the market place seeking customers, it divests itself of its *quasi* sovereignty *pro tanto*, and takes on the character of a trader, so far, at

least, as the taxing power of the federal government is concerned."
This was in the case of New York *v.* United States (326 U.S. 572).
I seized upon the occasion to refer to the inconsistency of a conception of sovereignty as applied to one of our own States which would
not be recognized under the same circumstances if it had been a
foreign government. In commenting editorially upon this situation,
in the *American Journal of International Law* for April, 1946, I
said:

"The importance of limiting sovereign immunity where the state
enters the arena of commercial business has only recently begun to
assume vital importance. The nationalization of all export and import business by Soviet Russia has now been followed, although to
a more limited degree, by the nationalization of certain industries by
Great Britain, France, and other countries. The significance of this
phenomenon in international life must soon be recognized as one
deeply affecting both economic and political relations. The fact that
the Supreme Court of the United States has wisely restricted the
immunity of State Governments to the exercise of essential government functions should not be overlooked in the conduct of our foreign relations. The principle is a corollary to the maintenance of a
system of free enterprise."

4. *The Nationalization of Private Industry*

When a state engages in commercial business, it enters the arena
of international competition not only with other states but with the
subjects of those states. This creates a new field of conflict which
eventually may lead to new threats to world peace. When the Soviet
Government took over the means of production and all property
used in foreign business, indeed, of all "big business" as defined by
Soviet law, it recognized no exemption of foreign-held property. We
are not thinking now of the question of compensation. This put the
government into business both at home and abroad. The example of
Soviet Russia has been followed, sometimes in whole, sometimes in

part, by other governments, both within and without the Russian orbit. In countries of a free economy, compensation was provided for in one manner or another. As governments carried on commercial activities abroad, they asserted their immunity as states from the jurisdiction of local courts, as we have seen when the Mexican Government went into the oil business.

When I made the analysis of the situation in the Mexican oil case, I could not have foreseen the precise manner in which the carrying on of commercial business by governments would lead to further international tension. It was plain that free enterprise would suffer. Since the nationalization of the oil industry by Iran and the taking over of the properties of the huge Anglo-Iranian Oil Company, two elements have entered into the problem which have made it more complicated. First, we have the tendency of weak and politically undeveloped countries to control their own natural resources even though they are without the capital or skill to develop and utilize them; second, we have the determination of stronger and more advanced nations to preserve their investment in the development of natural resources or in the carrying out of concessions previously given. Furthermore, the immense quantities of oil which are recovered, refined, and transshipped by the Anglo-Iranian Oil Company constitute an appreciable percentage of the world's production of an essential commodity on which many countries besides those directly interested are dependent.

When I made my first analysis of some of the problems of international law growing out of the conduct of commercial business by governments, World War II had come to an end, disorganizing the economy of many nations and impoverishing some of the strongest. Nations of the free world, such as France, Great Britain, and some others, had themselves resorted to the nationalization of certain of their industries. Here was a new impact on the generally accepted principles of international law, which recognizes the immunity of foreign-owned property from confiscation in time of peace. Accordingly, I continued my analysis of these new phenomena of international life in an editorial in the October, 1951, issue of the *Journal* in which I discussed the impact of nationalization of foreign-owned property on the legal structure of the international community.

"Foreign investors are now faced with an added risk and if the resources of the world are to be developed by foreign risk-capital under a Point Four Program or otherwise, a better basis than that now provided against the danger of nationalization must be established. Some supplementary principles of a political and economic nature must be developed to bring the undisputed rules of international law within the realities of international life. At the annual meeting of the Standard Oil Company (New Jersey) on June 8, 1951, President Eugene Holman gave an outline of what he conceived to be such a basis for the oil industry. He said that the oil companies producing oil in foreign lands recognize that the oil underground belongs to the people of those lands and that a foreign government which lets oil concessions may rightfully expect: that an adequate participataion in the proceeds should accrue to the government; that operations shall be so conducted as to contribute to the domestic economy of the nation; that domestic demands for oil be fully satisfied before any oil is exported; that there be no avoidable waste of the natural resources; that the enterprise give training and employment to local citizens at fair rates of compensation; and that oil and oil products available for export move to markets in fair volume at fair prices. On the other side, the foreign government should assure continuously for the period of the concession, security of title to the property or rights conceded; managerial control of the company's operations; and the opportunity to make a reasonable profit from the enterprise.

"We believe that eventually some regulation will be achieved either by non-governmental agencies or under the auspices of the United Nations for a compromise between the demands of national sovereignty and the international protection of foreign property in time of peace. If nationalization laws introduced as social reforms were to recognize full, adequate and prompt compensation, none could be carried out. A compromise in the method of compensation is not a compromise in the principles of international law; on the other hand, nationalization should never be permitted or recognized if the compensation provided for is so inadequate as to constitute merely a disguise for the spoliation of foreign-owned property."

The mid-century has seen a notable increase in the number of countries which have resorted to more or less comprehensive nationalizations of industry and property in order to solve financial crises. How much of this is due to a breakdown of previously existing standards of respect for financial obligation and the personal rights of individuals and how much is due to direct communist influence working from within, it would be difficult to appraise. The threat to international stability is in either case manifest. There are few countries indeed in which foreigners do not have some property interests.

In view of the increasing importance of nationalizations as matters of international interest, the Institut de Droit International created a special committee on "The International Effects of Nationalizations," with the eminent French jurist A. de La Pradelle as rapporteur. I was appointed a member of the committee. We presented our report to the Institute at its session in Siena, Italy, in April, 1952, at which I was present. The rapporteur had prepared a set of resolutions of which the first part dealt with the concept of nationalizations, the second with the rules affecting foreigners, the third with idemnifications, the fourth with procedure, and the fifth with sanctions. Perhaps the most outstanding characteristic of the report was a distinction which was recommended between nationalizations and expropriations. The rapporteur seemed to think that where a nationalization was intended to effect a general reform of the entire industrial or agrarian economy of a nation, the right of full indemnity must give way to the higher values of reform; but that where expropriation affected only certain categories of property or was limited only to a certain place or district, full indemnity might be expected. There was considerable support for this among the members of the Institute. I regarded the distinction as artificial, for I could not see any reason to separate the two concepts from the international point of view. There might be a *political* distinction, but where the question was as to the right of a foreigner deprived of his property to receive compensation there was no *judicial* distinction. The foreigner might well think that there was very little difference whether he was to be shorn for a sheep or a lamb. I laid stress on the importance of not defining either nationalizations or expropriations in such manner as to grant to either a sort of regularization. I insisted that each case must be considered according to the facts. I pointed out that the United States had presented claims in such cases upon the principle of a denial of justice.

The Institute did not get very far toward the adoption of specific rules, and it voted to regard the discussions as merely an exchange of views. This was to be expected, since the rapporteur was really breaking new ground in international law by attempting to make a legal system applicable to nationalizations at a time when there were few legal precedents upon which to build. The debate showed—for it really was a debate—that we were discussing a problem *de lege ferenda* rather than *ex lege lata*. For this reason some of the members were inclined to drop the subject completely, at least for the time being. I urged that it be retained, but I also said that the Institute should deal with specific problems of nationalization which had already occurred and which involved strictly legal questions of an international character. I pointed out that Mexico, which had expropriated the oil industry in which American citizens had a very great interest, immediately claimed immunity from the jurisdiction of American courts when its government-owned Petroleos Mexicanos was sued on contracts for materials to promote sales of the very oil which was taken from expropriated wells. I referred also to the immunity which would undoubtedly be claimed by governments which had nationalized industries because they themselves had had their property in the same industries nationalized. It all depends upon whose ox is gored. I brought these questions up not for the purpose of discussing the merits but to recommend that the Institute limit its discussions and action in the field of nationalization to specific problems like those I had mentioned, rather than to explore the entire field of a subject still in the development stage.

There is another consideration which enters into the nationalization of property and which brings it into the field of international law. The United Nations, in its Universal Declaration of Human Rights, approved by the General Assembly on December 10, 1948, pledged themselves to achieve "the promotion of universal respect for and observance of human rights and fundamental freedoms." While this protection is as yet neither clearly defined nor universally accepted, it nevertheless represents a new concept which cannot be ignored. In the Declaration (Article 17) it is provided: "I. Everyone has the right to own property alone as well as in association with others. 2. No one shall be arbitrarily deprived of his property." Here we have at least the beginnings of an international protection of the right of property, irrespective of the nationality of the owner or indeed of the possession of any nationality whatever. The large number of stateless persons living in the modern world has had a notable influence in the growth of public opinion in favor of the international protection of human rights and fundamental freedoms.

The effect of nationalization of property upon this human right was brought up in the debate, and whatever may be its immediate binding character it is fair to say that at least no fixed principles on nationalization can be adopted without giving it proper respect.

Pioneering in the law has always appealed to me strongly. The law is not an esoteric subject, but one that is constantly evolving and progressing to meet the needs of human life. I was glad to have had a small part in these early discussions. As a member of the committee, I had written to Professor de La Pradelle that I approved of taking the large view of the subject "as being not a mere judicial question but one which affects the whole economic and social life of the international community. From this point of view it is of the utmost importance to arrive at some normal procedure to deal justly between the states exercising nationalizations and states which regard such decrees as violating the liberty of the individual and destructive of free enterprise. . . ." I felt that a noteworthy step had been taken in what was practically a new field.

5. *Blockade of the Suez Canal and the Palestine Coast*

On May 15, 1948, the British Government withdrew from its Mandate over Palestine. Hostilities were in progress between forces of the Egyptian, Syrian, and Lebanese governments against the inhabitants of the formerly mandated territory of Palestine, who had proclaimed the new State of Israel on the same day. On May 17th and 19th respectively, the Egyptian and Syrian governments notified the American and other embassies at Cairo of a maritime blockade of Palestine. On May 25th the United States warned Egypt and Palestine that it would not recognize the validity of the blockade because there was no state of war in the Holy Land and because the United States considered such declared blockade as violating the freedom of the seas. The position taken by the United States was not supported by any detailed memorandum of the legal basis upon which the United States relied for its refusal to recognize the blockade.

In the following month I was approached by Mr. H. Margalith, a member of the New York Bar who also has an office in Palestine, representing the Lawyers' Committee for Justice in Palestine. He asked whether I considered the blockade valid and whether I would be willing to support my opinion with a detailed summary of the legal basis. I answered that I was willing to do so if one or more other qualified persons would be associated with me who, like myself, had not been connected in any way with Palestinian affairs. I had never been a Zionist; indeed, so long as the Mandate persisted under the broad humanitarian and unsectarian basis of the Balfour Declaration I had never believed the establishment of a Jewish state in Palestine to be either necessary or expedient. The widespread persecution and shocking brutalities and massacres of World War II and the withdrawal of the British Government from the Mandate had left open no other course.

The Lawyers' Committee had selected as my associate Mr. James W. Ryan, a distinguished member of the Bar who had practised extensively in admiralty law both in California and in New York.

On June 29, 1948, we issued our joint opinion, which was sent by the Lawyers' Committee to the State Department and other officials of our own and other governments. The issues involved continued to be unsettled even after the recognition of the State of Israel. The blockade of the Suez Canal by Egypt later came to be the subject of a bitter dispute before the Security Council, involving issues which will affect the Near East for years to come. I quote the following extracts from our opinion:

You have asked our opinion with respect to the legality of the action of the Egyptian, Syrian and Lebanese Governments in blockading the Palestinian coast and adjacent waters and seizing, or diverting by force, the cargoes of vessels of third States, including American vessels, engaged in trade with the seaports of Palestine.

After investigation, and after consideration of the available official reports and of the rules of law applicable, it is our opinion that the blockade is illegal.

On investigation of the State Department, Department of Commerce and United Nations, it appears that Egypt and Syria have been enforcing against vessels of third States at least a partial blockade of Palestine ever since issuance of notes by the Egyptian and Syrian Governments to the American and other Embassies on May 17, 1948, and May 19, 1948, announcing a maritime blockade of Palestine. The exact text of the notes has not been released for publication. The State Department, however, has issued Press Releases stating that in its protests filed in response to the notes, the United States Government has taken the position that the blockade was not valid because a state of war did not exist in Palestine, and because such a blockade against vessels of third States during peace violates the rules of international law as to freedom of the seas and of international trade.

Information from official sources indicates that Egypt and Syria have been able to enforce the blockade only to the extent of seizing and removing from vessels of third States touching at Egyptian or Syrian ports cargo bound to Palestine. They have been unable to enforce it against American vessels on the high seas with cargo and passengers bound directly to Palestine and not touching at an Egyptian, Syrian or Lebanese port. It is immaterial under international law whether lack of effectiveness of a blockade is due to lack of sufficient naval forces by the blockading State or is due to other reasons. The fact that the blockading State does not effectively maintain its announced blockade tends, under international law, to show its illegality and has no legal significance as an excuse for hostile and forceful measures during peace against vessels of third States which are merely touching at a seaport in a country which owes a duty to allow them to pass through peaceably and without interference. Indeed the interference with vessels to the extent to which it has been made by Egypt and Syria since May 17th and 19th, 1948, is clearly unlawful under international law as the effort of pacific blockaders to blockade or interfere with vessels of third States.

Egypt, Syria and Lebanon have no sovereignty over Palestine. It lies wholly outside their territory and political or legislative jurisdiction. No state of war has been declared or exists to which Egypt, Syria or Lebanon is a party. Their action against Palestine has been limited to what international law characterizes as military and naval hostilities or pacific blockade during peace. This, even when authorized, gives no right to intercept, seize or divert vessels, or their cargoes, of third States. No status of insurgency exists, because no *de jure* Government of Palestine is opposing the new State of Israel's claim to independence. Nor does Egypt, Syria or Lebanon have any pending and liquidated or unchallenged legal claim against Palestine, which some States, as acknowledged creditors, have in the past used as an excuse for resort to hostile action or pacific blockade as means of collection. Moreover, as members by treaty of the United Nations, and bound by its Charter and by the peaceful means of determining rights and adjusting disputes which it makes available to its members, the Egyptian, Syrian and Lebanese right to act unilaterally in engaging in military and naval hostilities is, to a substantial extent, restricted by their treaty or agreement. The Charter of the United Nations enjoins all members to refrain in their international relations, from the threat or use of force. (Article 2, par. 4). Only in the common interest may armed force be used. (Preamble, 2nd sec., par. 3). The only exceptions to the rule against the use of force are: (1) in relation to self-defense (Article 50); and (2) in relation to former enemies of any signatory of the Charter of the United Nations (Article 107). Any force otherwise used is an act against the Charter of the United Nations. Blockade, whether pacific or belligerent, is an act of armed force.

Turkey had *de jure* and *de facto* sovereignty over Palestine until World War I. Subject to confirmation on signing of peace treaty, the British Army tentatively acquired Palestine on behalf of all the Allied and Associated Powers by military conquest during World War I. On signing of the Peace Treaty, however, it, as former enemy territory, was put by the Allies with British consent under the Mandate System by the League of Nations in accordance with the Covenant, Turkish sovereignty over it was terminated, as well as any inchoate legal interest, as distinguished from special diplomatic or political interest, of Great Britain. On May 5, 1920, at San Remo, Great Britain was selected as Mandatory. The Mandatory Commission adopted a resolution that the Mandatory Powers do not possess "any right over any part of the territory under mandate other than that resulting from their being entrusted with the administration of the territory."

On May 15, 1948, Great Britain withdrew as Mandatory. The League of Nations had impliedly been succeeded in the year 1945 by the United Nations. The United Nations declared in favor of a partition, requiring establishment of an independent State in Palestine, of a delimited territory West of the Jordan, embracing almost all of the Jewish community. The ability of the people of Palestine to stand alone or govern themselves is a generally accepted fact. On May 15, 1948, a State known as Israel was established in the delimited area, with an effectively functioning government and army of its own, and has ever since been strictly complying with all international obligations of a State. Its *de facto* authority or status was promptly recognized by the United States Government. All *de jure* and *de facto* sovereignty over the part of Palestine now known as Israel, therefore, rests of necessity with the new State and Government of Israel or with the organized community known as United Nations, and the latter has renounced any claim to sovereignty by declaring for immediate partition and delimitation of boundaries, and the recognition of an independent State of Israel in a specified area.

In giving this opinion we have endeavored to avoid political questions and to restrict ourselves to the legality of the alleged blockade.

Our opinion was written and circulated to various governments before recognition of the State of Israel and its admission as a member of the United Nations. During the period of hostilities, neither the United Kingdom nor the other Powers made protests against the blockade. However, Israel brought the continuance of the blockade to the attention of the Security Council in August, 1949, and also appealed to the Mixed Armistice Commission. Later, on September 1, 1951, on motion of the three Powers, France, the United Kingdom, and the United States, a resolution was adopted by the Security Council calling upon Egypt "to terminate the restrictions of the passage of international commercial shipping and goods through the Suez Canal wherever bound, and to cease all interference with such shipping beyond that essential to the safety of shipping in the Canal itself and to the observance of the international conventions in force."

We have no intention of pursuing the question further here because it is now largely if not wholly political and will continue to be so as long as it is connected with the defense of the Middle East, indeed, of the whole free world. It suffices to say that in former periods, the free navigation of a waterway such as the Suez Canal would have been considered an issue wholly within the jurisdiction of a very few Powers, even though it affects the vital interest of the entire world. Fortunately, it is now within the competence of the United Nations, and will eventually be settled on moral and political as well as upon legal grounds in the interests of world peace and commerce and with due regard for the integrity and security of the nations contiguous to the waterways.

Epilogue

The second half of the twentieth century still finds us continuing the quest along pathways marked at the end of the nineteenth. Two destructive world wars have not deflected the direction of these pathways, but the problems have become more acute. This is due in part to the rapid increase in populations throughout the world, the shrinking of the relative size of this whirling planet on which we live, and the continued reliance upon the principle of absolute sovereignty inherited from a quite different period of the world community.

Along these pathways we have observed the downfall of some ancient empires and the loosening of moral sanctions. On the more hopeful side, we have witnessed the setting up of institutions of international cooperation. Unfortunately, this has not been accompanied by the expected resort to law and the decrees of law for resolving the competitive struggle inherent in the life of men and nations. There has, indeed, grown up in the free Western World a better knowledge of, and more respect for, the underlying forces which tend toward better relations between peoples and nations. However, without more regular recourse to judicial processes for the settlement of international disputes, there will be little opportunity for the practical functioning of what Nicholas Murray Butler called "the international mind."

Perhaps it is too much to expect that there should be equal regard for the supremacy of law over concentrated power. A long historical process was necessary before this supremacy was acknowledged and before it became entrenched in the constitutional structure of many modern states. In some others having control over vast territories and huge populations, the supremacy of law over political power has gained little, if any, foothold. This is a consideration often forgotten or neglected when surveying the functioning of the United Nations. One might have expected that continued diplomatic contact with nations which regard the principle to be fundamental would have created greater respect for judicial processes. Now one wonders whether the free nations have not themselves lost some of their confidence in legal processes by long association in parliamentary contest with the representatives of nations respecting only political power.

In pursuing these pathways, we have interpreted international law not merely as appertaining to the law between nations, which is its strict interpretation, but as comprising the whole field of relationships between states and the individuals of different states. The law and jurisdiction of one sovereign state cannot alone determine public or private international disputes. International law in its strict sense rests upon long-established and accepted custom or upon conventional agreement. At best the system is fragmentary. International justice is still administered for the most part by *national* tribunals. The parties litigating before the World Court are states and not individuals. To say that states have been created to serve the interests of the people and that the people do not exist for the state is almost to be a voice crying in the wilderness. The various interests, the multitudinous transactions, the infinite variety of injuries demanding redress which arise continually in international intercourse require the administration of justice, notwithstanding the territorial limitation of the state in which redress is sought. It would be easy to redress all grievances in the Procrustean bed of the local law. Some of the most advanced states, even England, did this in their primitive period. States which do this today show a reversion to the primitive. It is not commensurate with the highly developed state of society which modern technical science has brought into being.

Not all international disputes can be settled by judicial decision. Political claims must be left to negotiation. The United Nations, through its appropriate committees, can remove the acerbity of political contention, and new forms of reference may be devised so that even political claims may be subjected to the white light of truth. The possibilities of international legislation through conventional agreement should be continuously explored. It is here that the human and humane elements may come to fruition. The modern world, with its hazardous peacetime industries and its scientifically applied destruction in time of war, has tended to become callous to human suffering. Without compassion we shall never recapture the pathways of civilization which the eighteenth century thought to be inevitable and the nineteenth to have already arrived. Some day, perhaps, the ideal of the Psalmist may be realized, but though the act may be of God, the way must be of man before "He maketh wars to cease unto the end of the earth."

The contribution one person may make along these pathways may be small indeed, but at least salvation oft lies in the effort if not in the achievement. Viewing it in archaeologic perspective with Sir Flinders Petrie:

> Yet man does not thus vanish without trace,
> But like in some vast pyramid a stone
> Helps to build up the glory of his race.

Perhaps the best contribution that one individual can make in his own generation along the pathways of international law is to point out the hopelessness of merely improvising the solutions of world problems through political rather than through judicial methods. Dialectics should not take the place of legal proof nor should invective supplant legal discussion. Elihu Root expressed it most cogently when he wrote to Will H. Hays on March 29, 1919, in criticism of the Covenant: "International law is not mentioned at all, except in the preamble; no method is provided, and no purpose is expressed to insist upon obedience to law, to develop the law, to press forward agreement upon its rules and recognition of its obligations. All questions of right are relegated to the investigation and recommendation of a political body to be determined as matters of expediency."

The progressive development of international law is especially necessary in a period when historic destiny points the way to the federation of Europe and perhaps regional federation in other parts of the world. What is to be the cement which is to unite these states into an integrated body, and what is to regulate their relations one to another and to the world, if it be not through law? The success of our own Federal Union is to be sought in its reliance upon law through a Constitution which regulates both interstate and international relations through a Supreme Tribunal which early recognized that the law of nations is part of the law of the land. It is toward this goal of the supremacy of law that my pathways were directed. Some day the pathways of international law will emerge from this mid-century Inferno of world relations, and, like Dante, we shall then be able to say:

"Thence issuing, we again beheld the stars."

Index